Advance P

*When Kids Rule the School*

Written with passion, depth, yet ease of style, *When Kids Rule the School* is an inspiring affirmation of the natural greatness of children and humanity. A treat that combines explicit details about all facets of democratic education with practical applications and the shared philosophy of all members of the school community, *When Kids Rule the School* invites us to an education future of dignity, intelligence, and wisdom.

— Ba Luvmour, MA and Josette Luvmour, PhD, authors,
*Everyone Wins, 3rd ed.*, and cohosts, Meetings with
Remarkable Educators www.remarkable-educators.com

This book reads in one breath. I highly recommend it for teachers, parents, prospective students, all kind of educators, and general public.

— Eugene Matusov, PhD, Professor of Education,
University of Delaware

This book is the clearest, most complete explanation of self-directed democratic schooling that I have seen. Whether you are brand new to the idea of democratic education or have long been immersed in it, you will find much to think about here. I recommend this book to everyone interested in education and child development, whether that interest comes from concern for their own children or all the children of the world.

— Peter Gray, research professor, Boston College,
and author, *Free to Learn*

If you're not keen on sending your kids to a "regular" school, but don't feel homeschooling is the answer either, relax — and gear up. You've got another potential path right here.

— Lenore Skenazy, president, Let Grow,
and founder, Free-Range Kids

*When Kids Rule the School* is an in-depth look at the nuances of democratic education. Jim Reitmulder peppers his beautiful personal stories among the history and exploration of what it is to REALLY trust children and their school communities. As a fellow school founder, I am proud to say that Jim's descriptions are a thoughtful and honest look at what could be possible if we gave all of our children an opportunity to thrive in democratic self-directed environments.

— Dr. Jen Schwartz PhD, CFLE, Founder, Sego Lily School

This is a fresh look at how learning works at The Circle School, and how it could be applied to education everywhere. No matter where you are on the education spectrum — student, parent, teacher or school founder — you will find important new insights from this book.

— Jerry Mintz, Director,
Alternative Education Resource Organization

*When Kids Rule the School* makes an important contribution to the field of education. Jim Rietmulder's advocacy of self-directed education and democratic schooling is compelling, and his skillful application of integral philosophy to education makes this book a must-read for every educator.

— Steve McIntosh, author, *Integral Consciousness and the Future of Evolution*,
and cofounder, Institute for Cultural Evolution

This wonderful book vividly captures what life is like within our self-directed democratic schools — funny, passionate, profoundly serious, mischievous, compassionate, just, full of intense conversations, a lot of voting, and endless learning.

— Lisa Lyons, co-founder, Evergreen Sudbury School

# WHEN KIDS RULE THE SCHOOL

## THE POWER AND PROMISE OF **DEMOCRATIC EDUCATION**

### JIM RIETMULDER

new society
PUBLISHERS
www.newsociety.com

Cover design by Diane McIntosh.
Cover images: ©iStock; Digital composite: Diane McIntosh

Printed in Canada. First printing May 2019.

Inquiries regarding requests to reprint all or part of *When Kids Rule the School* should be addressed to New Society Publishers at the address below. To order directly from the publishers, please call toll-free (North America) 1-800-567-6772, or order online at www.newsociety.com

Any other inquiries can be directed by mail to:
New Society Publishers
P.O. Box 189, Gabriola Island, BC V0R 1X0, Canada
(250) 247-9737

LIBRARY AND ARCHIVES CANADA CATALOGUING IN PUBLICATION
Title: When kids rule the school : the power and promise of democratic education / Jim Rietmulder.
Names: Rietmulder, Jim, 1953- author.
Description: Includes index.
Identifiers: Canadiana (print) 20190057084 | Canadiana (ebook) 20190057157 | ISBN 9780865719040
   (softcover) | ISBN 9781550926972 (PDF) | ISBN 9781771422932 (EPUB)
Subjects: LCSH: Democracy and education. | LCSH: Student-centered learning. | LCSH: Active
   learning. | LCSH: Education—Aims and objectives. | LCSH: Education—Philosophy.
Classification: LCC LB14.7 .R54 2019 | DDC 370.1—dc23

Funded by the | Financé par le
Government | gouvernement
of Canada | du Canada

 Canada

New Society Publishers' mission is to publish books that contribute in fundamental ways to building an ecologically sustainable and just society, and to do so with the least possible impact on the environment, in a manner that models this vision.

MIX
Paper from responsible sources
FSC
www.fsc.org    FSC® C016245

Certified
(B)
Corporation

new society
PUBLISHERS
www.newsociety.com

# Contents

# Stories

# Prologue: Taming the Wild

MAYBE WE ARE A BIT WISER NOW, 500 years into science, reason, and the modern era. After the first few hundred years, we started getting giddy. Who could blame us after so many miracles of medicine and technology? And after the Industrial Revolution — well, there was no limit to what we thought science and engineering would do to improve on nature. In the age of machines, we even thought to engineer children's minds in mass education factories.

Human beings are afraid of the dark, so it's no wonder we welcomed electric light and all that followed. It's not just darkness we fear. By nature, we fear nature itself: wildness, disorder, chaos. To this day, you can evoke a subtle fear response in human beings if you show them pictures of nature in the wild, or even an unkempt suburban lawn. It's true, a human thing. Our genes encode the dangers of our primordial home in raw nature. It's a jungle out there.

Our infatuation with technology didn't seem overzealous until the second half of the 1900s. Then we started to worry about unforeseen consequences like thalidomide babies and a silent spring without peepers. Now we've learned about the dark side of technology, and we have many apocalypses to worry about.

After those sobering lessons, nature doesn't look so bad after all, and we want to get back to it. Walks in the woods. Organic foods. Natural fibers. Stone-age diets. Even science has gone natural, scouring the jungle wilds for nature's own problem-solving methods and medicines. Turns out, nature's not just wild, but wise, too.

So now we balance our inborn fear of nature with our acquired fear of technology, and our addiction to technology with our attraction to nature. Instead of dominating nature, we want partnership. Instead of thinking we can do better with brute force, we want to engineer with elegance, intelligence, and a light touch. We want to tap the powers of nature, managed by creative human invention for the sustainable good of all.

Self-directed education, such as democratic schooling, rests on a power of nature: children's inborn impulse to strive, thrive, and grow. Spend time with children and you see it in their boundless energy, fits of frustration, inspired mischief, and radiant joy. It's the sustainable energy of education.

But the thought of setting children free to run amok, powered by untamed nature, evokes those fears of the wild. And with good reason. Children raised in the wild by wolves are unlikely to grow up to be president, or even happy. Eeek.

And yet the industrial era education machine isn't working. Its bulldozing approach thwarts the power of children's nature, sometimes devastating that environment. We need to stop with the brute force. We need elegant engineering, a technology to harvest the energy of human nature for the good of children, families, and society.

Self-directed democratic schooling is that technology: a human invention to manage the raw energy of children's nature without dominating or devastating. We've scoured the jungle wilds of children and found that their nature is to learn fast and well what they need and want. We've scoured the jungles of society and found that what works to manage adults works for kids, too: the constraints of community and lawful society. The democratic school is a real world scaled down.

So we say to kids: Come to school and do what brings you joy of life, and be mindful or reminded of the community around you.

And we say to parents: Take a look. You'll see the spirit and sparkle of children practicing life, growing into the world as though they own it.

And we say to teachers: School can be fulfilling for you, too, as steward, resource, guide, companion, and living example in community with children.

Self-directed democratic schooling is proven and growing, but not yet widely adopted. Are you ready? Straying from the conventional herd makes you vulnerable on two fronts: exposure to the unknown at the edge of the crowd and maybe shunning by your tribe. Put your kids in an edgy school and what if it doesn't work? And anyway, how will you explain it to the in-laws?

But the old education system is exhausted, and our children need not pay the price of diminished life. Truth is, if we feed, clothe, secure, and love our children, they naturally seek knowledge, understanding, wisdom, and high purpose. One way or another, we all seek infinity. It's a human thing.

# Introduction

IN SELF-DIRECTED DEMOCRATIC SCHOOLS, kids practice life in a micro-cosm of society, empowered as voters, bound by laws, challenged by choice, supported by community, and driven by nature. In this book, I'll tell you all about it: philosophy, theory, and practice. I'll tell you how schools are governed by students and staff together, and what happens in school day to day. I'll tell you why it feels morally right, practically effective, and deeply satisfying. Along the way, I'll tell you dozens of personal stories.

## Agency in Community

"Agency" is a word coming into its own these days. Agency is the capacity to choose and act on your own behalf, and may be a hallmark of life. A rock just sits there, but living creatures can do things, can take actions. Even bacteria detect and move toward nutrients, taking action in a primi-tive sort of agency.

In human beings, agency is conscious and even self-conscious: we can reflect on our choices, actions, and experience — and learn. We can retain what works, and drop what doesn't, adapting and evolving ourselves in a lifelong practice of self-authorship. If agency is a distinguishing feature of life in general, reflective agency may be a distinguishing feature of humanity.

Agency is like muscle: stronger with work, weaker without. Just as physical inactivity weakens muscles, chronic restraint of children's choice and action weakens their ability to choose and act. Inactivity and restraint are sometimes necessary or wise, but greatest growth is prompted by conditions in which choice and action are exercised, constrained by limits of safety and society.

That last part — constraints — is worth emphasizing. Agency is biologically installed, but its actions may or may not lead to good outcomes. Unbridled pursuit of inborn impulses is unlikely to work out well in the long run. The opportunities and taming influences of community and societal structure are crucial and central in human experience. Just so, at the heart of self-directed democratic schooling is the bounded freedom of agency in community.

In this setting, nature and culture mix and merge, stirring a uniquely personal stew of existential and situational challenges, stimulating satisfying growth. Instead of the brute force of conventional education, democratic schooling channels natural forces to drive development.

## Transcending Culture Wars

Education is a frontier in the culture wars of values and public policy. Schools are in the crossfire. Each of the several cultural movements hopes to embed their own favored values in curriculum, methodology, and policy, to be imposed on all children and families. In contrast, the democratic schooling discussed in this book might be called post-curricular. It stands entirely outside the current debate, and implicitly suggests a new policy direction and a new role for government in education.

Democratic schools impose no curriculum at all, and no particular teaching-learning methodology. Instead, democratic schools are more like a venue — hosting any curriculum and any teaching-learning methodology, while imposing none. One could argue, with some merit, that this is just another set of values vying for dominance. But democratic schooling is not just another flavor of curriculum and methodology. Instead it is the first to integrate *all* flavors, first to include and accommodate all of the competing value sets, while also transcending the limitations of coercion and a one-size-fits-all approach.

Instead of government picking favored curriculum to be applied universally, I imagine a world in which government's role is to ensure universal access to a wide array of possibilities in schools. This is not about charter schools, vouchers, privatization, or the politically charged versions of school choice. My wish is simply that education policy would catch up with science, scholarship, and common sense — which all recognize the significance of diversity in values, socioeconomic circumstances, family composition, and especially individual developmental paths. There is no one flavor of schooling that is right for every family and every child, and there is no good reason that schools cannot better accommodate human variety and children's individuality. The one-dimensional homogenizing function of schooling a hundred years ago is out of sync with today's multidimensional diversity, and no longer serves (if ever it did) to equalize opportunity and cultivate personal fulfillment and societal engagement.

Although self-directed democratic schools today are not part of public schooling (which is ironic in democratic nations), they very well could be, and that is what I hope for. Alas, it doesn't seem imminent.

I will not pursue this thread any further in this book. I mention it mostly to help situate democratic schooling in the current education landscape.

## About Me

I'm in a good position to tell you about democratic schooling. I'm a staff member and founder of The Circle School (Harrisburg, Pennsylvania), which opened in 1984, and I'm the father of two now-adult Circle School "lifers." The school's students, mostly 4 to 19 years old, have brought every sort of joy and challenge we could imagine — and almost every day they bring yet another surprise, something entirely new, even now, 30-some years later. We have consulted with dozens of other self-directed democratic schools and their founders, some during their founding period, and learned much from cross visits, conferences, and daily interactions within the national and international community of democratic schools. We have conducted and published two statistical and analytical studies of one particular brand of self-directed democratic schooling (Sudbury schools). We have been visited by hundreds of educators and examined closely by dozens, including years of sustained deep dialogue with professors of education from several universities.

My interest in schooling extends back to my teenage years. For 11 happy years, I was a compliant A student in conventional government-run public schools. Then an itch, an opportunity, and a whim landed me in a partly democratic school for my last two years of high school, back in the era of the "free schools" movement. There I found two lifelong loves: democratic schooling and my wife, Beth L. Stone, who is also a Circle School founder and staff member.

As a teenager, I studied alternative schooling as a hobby. I volunteered as a classroom tutor and later, in college, a Big Brother. I aspired to be a 5th-grade classroom teacher, but that never happened. (It was specifically 5th grade. Now I wonder if that's because part of me happily "locked in" at that age — something I suspect now, as I rejoice in the adventures and mischief of 10-year-olds.) After high school, I attended Yale, dropped out, and later attended night classes at Penn State for a few years. Early in fatherhood, I established and staffed a playgroup for babies and toddlers in our local library. My training and nine years of volunteer work as a telephone helpline counselor awakened me to the amazing power of people, when given the opportunity and support, to navigate difficult situations and personal transformation. Before and overlapping with The Circle School's early years, I enjoyed 5 to 10 years each as a history magazine editor, business analyst, independent software developer, and management consultant to manufacturers.

In this book, my point of view is that of a practitioner, rather than, say, a journalist, academic, or social commentator. I'm speaking from my perch in a school and a movement of schools, drawing mainly on my firsthand experience here, my own years as a student, and a lifetime of learning. Although I'll refer to ideas from beyond my world of democratic schooling, I have not systematically studied the canon of education and developmental psychology. Maybe I have it all wrong. I'm an expert about my own experience, but nothing else.

## About This Book

In this book, I'll present democratic schooling as articulated and practiced by The Circle School, because that's what I know best and can describe from firsthand experience spanning four decades. Sometimes I'll highlight similarities and variations among democratic schools, to the best of my knowledge, but I do not speak for them. My aim is that you will experience the flavors of democratic schools in general, partly by tasting the particulars of one. Although The Circle School is not typical in some ways — such as checks and balances in its legal structure — it is typical in the most important way: students experience personal and community self-determination in democratic freedom, responsibility, and authority.

This book is especially for three overlapping groups. First, I hope to feed hungry parents, teachers, and students seeking a better way, perhaps from hopeful anticipation or disappointing experience. May this book point you in a fulfilling direction and help you develop realistic expectations of what is possible. Second, I hope to challenge and inspire those who are already involved in democratic and alternative schooling, who want to deepen their understanding of what's going on. I'll be especially pleased if this book helps guide you in founding or refining a school. Let me know. Third, I hope to inform and provoke response from scholars, commentators, integral theorists, citizens, and policymakers who are on the lookout for promising developments that could help transform schools.

More generally, this book is for anyone who wants to learn more about democratic, Sudbury, and integral schooling, including philosophy, theory, structure, administration, daily practices, and personal stories.

Part One introduces self-directed democratic schooling generally, and The Circle School in particular, drawing on the school's literature to outline school structure and philosophy. Here's an important caveat. Other democratic schools are similar in program structure, daily practices, and personal stories. Colleagues tend to accept our descriptions of these as similar to their own, and smile knowingly when we tell our stories. On the other hand, The Circle School's statements of philosophy, theory, and beliefs are specific to The Circle School. Other democratic schools and individual practitioners might or might not agree. Indeed, practitioners within any school might disagree with one another. Such is the nature and strength of democracy.

Part Two builds a case for democratic schooling: half a millennium of cultural, social, and economic trends; elegant alignment of democratic schooling with society, children's lives, and basic aims of education; science and scholarship in education and human development. This is not intended to be the definitive or comprehensive case for democratic schooling, particularly as it omits some matters that have been well covered by other writers. Part Two also situates democratic schooling as the first (and so far only) developed school paradigm of integral education — so-called for integration in three dimensions, and also alluding to Integral Theory.

Part Three addresses two questions in education theory. First, how do children learn in democratic schools? More specifically, what new methods and modes of learning are enabled by democratic schooling? Second, how can we account for the frequent observation that democratic schools cultivate critical thinking? Specifically, by what mechanisms do students develop cognition and higher thinking skills?

Part Four moves from philosophy and theory to daily practice, describing a typical day (although there's no such thing), details of school government, law enforcement, Judicial Committee, legal structure, housekeeping, safety, and college.

Part Five answers Frequently Asked Questions with summaries and abbreviated material, good for grazing but also covering a few ideas that are not discussed elsewhere.

Appendix A presents the table of contents of The Circle School's Lawbook (listing the "short title" of every law) and the operations manual (listing elected officials, committees, corporations, and certifications). Appendix B presents most of The Circle School's bylaws, detailing the school's legal structure as a nonprofit corporation. Appendix C lists colleges attended by Circle School graduates.

For your ease and mine, I'll now mostly drop "self-directed" and instead refer to "democratic schooling" to mean the kind of schooling this book is about. Keep in mind, though, that other schools have democratic features or call themselves democratic, but are not the self-directed democratic schools of this book. I'll point out the differences and defining features in a moment.

# Part One:
# Self-directed Democratic Schools

Jyles was ten when he first came here. After a day or so, he thought it was like kindergarten: no required classes or homework, lots of things to do, busy children moving about, and friendly adults.

Time passed and Jyles changed his mind. It's not like kindergarten, he thought. It's like college: demanding rules and requirements and voluntary commitments, but no nagging parent types; each person responsible for their actions; groupings based on interest and attraction rather than age; diversity in kinds and levels of skill and ability, freely mixing; scholarly respect for each voice and point of view.

More time passed and Jyles changed his mind again. No, it's not like kindergarten, he thought, and it's not like college either. It's like life: we're free and accountable citizens in a democratic society. We make laws and we live by them, change them, or get taken to court for breaking them. We make our own decisions about what to do today, and we find our own best ways of dealing with the world, with all kinds of examples to learn from.

That's it, thought Jyles: I just come here and I live my life.

Chapter 1:

# What's a Democratic School?

T HOUSANDS OF SCHOOLS CAN CLAIM TO BE DEMOCRATIC in one way or another. I suppose you could even say all of America's 130,000 schools are democratic simply because they are run by democratic governments serving a democratic nation, or because school boards are elected by voters. But in this book, I'll narrow the focus to schools that are themselves small-scale democracies.

In the narrower meaning, there may be dozens or hundreds of democratic schools in North America and around the world, and new ones are sprouting all the time. Just as no two democratic nations or towns are quite alike, no two democratic schools are quite alike either. Each is uniquely situated geographically of course, inheriting some of the culture and demographics of the surrounding area. As with any small community, each school has its own character, social norms, traditions, and values. Beyond such cultural variation, there are also differences in governance, philosophy, and theory of education.

Almost all democratic schools have been founded in grassroots efforts, rather than within state school systems. Democratic schools do not easily fit in today's government-run school systems, which generally focus on curriculum, classrooms, and top-down control. In contrast, democratic schools operate bottom-up, like democratic societies.

What the various democratic schools share in common is that students experience free, responsible citizenship in a formal democracy and democratic society. A 17-year-old boy put it this way: "I like that the kids and the teenagers have power here, and it's not just some kind of mock thing. This is real."

## Small-scale Democracy

The term can be misleading, so let's clarify further. For our purposes in this book, a democratic school operates as a free society and democracy of staff members and students, embracing student civil liberties, rule of law, due process, one person one vote, and absence of mandatory curriculum. Specifically, laws and executive actions are proposed by any student or staff member, voted by students and staff who choose to participate, and not generally subject to veto or override. Laws and executive actions are limited by constitution or tradition to protect student civil liberties, the democratic structure of the school, and the school's long-term assets such as real estate. Participation in governance is voluntary. School offices are filled by elections. Allegations of rule infractions are settled in open judicial processes with careful regard for defendants' rights. Students are generally free in school to pursue lawful activities as they choose, subject to civic duties such as house-keeping chores, fire drills, and jury duty. Students are typically required by state law to attend school for a certain number of days and hours, but within the school they are free of curricular coercion such as mandatory studies.

Does this sound familiar? Except for the bit about compulsory school laws, this roughly describes national democracies in North America and Europe, and increasingly elsewhere. That's the point: immerse kids in a scaled-down version of the world beyond school, complete with liberty, community, and constraints. Children's innate tendencies drive them to explore the world, adapt to it, acquire knowledge, and strive for fulfillment. Practicing life, as we say.

---

### *Sense and No Sense*

Rasheeda had recently heard of self-directed democratic schooling. Her daughter Riane, in a standard school, got good grades and conformed as a good student is supposed to. But son Brady, 8 years old, wasn't motivated, she said. He was doing okay, but not thriving and not happy, and that worried Rasheeda. She wanted to come see this new kind of school for herself, so she made an appointment to visit, along with Riane and Brady.

Rasheeda had read the school's literature before visiting. She was intrigued by the idea of school as a scaled-down version of the larger world, but didn't understand how it worked. She had been a conscientious A student through all her schooling and right on through college. As a parent, she made sure her kids did their homework. If their grades faltered, she'd worry they were falling behind.

Twenty minutes into our conversation, Riane and Brady were beaming. No required classes? No required testing? No required homework? They were sold. I hadn't yet told them we have 200 laws in our Lawbook, and they are responsible for helping to enforce them, but I knew from experience that wouldn't diminish their thrilled reaction.

"Is there a dress code here?" was 11-year-old Riane's first question — understandable for someone approaching adolescence and subject to a strict dress code in her current school. "Well, you have to wear clothes," I said. Riane looked at her brother, and both laughed nervously. "Yes," I continued, "but you can probably wear what you like. Mahlyn likes to wear a wolf tail, and sometimes ears to go with it, and Ashley once wore a long skirt she made entirely with colorful duct tape."

There's a little more to it, I told them, launching into my "community standards" speech. I mentioned our laws and social norms related to the three big hot-button topics — sex, drugs, and violence — and how those standards relate to clothing and other forms of expression. Dress as you choose, but if it makes people uncomfortable — perhaps because it's too revealing, or the tee shirt humor is too vulgar — then you might get charged with breaking a school law, and you will have to stop dressing that way. Or you can plead "not guilty" and argue your case before a jury. Basically, I concluded, it's like freedom of speech in the world beyond school: a balance of personal rights and public standards, calibrated to our community of people from 4 years old to 19 years old, and adults.

By this point, Rasheeda was almost bursting. "This makes perfect sense!" she exclaimed, "but it makes no sense!" School that works like the real world makes perfect sense, but how do they learn? How do they get what they need? How do they get into college? What do they do all day? We talked for two hours, and they left with a lot to think about. Perfect sense and no sense.

A few weeks later, Rasheeda brought her husband in for a visit. They had decided to enroll daughter Riane for the coming school year, but not Brady, because they weren't sure he could "handle the freedom and the responsibility." I didn't remind her that it was Brady's unhappiness that led Rasheeda to the school in the first place. Again we talked for a long time. Near the end of our conversation, Rasheeda sighed and commented to her husband that maybe Brady needed this more than Riane. They enrolled Riane a few days ago. I think Brady won't be far behind.

---

In addition to the self-directed democratic schools I know, there are thousands of other schools that have democratic features, but do not count as democratic schools in my meaning. For example, in some schools, the chief administrator or the board of trustees is elected by parents. This does not make the school democratic in my meaning. Nor would I count as democratic a school that imposes curriculum, classes, learning projects, or religious practices. Nor would I count a school in which students vote on a few limited matters, as student councils commonly do, but not on the basics of governance, such as legislative, judicial, and administrative actions.

I do not disvalue those other schools. To the extent their democratic practices support students' personal and collective self-determination, they share some of the basic values of democratic schools. In fact, they represent a tidal shift in cultural values: greater enfranchisement of all human beings in self-determination, and less reliance on coercion and autocratic control. I applaud and celebrate the spread of democratic values and practices in schools, and offer my sincere encouragement to teachers, administrators, parents, and students in schools of all kinds.

I find that what I most appreciate in democratic schools — power to ignite joy of life and its attendant development of personal potentials — is rooted in children's genuine liberty, responsibility, and authority. I find that informal and isolated democratic features in classrooms and schools merely soften and gloss over the sting of coercion, and sometimes the teacher's misgivings about being an agent of coercion. For example, student selection from multiple choices of mandatory assignments arguably provides a measure of self-determination, but a meager measure only, and unlikely to ignite much joy. Moreover, isolated and informal democratic features may be regarded cynically, as though intended to give the illusion of democracy, too often leading to alienation and feelings of powerlessness.

I am not suggesting that coercion is bad and always to be avoided. To be clear, democratic schools apply school laws with the school's full force, in a small-scale adaptation of American judicial practices. I'm also not arguing against compulsory education; I hold that a democratic society can reasonably require some level of development of its citizens. I'm simply reflecting commonsense truths, both practical and moral: self-motivation outperforms coercion in its power to educate and fulfill; and coercion is generally a moral last resort. Pushing children through a lockstep curriculum is suboptimal as educational strategy, and unnecessary coercion is out of sync with today's values.

## Sudbury Schools

Sudbury Valley School (Framingham, Massachusetts) was founded in 1968 and is among the oldest and best known self-directed democratic schools, still thriving today as a flagship. Sudbury Valley School has been a vitally important influence and support in the history of my own home base, The Circle School. It is also the inspiration and template for the democratic schools I know best. A few years after its founding, The Circle School adopted and adapted many structures, methods, and terms we first encountered at Sudbury Valley School. We gratefully celebrate their pioneering work and generous support. Although The Circle School does not identify itself as a Sudbury school — having significant differences in philosophy, theory, and governance — I believe the two schools are both entirely democratic in the meaning of this book, and similar in student experience.

Some schools associate themselves with Sudbury Valley School, indicating their similarity by using the word "Sudbury" in their name or describing the school as a "Sudbury school" or "Sudbury model school." Many but not all of the Sudbury schools I know are democratic in our meaning, and this book is about them. A growing number of self-designated Sudbury schools incorporate selected features of the Sudbury model combined with other features, including some that are incompatible with Western-style secular democracy, making the school an innovation, a hybrid, or a monster, depending on your point of view. Thus the term "Sudbury" does not reliably indicate a democratic school for the purposes of this book.

## Summerhill School

Summerhill School (England) was founded in 1921, is still going strong today, and calls itself the "oldest children's democracy in the world." Summerhill is neither a democratic school in the meaning of this book nor a free school (discussed below), but inspired both and remains an esteemed colleague school.

## Integral Education

"Integral" education points to the possibility of a new era to emerge as the next generation beyond traditional and modern education. Although nobody knows just what it will look like, some of its principles and properties are coming into view, and may be exemplified in democratic schools. Integral education, in my conception, better integrates children's and teens' lives in school, better integrates schools in society, and draws on Integral Theory in ways to be mentioned later (although Integral Theory itself is beyond the scope of this book).

For now I just want to outline the relation between integral education and democratic schooling. Most of the theory and practice of integral education so far involves the classroom setting in conventional schools, and particularly the dynamics of teaching and learning in the classroom. In contrast, this book explores a different context — the structure of the school itself — and proposes that democratic schooling may be the only developed paradigm of integral education at the school level: governance, administration, structure, culture, and daily practices. In my view, democratic schools and many Sudbury schools are integral schools because they are in harmony with society and children's lives, because integral teaching-learning practices are inherent, and because the integral world-view is better satisfied. I anticipate other kinds of integral schools in the future. In any case, I believe democratic schools can lead the way into a new era in education, perhaps with the ripening of postmodern values and thought, or maybe moving beyond to post-postmodern.

## Free Schools

The democratic schools in this book stand apart from the "free schools" movement of the 1960s and 1970s. Free schools emerged from that era's social revolution, counterculture, and liberation movements, rising against social injustice, abuse of power, and repression of the individual. Free schools were less about education and more about the values of the social revolution: rejection of authority and structure, and building a just society — values of hippies and civil rights activists, respectively. Free schools were part of the grassroots social movement to undermine the established order and bring about a vaguely conceived new society. As such, the free school movement had little to say about education per se. Children were swept along as the adults around them found new empowerment and pioneered new cultural norms.

Reflecting the social movement, many free schools sought to eliminate power, structure, and authority generally, sometimes tending not to distinguish the real targets of the revolution: *abusive* power, *oppressive* structure, and *illegitimate* authority. The result was not usually *anarchy*, but instead pervasive informality: *informal* power, *informal* structure, and *informal* authority. Some free schoolers tended to gloss over or "not see" the presence of power, structure, and authority in their schools. In contrast, the democratic schools in this book are about *formal* structure and *formal* authority — meaning structure and authority are visible, valued, acknowledged, and documented.

In free schools, with wide variation, teachers improvised curriculum, rules, and administrative policy. Curriculum tended to be more or less conventional, and more or less imposed as mandatory. Teachers engaged students in informal decision-making in a spirit of democracy and empowerment. The student experience varied widely, but tended to be one of relaxed community, subject to adult direction and school administration. Thus, free schools continued the tradition of top-down control, softened with group decision-making; and continued the traditional curriculum, relaxed and taught with flexibility in method, sequencing, and assessment.

In contrast to free schools, the democratic schools described in this book explicitly embrace structure and authority within a constitutional democracy of students and staff. Legislative, judicial, and administrative matters are decided or overseen by the governing democracy, following Western principles of rule of law, civil liberties, due process, one person one vote, and so on.

Today's surviving free schools and their descendants have collectively matured from expressions of a social revolution to respected educational choices. Some retain countercultural values, structural informality, and community decision-making. Others bear little resemblance to the free schools of history.

The term "free school" has thus come to have various meanings today: sometimes indicating roots in the historical movement, sometimes signaling a free-spirited rebelliousness, sometimes reflecting the ongoing struggle for social justice, and sometimes simply alluding to free citizenship in Western democracy. Some may blur the lines between free schools and democratic schools, and occasionally the terms are (mis)used as synonyms.

I value free schools and many hybrid species as cousins and colleagues in promoting democratic values and self-directed education. I celebrate them and also the innovative educators who introduce features of democracy and self-determination in schools of all kinds.

In my meaning in this book, democratic schools empower students in a formal democracy of its students and staff, with primary authority for the substantial matters of running the school and governing the daily community. By whatever name, democratic schools immerse students in something like the adult experience of lawful citizenship in a secular democracy. Keep reading and you will see in detail how it plays out, and why it is good for children, families, teachers, schools, and society.

## The Most Wonderful Thing

It's your first day in a self-directed democratic school, and you are Alice down the rabbit hole. You are in a strange new world: fascinating, mysterious, confusing, but somehow the most wonderful thing. You signed in, like someone told you, copying the numbers from the clock with lots of people and noise all around you. You put your lunchbox on a shelf where other people were putting theirs while someone said helpful stuff that you didn't understand but said you did. Then two kids took you around the school and talked fast while you nodded a lot. But what were they talking about? Then you were alone. You found yourself lost. Someone asked who are you looking for, and you mumbled something and walked away. Later you met someone and joined a group, and stayed with them for a long time. An adult came in, and you thought they were going to tell you what to do but they didn't. They just said hi and asked you how is it going? Later someone said it was chore time, and you sprayed and wiped some doorknobs. A big kid looked at the doorknobs and said okay you're checked. And then it dawned on you. They are treating you like a regular person, like they don't know you are a kid, four and a half years old. It was a strange feeling but very nice, the most wonderful thing really. And at the end of the day, it was nice to go home, a relief sort of, and tomorrow you want to come back.

---

Chapter 2:

# The Circle School

F OUNDED IN 1984 BY EDUCATORS AND PARENTS, The Circle School is located in Harrisburg, Pennsylvania, and enrolls 80 to 100 students from four years old through high school. Most students are from low-income and middle-income households, most receive substantial financial aid, and the school receives no government funding. Family demographics, including household income, roughly match those of the surrounding area, with students split more or less evenly by gender and age. Graduates attend college and earn degrees at higher rates than high school graduates generally. The school is nonprofit, tax-exempt, and licensed by the Pennsylvania Department of Education.

At The Circle School, children practice life in a scaled-down version of the larger world. Children experience freedom, responsibility, democracy, and community:

- freedom to explore the world, guided by personal choice;
- responsibility for self, others, and the school;
- democracy in school governance, free market, and access to resources;
- community in fellowship, social standards, and shared challenges.

Students decide for themselves what they will do at school, prompted by their own interests, abilities, aspirations, opportunities, priorities, and preferences, as they develop from day to day and year to year. Life and schooling are blended and fused, thoroughly integrated, serving the highest personal aims of education: self-awareness, self-direction, developed knowledge and skills, general intelligence, and individually effective ways of being and relating.

In structure, culture, and governance, The Circle School echoes the wider world beyond school. By thus integrating school and society, the broadest social aims of education are well served: thoughtfully active citizens, individual self-responsibility, vibrant culture, supportive community, continuity of technology, and responsive evolution of societal institutions.

Thus the school achieves what we deem to be education's two basic aims: supporting students' personal fulfillment and bringing young people into society's fold as productive members. Thus, too, the school realizes essential values of integral schooling as we conceive it: self-satisfying expression in many dimensions of personal development; self-organizing community; pathways and invitations to higher orders of being, thinking, and doing; social structures for co-existence of divergent perspectives.

Given freedom to explore and practice as citizens in a manageable world, students find individual paths and ways of being effective. Democratic education cultivates wholesome self-reliance, responsible freedom, original exploration, critical thinking, and active community awareness. Children become experts at life, liberty, and pursuit of happiness.

## Scaled-down World

Think of the school as a self-governing society of children, teens, and staff adults, in some ways comparable to American society scaled down. Students and staff together, in School Meeting, govern the school community and manage school business, including funds, campus, staff, and more. A Board of Trustees preserves the school's democratic structure, students' civil liberties, and the school's long-term assets.

Adapting principles of democratic government, the School Meeting manages executive, legislative, and judicial functions. Weekly sessions of the School Meeting are conducted by formal parliamentary procedures. Actions generally require a simple majority vote. Each staff member and each student, regardless of age, is entitled to one vote. Staff members hold no veto power.

Together, students and staff enact and maintain hundreds of laws and policies governing the school. Elected officials and committees perform administrative functions. "Corporations" manage designated equipment, space, and activities.

The school's judicial system is founded on cherished American principles of individual rights, due process, and rule of law. In hundreds of cases per year, students and staff together methodically investigate allegations, gather evidence, take testimony, make findings of fact, issue indictments, arraign defendants, negotiate pleas, impose sentences, and conduct formal trials when defendants plead "not guilty." The School Meeting hears appeals.

Within this distinctly democratic milieu, students pursue activities of their own choosing or creation, constrained by imagination and school laws, but not by curriculum or adult demands. For example, they may hang out with friends, build a fantasy world with wooden blocks, organize a math class, work at a community externship, do "nothing," play Capture the Flag outdoors, browse the web, build a virtual world in a cyber simulation, take a nap, earn money doing extra chores, obsess over social media and pop culture, write a blog post, attend Spanish classes, produce a video, run a committee meeting, organize a blues band, paint a mural, take apart a microwave oven, operate a business, teach a friend to apply makeup, learn chess, make and sell baked goods, create a school corporation, prepare to take college entry exams, advocate for legislation, give an election campaign speech, put on a play, organize a week-long backpacking expedition, build a Tesla coil, and so on from daily novelty to creative infinity.

Furthermore, students may spend mere minutes on an activity, or an entire day, or they may immerse themselves in a passionate interest for months on end.

Importantly, students also break school laws, get in trouble, experience rudeness, try out dishonesty, cause damage, experiment with vulgarity, test limits, and so on from frequent novelty to transgressive infinity — a scaled-down rendition of the larger world, indeed.

---

## Astronomical Planning

As I write this sentence, nine of our students and two of our staff members are making their supper over a campfire far away from here, anticipating an extraordinary event tomorrow. In their nearly two years of preparation, they conducted more than a hundred meetings. Meticulously they planned every detail of their 16-day adventure on America's west coast: hour-by-hour itinerary with route maps to guide them in a rented 15-passenger van; reservations at a dozen campgrounds and sightseeing attractions; presentations to families; lots and lots of paperwork. They conducted dozens of fundraising efforts, including two online campaigns. They sold milkshakes, spaghetti lunches, dinners at evening events at school, and on several weekends, they sold hotdogs outside Walmart. Two restaurants — Friendly's and the Sweet Frog frozen yogurt store — sponsored donation days. In all, they raised almost the entire $10,000 cost of the trip.

To test their equipment and their ability to work together, they conducted two practice events: a schoolyard overnight campout (which proved the inadequacy of a leaky tent), and a 3-day road-and-camping trip to the Niagara Falls region.

Now they are at the climax of their adventure, poised to see something most people never see, or maybe once in a lifetime. Tomorrow morning, under a cloudless desert sky in Oregon, they will see, in its path of totality, the Great American Eclipse of the sun.

---

In addition to general expectations of compliance with school laws and responsibility for enforcement of school laws, the School Meeting imposes a few other civic duties, such as judicial system service, jury duty, giving testimony, and daily housekeeping chores. Students are not required to attend classes, which typically happen only when initiated by students. Homework, testing, and grades are assigned only as part of studies initiated by students, and there is no requirement or expectation that students will initiate formal studies. The school does not issue report cards and does not routinely report to parents about their children's activities, behavior, or development.

Students are citizens making their way in a free society, subject to the authority of legitimate government in which they share equally, and entitled to its protections. Thus the structure of the school echoes the "real world" and places real authority in the hands of children and teens. This essential aspect of the school engenders extraordinary power to educate.

## Foundation Principles

Education is about developing self and society. Across time and cultures, scholars and thinkers have said so in many ways. The Circle School agrees, committing itself to children's personal fulfillment and engagement in the world.

We hold that children are born with a tendency to grow, to develop their potentials, to strive and thrive, to self-actualize as psychologists say. The impulse is universal, durable, and motivating. Given the opportunity, children find individually effective growth paths.

Thus the school is committed to ideals of trust and respect: trust in an inborn tendency to self-actualize and respect for self-determination.

## Seeking Infinity

The school is founded on the principle that we each embody grand possibilities, and we grow towards their realization. Children are born with a tendency to self-actualize; to strive, thrive, and grow. Children are driven by natural impulse to seek increasingly effective ways of understanding the world and taking action, in response to never-ending existential and situational challenges. We are born with this inclination to strive, and this power to develop our abilities. These vital gifts of nature are highly adaptive, a form of instinctive wisdom.

This notion of growth driven by inborn impulse and potential is common, perhaps universal, with expressions both sacred and secular. On the *sacred* side, the world's major spiritual traditions include belief in a latent or potential higher human nature, the grandest possibilities that are sought after. Each tradition has its own prescriptions for how to realize higher nature, and warnings about pitfalls along the way. Each tradition holds out the promise of realization of grand possibilities through exercise of inborn powers.

On the *secular* side, developmental psychology is the study of progressive possibilities of the mind: stages of growth, common pathways to their realization, and pathologies along the way. Children's growth proceeds along many lines of development, with increasing abilities and higher stages emerging in common patterns and individual variations.

Thus both religion and science, each in its own way, recognize innate possibility and its essential role in human fulfillment. Each recognizes inborn potential, impulse to seek, power to find, and patterns in growth.

Each suggests a natural compass pointing in the general direction of well-being and wholeness. In any particular occasion, the compass reading may be imperfect or obscured or overwhelmed by other signals. Across time and experience, though, the cumulative influence appears as a tendency to strive, thrive, and grow.

This cycle of expanding capacity appears not only in growth of individuals but also in societies and even the cosmos. In all three dimensions — self, culture, and nature — development proceeds unevenly, this way and that, sometimes seeming random. Yet a story line unfolds across billions of years in the cosmos: a progression from void to matter to life to mind; from nothingness to rocks to plants to animals to self-aware consciousness.

A parallel story echoes across millions of years in human society: progressing from family to tribe to nation to planet-spanning community. And across thousands of years in human culture: the march of technology from ages of stone and metal to ages of industry and information.

Yet again a parallel story of unfolding echoes across tens of years in each human life: oblivious infant to naïve toddler to concrete child to idealist teen to reasoning adult to transcendent sage.

In all three dimensions — nature, culture, and self — each stage brings greater complexity, enlarged awareness, and extended range of expression, both "good" and "bad." Earlier stages are not wrong or evil, but simply partial. Later stages are not right or virtuous, but rather more inclusive, more whole, more capable. Each stage brings deeper truth and grander possibility. Each stage brings humanity new joys, burdens, opportunities, setbacks, capabilities, and pathologies.

In all three dimensions, the stories are animated by inherent wisdom: an impulse toward wholeness, an imperative of nature to seek infinity. Thus animated from birth, children enact the human story of growth in body, heart, mind, community, and spirit, each by an individual path and a unique expression of nature. Thus animated from birth, children joyfully seek growth towards infinity. Enabling that growth through children's agency in community is the heart of the school.

## Self-determination

The school holds that society ought to treat all persons with respect in equal measure without regard to age. A school, as an agent and microcosm of society, ought to do no less. We use the word respect here in its common meaning, "to show deferential regard for." We want to suggest a principle and moral value not to needlessly repress natural autonomy and personal self-determination.

The American Declaration of Independence expresses the school's view, asserting that each person is born with certain inalienable rights, including rights to life, liberty, and pursuit of happiness. We hold that children in school are entitled to exercise of inalienable rights endowed at birth.

We do not propose exaggerated freedom for children. We simply propose that schools can perform their societal functions best by respecting and promoting children's practice of life, liberty, and pursuit of happiness.

## Moral and Practical

The school is committed to ideals of trust in an inborn tendency to self-actualize, and respect for self-determination. There are both moral and practical components to these commitments.

The moral component holds that we are each entitled to personal and collective self-determination as a birthright, simply by dint of our humanity. The school respects that birthright because it is morally the right thing to do.

The practical component holds that respect for self-determination leads to the best outcomes of education. Self-determination tends to lead to self-actualization, and actualized individuals tend to lead to actualized society. The school values self-determination for the practical reason that it maximizes benefits both for the individual and for society generally.

## Melting Pot of Values and Worldviews

We regard the school as a public domain for children and teens, rather than an extension of family and parenting. Parents are not expected to adopt the school's values, rules, and practices at home. Conversely, the school does not take on a duty to instill in children the worldview and values of their parents. Nor does the school have any mechanism for enforcing parents' wishes about what their children do at school. Students are independent citizens practicing life in school society.

Parents need not hold the school's beliefs as their own, nor commit to any particular childrearing practices at home, in order for their children to get the benefits of democratic schooling. Indeed, within the school community, we find great variety in family ideals and practices. We value the school's ready accommodation of various worldviews and lifestyles, some in striking contrast to one another, and the cultural pluralism it brings. Democratic schooling is well-suited as a paradigm for education in democratic nations.

## Privacy and Independence

Children's journey from dependence to independence is often more difficult for parents than children. Supporting your child's growing independence — from you — is surely among the most tender and trying of parents' duties. Democratic schools serve this crucial function, helping parents give their children experience of independence from home and family, in a larger world. Think of the democratic school as a halfway house between home and world, between dependent childhood and independent adulthood.

As with other civil liberties, the school applies standards of privacy that are adapted from general social standards. For example, the school does not disclose students' birthdays. School law requires consent before posting photos to social media. Tests and grades, which are part of some students' studies, are for the student's own purposes and do not become school records. The school does not issue report cards to parents, nor other academic assessment. Judicial infractions are also not generally reported to parents.

Exceptions are made when health or well-being are seriously threatened; when School Meeting votes to suspend or expel; and during the "practice period" of four weeks at the beginning of each new student's enrollment.

Absence of parental reporting supports growth of independence in two ways. First, knowing that the school does not generally report to parents, children are partially released from the habits and expectations of family life. They are freer to think expansively about themselves and their place in the world, and freer to overcome limitations and assumptions developed in family life. In their independence at school, children try out new ways of interacting with people, new areas of knowledge, new mental models of how the world works, new physical feats, and a host of other personal innovations. The school functions as a laboratory for self-experimentation and self-authorship.

Second, knowing that staff members are not here to assess and report, children are freer in self-disclosure with them. Combined with other social leveling factors, children freely develop trusting personal friendships with staff members, providing exquisite opportunity for close-up study of how to be an adult and what makes them tick — vital curriculum for every child, and especially for teenagers.

Student privacy also promotes learning efficiency. Assessment, reporting, and surveillance undermine self-motivation, thus reducing interest, learning depth, and retention.

The educational and developmental benefits of student privacy are significant, but its most important basis is simply common human respect. The gift of independence, enabled by respectful privacy, is an important reason that parents choose democratic schools. Even parents who have been accustomed to micromanaging their children find deep benefits, and sometimes personal liberation from worry, as children assume increasing self-responsibility.

On the other hand, parents naturally attend to their children's well-being. Student privacy notwithstanding, we invite parents to discuss with staff members their concerns related to their children, especially when parent-child communications haven't resolved the concern. Staff members can usually provide helpful information and perspective without undermining privacy, independence, and trust. Parents can also post questions, with due respect for personal privacy, to the school's online forum for parents, students, staff, alumni, and alumni parents.

Student experience of the school is strongly influenced by parents' experience of the school, so we encourage parents and students to make every effort to address parents' questions and concerns.

## Ends We Seek

Extending principles into practices, The Circle School highlights a dozen ideals or "ends we seek." Most of the democratic schools I know hold similar values, with significant variations, but The Circle School is unusual in making them explicit and incorporating them as binding aims of the school:

*Opportunity.* Students have abundant opportunity for personal fulfillment and societal engagement.

1. **Community.** Students experience fellowship, common culture, collective self-governance, and shared responsibility.
2. **Order.** Students experience safety, order, and access to community resources.
3. **Knowledge.** Students have opportunity to develop knowledge and skills in self-chosen domains.
4. **Staff.** Students experience adults who dependably steward the program's facilities, finances, and business; facilitate student access to resources; exemplify mature practice of personal fulfillment and societal engagement; and anchor school culture to values of interpersonal respect and trust in the natural impulse to self-actualize.

*Growth.* Students grow in many dimensions, such as physical, intellectual, emotional, social, and spiritual.

5. **Personal fulfillment.** Students increasingly actualize personal potentials, and seek satisfaction in self-chosen domains of activity, knowledge, and skill.
6. **Engagement in society.** Students develop increasingly fulfilling ways of participating in culture, community, and society.

*Self-determination.* Students enjoy natural rights of life, liberty, and pursuit of happiness, paralleling adult experience in the community beyond school.

7. **Civil liberties.** Students enjoy civil liberties such as freedoms of speech, press, thought, attention, religion, privacy, movement, association, and peaceable assembly.
8. **Curriculum.** Students are free of curricular coercion.

*Governance.* The daily school program is self-governing, with authority and responsibility shared among the governed, students and staff alike.

9.  **Voice.** All members of the daily school program — students and staff — enjoy equal rights of voice and vote in matters of governance and the common good.
10. **Rule of law.** All members of the daily school program are subject to the authority of school government according to duly adopted laws that are publicly disclosed in writing.
11. **Responsibility.** All members of the daily school program share responsibility for the common welfare.
12. **Protection.** All members of the daily school program enjoy equal protection and due process under school law.

The Circle School thus lays out broad beliefs, general philosophy, operating principles, and ideals in practice. Now let's turn to evidence and reason in support of democratic schooling.

# Part Two:

# A Case for Democratic Schooling

Most of us share in common some basic values about public life. We argue about how to apply these values, how to balance them, and what to do when they conflict with private interests. By and large, though, these common values are regarded today as social bedrock in Western democracies.

What are these shared values? Here are four fundamentals:

- Personal freedom
- Mutual toleration
- Public government
- Free, responsible markets

These account for much in human civilization, as the foundation for a satisfying life, and in the gradual perfecting of self and society.

Other cherished principles follow from these four fundamentals. Personal freedom, most would agree, includes protection from arbitrary power, usually achieved through rule of law. Public government, most would agree, means accountability to the governed, usually achieved through voting, affording every citizen equal voice in public affairs.

You get the idea. If you are an adult, you have quietly enjoyed the fruits of these values. You have entered into an implied social contract in which you give up a measure of personal sovereignty in exchange for social order and access to resources.

Democratic schools extend this invitation to children and teenagers — to enter into a social contract, to grow into ever-expanding freedom and responsibility, to forge the future of self and society. Democratic schools immerse students in a school society based on fundamental values. The result is daily practice of life, liberty, and pursuit of happiness.

## Chapter 3:

# Integral Education: An Emerging Era

B Y ELIMINATING THE DISSONANCE of *autocratic* schooling in *demo-cratic* society, and by incorporating fundamental values of society, democratic schools tend to unify and harmonize education with the world beyond school. Democratic schools transform education, making it more integral to life and society. I use the term "integral education" partly to indicate these qualities. Later I'll point out other unifying and harmonizing qualities of democratic schooling, giving further meaning to the term. In addition, the term alludes to Integral Theory, which is beyond the scope of this book. Integral Theory is relevant partly because it highlights progressive transformations brought about by transcending exhausted systems, such as traditional and modern education, while retaining their essential innovations.

Most pioneering of integral education based on Integral Theory is happening in classrooms in conventional schools. There the aim is generally to teach the standard curriculum more effectively by attending to more dimensions of teaching and learning, and by designing activities for a broader range of developmental levels, kinds of intelligence, and learning styles. In seeming contrast, this book proposes to achieve integral aims by replacing the conventional structures of curriculum-classroom-control with agency-in-community: fostering a school society that better satisfies an integral worldview and aesthetic. This is an unfamiliar approach to most integral education practitioners, and mostly irrelevant in their conventional classroom setting. Nevertheless, the two approaches to integral education are entirely compatible and even synergistic, since integral teaching-learning is easily accommodated (and enhanced) in the integral structure of democratic schooling.

Integral and democratic values are also growing among conventional educators. Many school teachers are uncomfortable with coercive aspects of their work, or recognize in their students a capacity and desire for greater self-determination. Such teachers seek to increase the air of collaboration and democracy in their classrooms. They offer increased choice of assignments and multiple modes of learning. They stretch the curriculum as they can to accommodate students' interests and various kinds of intelligence. They advocate for student choice and involvement in school policymaking. Although these efforts can only go so far in the conventional school setting, they may nevertheless reflect integral values, and set the stage for deeper change.

There is much disagreement about how to reform education, but most voices agree on the need for reform, rooted in changing values, lifestyles, mobility, demographics, technology, economy, and globalization. Integral education is the term I use to indicate emerging and yet-to-emerge paradigms that better align children's education with their development and with the rest of the world. Specifically, I mean potential successors to traditional and modern schools. Democratic schooling clearly qualifies as a good candidate.

Democratic schools are the only well-developed integral school paradigm I know. But just as there are many kinds of traditional and modern schools — such as college prep, Reggio Emilia, Montessori, Waldorf, progressive — there may someday be other paradigms in the integral category, or democratic schools may develop distinct variations. In the meantime, there is widespread interest and experimentation in aspects of integral education in the standard classroom, but only democratic schools are integral at the school level: in structure, governance, administration, culture, and daily program. Democratic schools are alone in a category of schools that are administered bottom-up rather than top-down, and self-organizing rather than command-and-control.

One way of highlighting the categorical difference of integral schools is to notice that traditional and modern paradigms in education, such as Montessori and progressive, prescribe aspects of the *classroom* milieu: teaching, learning, curriculum, and activities. In contrast, the democratic model prescribes aspects of the *school* milieu: structure, governance, rights, and limits. Traditional and modern models are mostly silent about structure-governance-rights-limits, and assume the familiar hierarchical school structure of administration, teachers, and students. In contrast, the democratic model is mostly silent about teaching-learning-curriculum-activities, and assumes the familiar *civil* structure of democratic society. The difference in focus — school versus classroom — places democratic schools alone in a new category of schooling paradigms.

Democratic schools thus represent more a theory of *schooling*, and less a theory of education, teaching, or learning. As we will see, democratic schools accommodate many theories and paradigms of teaching and learning. Instead of prescribed curriculum and teaching methodology, the school supports students in self-chosen pursuits and teaching-learning formats. The democratic school is more a container or venue than a prescription or pre-planned program. Democratic schools might be called curriculum-neutral or post-curricular. This is a categorical break from the past, bringing a windfall of fruit that has been ripening for centuries.

## Traditional to Modern to Integral

Widespread formal education has a short history, dating only to the mid-1800s in the U.S., with high school catching on only toward the end of the century. During that 150-year history, two models of education have dominated: traditional and modern.

*Traditional education* methods include drill-and-practice, rote memorization, recitation, and absolute authority of the teacher. Children are regarded as empty vessels, education as the process of filling those vessels, and teachers as the source of knowledge and discipline. The emphasis is on culturally normative lore: facts, traditions, skills, and beliefs that are presumed to be universally shared and valued.

*Modern education*, becoming widespread in the latter half of the 20th century, emphasizes the linking of subject matter to student experience ("relevance") and the importance of student-teacher interactions. Widely accepted as an advance over traditional, modern education appears in a variety of forms sharing the same essential model: a skilled teacher artfully excites student curiosity and interest, and leads students to prescribed knowledge through preplanned activities.

Note that traditional methods, such as drill-and-practice, are incorporated in the more humane environment and broader scope of modern schools. For example, some studies are best accomplished using rote memorization — think of multiplication tables — and modern schools do not hesitate to use traditional methods when appropriate. Study of elementary science, on the other hand, is sometimes accomplished in modern schools through guided discovery in hands-on activity, aiming to stimulate prescribed personal insights. Thus, modern education includes aspects of the traditional model, and adds its own new possibilities.

*Integral education* is the successor to modern education. As exemplars of integral education, democratic schools are the natural successor to modern schools, a categorical upgrade. Just as modern schools incorporated traditional methods, democratic schools incorporate traditional *and* modern methods, integrating the two with new methods that are distinctly integral. For example, democratic schools include rote memorization (a traditional method), guided discovery (a modern method), and near-stage transmission (an integral method I'll discuss later).

We can loosely characterize aspects of the three movements with the following suggestive themes. These are abbreviated generalizations rather than crisp defining statements, conveying flow and flavor at the cost of depth and precision. Notice the tendency for modern themes to *envelop* and *include* traditional themes, and the tendency for integral themes to include *both*, each era more inclusive than the last:

## Suggestive Themes in Education Movements

|  | Traditional → | Modern → | Integral |
|---|---|---|---|
| Target: | Facts | Insights | Development |
| Method: | Telling | Doing | Living |
| Imperative: | Obey | Think | Explore |
| Curriculum: | Static | Prescribed | Open-ended |
| Student rights: | Inmate | Patient | Citizen |
| Teacher's role: | Master | Director | Resource |

The advance from traditional to modern to integral in education flows in deeper currents of history. For half a millennium, the Western world has trended toward increasing realization of *individual autonomy* and *self-determination*, and decreasing emphasis on *social conformity* and *autocratic authority*.

Thus, integral education follows the rise of personal autonomy in roughly the last 500 years: emergence of the individual from the collective, exemplified by modern science and the Enlightenment (1600s, 1700s); political revolutions and large-scale democracy (1700s); abolition of slavery (1800s); women's enfranchisement (early 1900s). Since the mid-1900s, individual empowerment has expanded rapidly: civil rights, liberation movements, hippie movement, self-help industries, personal technologies, and historic spread of democracy. More recently, the rise of personal spirituality at the expense of traditional religious institutions indicates continued realization of personal autonomy and individual capacity for self-transcendence.

Integral education flows from this centuries-old stream of thought, including children more fully in society's embrace by applying principles of personal autonomy and self-responsibility in schools. Basic educational aims remain the same: actualization and socialization, sustenance of the individual and society.

Historians observe that new paradigms often emerge in response to changes in the techno-economic base of society. Such is the case now in education. Just as traditional education served primarily agrarian society, and modern education served primarily industrial society, now comes integral education serving society in the post-industrial information age.

Rather than reject what came before, democratic schooling embraces a legacy of strengths. From traditional worldviews, democratic schools inherit values of law and order, civic duty, and tradition. From modern and progressive worldviews, democratic schools inherit values of progress, science, technology, and individualism. From the postmodern, democratic schools inherit values of inclusion, cultural pluralism, compassion, global community, and renewed spirituality.

Democratic schooling takes to heart the best of the past, while adapting to profound changes in technology, society, and family. The integral result combines structures, systems, and practices to make a home for all worldviews, stigmatizing none and holding to global ideals of self-determination, co-existence, and collective responsibility.

## Fill a Bucket, Light a Fire, Fan a Flame

"Fill a Bucket" could be a guiding metaphor for traditional schooling, typically serving agrarian times and places. Teachers poured knowledge into students. But a century of science debunked that idea: knowledge is not a substance, and learning is nothing like filling an empty vessel. Now we know that knowledge is constructed by the learner, the outcome of an internal process. The child must be engaged to build knowledge, and engagement is best when secured by the child's personal interest and intrinsic motivation.

In modern schooling, the metaphor of filling a bucket was replaced with another: "Light a Fire." Perhaps you have heard the William Butler Yeats quote: "Education is the lighting of a fire, not the filling of a pail." The idea has inspired millions of teachers and shaped classroom practices in modern schools. As suggested in this metaphor, the teacher sparks interest in a curricular objective — lighting the fire — and then leads students to construct the prescribed knowledge and insights. Then the teacher repeats the process, lighting another fire for the next curricular objective, and so on for 12 years through a predetermined chain of curricular objectives. The aim is to harness the power of children's curiosity, an essential condition for meaningful learning.

You may already know the problems with that. Too often the student's fires fizzle, and too often the teacher burns out.

Putting a teacher in front of a classroom of students may seem an efficient way to teach, an efficient use of the expensive "human resource," but motivating and synchronizing a roomful of students, day after day, is nearly impossible even for talented teachers. Crucially, whether or not it's an efficient way to deploy teachers, it turns out to be a poor way for students to learn.

Perhaps worse, children come to ignore their own interests, hopes, learning styles, internal states, and even physical needs. With a teacher's constant direction, children's introspective skills are undermined and tend to deteriorate or fail to develop. After 12 years of such conditioning, many enter adult society with little sense of purpose, direction, or initiative. Some seem to be waiting, as they have been trained, for someone to tell them what to do next. Rigid curriculum and teacher-directed schooling tend to produce apathy, passive compliance, and dependence on authority — not helpful in today's economy, out of step with today's values, and not conducive to fulfilling life.

In summary, the metaphor "Light a Fire" suggests too dominant a role for the teacher, and too submissive a role for the student.

Today's standard school systems originated in the ideas of the Industrial Revolution. Schools were thought of as factories. Children are the raw materials. Teachers are the machines. The raw materials are processed through grades of refinement and subjected to quality control testing along the way. The final product is standardized young adults who meet the predetermined specifications.

The idea was to produce workers who are interchangeable, like manufactured goods, to operate in factories and offices like cogs in machines; workers who were punctual and obedient. That was the mode of thinking that prevailed in the fervor of the Industrial Revolution of the 1800s and early 1900s when today's school systems and structures were laid down. That was the vision for American education, strangely incompatible with the nation's founding values. The vision has changed now, but the structures remain.

We no longer seek that sort of uniformity. Values have changed, and knowledge of human development has advanced. Today we know that each child is one-of-a-kind and in constant flux. Each child embodies a unique character and changing configuration of personal factors; a unique and changing mix of interests, abilities, motivations, and patterns of learning.

We know that children generally develop through characteristic milestones and lines of development, with important individual variations in sequence, timing, and potential. There is no standard or best developmental sequence or timing, and there is no universal standard or best way to teach or learn. Science now confirms what parents have known all along: each child is unique.

In "Light a Fire," we got the fire part right: the importance of children's spirited engagement. What we got wrong is thinking the teacher has to ignite it. Children are born with fires ablaze, passionate and persistent in pursuit of their universal agenda: strive, thrive, and grow. It's the sustainable energy of education.

Embracing what we now know about children's development, integral education suggests a new metaphor: "Fan a Flame." The fires are already burning. Democratic schools engage children's natural curiosity and tendency to strive, thrive, and grow. Instead of trying to stimulate the same interest in a roomful of children all at once, democratic schools set each student free to follow their interests like stepping stones. Just like life beyond school, each student picks out a path determined by their interests, needs, abilities, opportunities, and choices, powered by fires burning from birth.

Self-powered and immersed in community, rather than goaded by teachers, children's lives and learning in democratic schools are more fulfilling and meaningful from day to day. Life satisfaction is not postponed until tomorrow and tomorrow and tomorrow, nor subordinated to a curriculum that may or may not be relevant in an unpredictable future.

Furthermore, the self-knowledge and skills acquired while building a satisfying life in school extend seamlessly to a lifetime of fulfillment and engagement beyond school. Democratic schools integrate school and life.

## The Radical Difference

Fill a Bucket, Light a Fire, Fan a Flame. Do you see the trend in these metaphors for the teacher's role? With better understanding of human development, the focus shifts from the teacher to the child, from top-down to bottom-up, from command-and-control to individual agency and self-organizing community. This trend parallels larger social transformations from farming economy to manufacturing economy to knowledge economy. Fill a Bucket was the dominant metaphor in agrarian times. Light a Fire is associated with industrial economy. Fan a Flame is more recent, emerging with the knowledge economy and growing up with Google.

Democratic schools replace top-down, centrally planned management of the school with bottom-up democracy. The American nation began with just such a bold inversion into democracy: a constitutional formalization of individual empowerment. In addition, global economies today rest on the economic democracy of free enterprise and free markets. Extension of democracy to children in school resonates with national ideals and global economy, and also with hundreds of years of advance towards universal enfranchisement and self-determination.

The promise of democracy, in both government and economies, is the capacity to self-organize and self-renew, to adapt to changing conditions, to evolve higher solutions to increasingly complex problems. Democratic schools thus adapt more quickly and more effectively to societal, cultural, and economic changes than other schools with their massive inertia of entrenched bureaucracy and economic interests.

While children's enfranchisement in school governance is a striking innovation — and an elegant way to bring young people into society's fold — it is really an incremental extension of the past, and a hopeful next step. Democracy is old news, newly applied in schools, but only half the story.

The radical difference of democratic schooling lies in the activation and acceleration of children's innate tendencies: to strive and grow, to seek and master new knowledge, to leap to higher orders of thinking, to join in community, to transcend self, to perfect society, to seek infinity.

In democratic schools, this radical difference originates in freedom, authority, and responsibility, practiced on two levels: personal and collective, or individual and societal. On the personal level, children experience *freedom* to follow curiosity, *authorship* of their own lives, and *responsibility* for their actions. On the collective or community level, children experience *freedom* to collaborate in culture, *authority* to govern public society, and *responsibility* for the common welfare.

The radical difference is in the school's binding of freedom, authority, and responsibility: the practice of personal and collective self-determination in a child-scale rendition of the larger world, reflecting its beauty and its imperfection. The democratic school is a living library and laboratory for personal and social experimentation, a microcosmic world in children's hands and minds.

Integral education and democratic schooling arrive at the intersection of historical trends: the rise of individual empowerment and the shift from industrial to informational economy. Democratic schools may herald an emerging era of basics: supporting children's growth in personal fulfillment and engagement in society. That's education.

Chapter 4:

# Democratic Schools: A Better Fit

AS I WILL SHOW, DEMOCRATIC SCHOOLING TRANSFORMS education by improving alignments on three levels: between school and society, within school, and between children and school. Along the line from society to school to child, democratic schools offer practical continuity, purposeful consistency, and greater life satisfaction. With improved alignment, society's purposes are more fully served, schools operate with greater harmony and efficiency, and children launch fulfilling lives. Let's look at these three, one at a time: society, school, and child.

## Aligning School with Society's Ideals

Most children's experience of school is shockingly disconnected from their later experience as adults in society. In school, most children do not experience fundamental ideals of freedom, law-abiding citizenship, due process, free enterprise, and equal voice in governance. American schools mostly deny children the ideals on which the nation is founded. From a child's perspective, school looks like a rigidly controlled society run by unelected dictators. Why would we want to expose children to 12 years or more under a repressive political system so contrary to our ideals for adult society?

Instead, democratic schools immerse children in *freedom, responsibility,* and *community,* such as we hope they will know as adults. Democratic schools are built on the bedrock human rights of life, liberty, and pursuit of happiness. Governed in harmony with principles of Western democracies, democratic schools practice what we preach as a nation, empowering children as active, responsible citizens from an early age.

Furthermore, in a free and rapidly changing economy, school-as-microcosm keeps pace with a world of rapid change, and better prepares children for entry into that world. Conditions today favor those who are self-directed, quick-learning, resourceful, and original. Children and society are better served by schooling for adaptability, creativity, skills of access, critical analysis, divergent thinking, initiative, leadership, self-awareness, and community awareness.

Democratic schools better align students' experience of school with ambient society, culture, government, and economy: enfranchising students, bestowing citizenship, and prompting engagement. The result is greater grace and continuity as children graduate from school into the world at large. Children are primed for a fulfilling adulthood.

Importantly, alignment of democratic schools with society is not merely a calculated educational device, but rather a genuine expression of the underlying ideals. Democratic schools efficiently transmit values and sustain society and culture, by embodying the values we seek to transmit.

## Alignments Within the School

Democratic schooling elegantly combines essential practices of traditional and modern schools, places them in a broader school context, and adds vital new practices, previously unavailable in schools. Specifically, the democratic school integrates *learning methods* (traditional, modern, integral), *social classes* (student, faculty, administration), and *daily functions* (learning, teaching, managing).

### Learning Methods

Democratic schools embrace essential learning methods of traditional and modern schools, and add new (integral) methods, previously unavailable to children in schools.

Modern schools introduced modern teaching-learning methods but also employ traditional methods, such as drill and practice, when those methods best address the needs at hand. In similar fashion, democratic schools introduced integral methods but employ traditional and modern methods when they best address the needs.

For example, learning a foreign language typically includes memorization, a traditional method. Mastery of cursive writing may be best accomplished with drill and practice, also a traditional method. Science studies might call for lab experiments guided by a skilled teacher and designed to evoke the ah-hah experiences that are a goal of modern education. All of these examples are commonly seen in democratic schools.

Democratic schools also accommodate a range of roles for the adult teacher, adopted freely between student and teacher, in harmony with personal learning styles and the demands of the subject matter. The teacher might serve as drill master, information provider, collaborator, tutor, advisor, mentor, co-learner, or supportive friend. Some of these roles are uniquely enabled by democratic schools.

Democratic schools include classroom teaching, tutoring, independent study, and the whole range of learning mode possibilities employed in other schools.

Democratic schools also add powerful new modes and methods, previously unavailable in schools, such as fully deployed integrated curriculum (discussed below), systemic or meta-message learning, public process, accelerated culture, near-stage transmission, multiple lines of development, self-balanced development, functional apprenticeship, and more. I'll discuss these and others later, in Part Three.

## Social Classes

In democratic schools, students and staff mix freely. Groupings form spontaneously or by design, often coalescing around shared interests, abilities, opportunities, and friendships. All students and staff are members of the school's primary governing body (typically called School Meeting), and all are subject to its authority, including laws and judicial processes. All are required to perform certain civic duties, such as daily housekeeping chores and judicial service. (My daily chore this year is to tidy and vacuum the Conference Room.)

All enjoy equal rights of voice and vote, and equal protection under the law. There are no privileged classes who are *above* the law or can make up rules unilaterally, such as teachers and administrators in traditional and modern schools. And there are no underclasses who are *excluded* from governing authority, such as students in traditional and modern schools.

Staff members, who are paid employees, and students, who are paying customers, clearly stand in different relation to the school, and have different legal and moral duties. Nevertheless, the two groups are generally equal in the eyes of school law and equal in governing rights. Being a staff member does not confer civil authority over students. Civil authority and public responsibilities are assumed by election to public offices, many of which are filled by students.

Of course, some functions are more effectively performed by adults than by children. For example, staff members (usually the only adults present) often prevail in policy debates during sessions of School Meeting, partly because adults more often have relevant experience, partly because adults tend to have greater skill in political persuasion, and partly because kids have a tendency to defer to adults. Regarding this last factor, staff members are usually sensitive to such age-based deference and sometimes back off, call attention to the dynamic, or encourage speaking up.

Adults also stand apart in service as school officials. At The Circle School, for example, certain elected offices, such as Admissions Director and Business Manager, have always been filled by staff members. Although students and staff are equally eligible to run for election to all offices, students are usually not attracted to some offices, and voters tend to prefer adults in certain positions. Candidates tend to self-select realistically.

Also widely recognized is a hallmark of the information age: students often surpass adults in knowledge of current technology and culture. The point is that differences in age, experience, maturity, and knowledge are significant in context, but do not disenfranchise anyone or lead to divisive social classes. Authority is shared by all, and flows from the governed populace to its designated officials, some of whom are grown-ups.

Social leveling of this kind creates a climate in which children can relate to adults with ease, free of fear and without the burdens of power imbalance. Unburdened relationships between staff and students are vital, paving the way for deeper self-disclosure, greater trust, and safer community. Students more freely seek knowledge and advice from grown-ups, and closely study adult knowledge and ways. Staff members are in an ideal position to convey their adult perspective and evaluative judgments to students, in the same sort of context that a mature adult talks with a same-age friend: sensitive to the friend's need and receptivity; sensitive to the friend's history and aspirations; sensitive to one's own degree of concern and need to speak up; and sensitive to privacy and confidence.

In relative absence of social classes, traditional teacher-student power imbalances vanish, and with them barriers to adult-child and mixed-age friendships, making for a more unitary, integral society.

## Daily Functions

Learning, teaching, and school administration are also integrated. In the busy flow of the daily culture, every person is both student and teacher at various times, perhaps learning *by* teaching as often as not. This happens constantly, fluidly, and informally, without planning and typically without remark or even awareness. As in any active culture, parties to the give-and-take dialogue are learning and teaching, back and forth, reversing roles or simultaneously engaged in both. The blurring of boundaries, shifting of roles, and mixing of ages powerfully integrate and accelerate transmission of information, knowledge, principles, values, ideas, theories, skills, and local lore.

In contrast, traditional and modern schools tend to sharply define the roles of student and teacher, the postures of learning and teaching. Traditional and modern schools also limit the free-flowing nature of human culture and collaboration, by imposing noncollaborative methods, and by parsing the day into isolated pockets of time and subject domain, thus inhibiting integration.

Democratic schooling embraces essential traditional and modern values and learning patterns, and embeds them in the stew of human culture in free society. The contributions of traditional and modern education are not lost or ignored, but are subsumed in the larger whole of democratic education, which adds culture and social interaction as constructive educating influences.

In addition, administration of the school represents a profoundly significant domain of teaching and learning opportunities. The School Meeting, comprising all students and staff, manages the school's business and daily affairs as its chief executive. Administration is an integral part of the student experience. Employees of the school, regardless of credentials and job functions, are hired and managed by the School Meeting. Staff and students together, by majority vote in formal parliamentary procedure, make executive and policy decisions about facilities management, hiring, employee benefits, budget, appropriation of funds, suspensions and expulsions, deployment of staff, committee structure, and so on.

The School Meeting commonly relies on adult experience, and delegates substantial authority to its officials, particularly adult staff members, but nevertheless retains authority to overrule, intercede, or amend policy at any time. In addition, students serve in many roles and elected offices with real authority for school administration. Shared responsibility for the business and management of the school involves all members in real-life matters that are beyond children's reach in other kinds of schools.

Thus, daily functions of learning, teaching, and administration are integrated, one function blending into another, one role disappearing into another, fluidly from moment to moment, day to day, year to year.

---

In summary, at the institutional level, within the school, democratic schooling introduces new integration of *learning methods, social classes,* and *daily functions.* The result is vibrant culture, ready friendship, immersive community, transparent administration, social responsibility, personal efficacy, and vastly expanded opportunity. Entirely new dimensions of possibility open up to provoke and support children's learning and growth.

---

## Homework

There are three 10ish-year-olds at the Kitchen booth doing homework. "I have so much homework," they keep saying. They've made two bags of microwave popcorn between them, covered the table in paper towels, and poured the popcorn out into a huge pile. They are munching on popcorn, busily and happily chattering about Español, math, and first aid. Every so often, one of them asks a question about how to say or spell "I speak" or "I don't understand" in Spanish, and the others respond with their partial knowledge. They talk through it, but don't ask me, sitting a few feet away, though they know I have the answers. Once, when I hear    them say, "We'll ask Beth later," I can't help but interject with the spelling of the Spanish word for English. They thank me politely, and their pencils scurry across their papers, but they don't ask me the next question, either. After I walk away, I realize I got it wrong, combining French and Spanish, and return to tell them of my error. They thank me politely again, and, having moved on to multiplication, pull out their Spanish pages to make the correction. Then back to the math, up on their knees and toes on the benches, huddled over the worksheets with interest and excitement and, for some reason, a twinkle of mischievous delight over their faces.

I realize after watching for a moment that the twinkle is not mischief, but the sparkle of play. They're playing homework. It is a real study session, but they're also using their voluntary homework as a prop in a fantasy scenario, acting out what they must imagine "real" homework to be like. It looks to me something like a college study session, but just as playing house is a lot more fun than doing the dishes and mopping the floor, playing homework is a lot more fun than memorizing multiplication tables. Then again, they really are memorizing multiplication tables, even while they're playing. This is the thing parents and teachers everywhere dream of and work for, that elusive intersection between learning and fun, but here it didn't require any intervention. Just the opposite.

*— Circle School staff member Julia James ('98)*

## Aligning School with Children's Lives

From a child's perspective, democratic schools present a more seamless (integral) fit between school, home, life, and the world. At school, children pursue their own agenda on their own schedule or no schedule, engaging people and resources, supported and constrained by community.

When the purposes of school are aligned with children's own aspirations, school becomes downright exciting: a place for conducting the business of childhood; a marketplace of ideas, activities, experiences; an adventure in independence from parents; a real world, a child's proprietary domain.

In democratic schools, interests are awakened and intrinsic motivation is engaged more often and more deeply than in forced-curriculum schools. With time, people, and resources to follow interests, students in democratic schools pursue the same intense process of task selection, learning, and growth that they have pursued since infancy and can sustain for a lifetime. When the interest is satisfied, or a greater interest emerges, the whole process begins again. This is the cyclical process of human growth, and children are born experts.

Of course, alignment with children's interests can also happen in traditional and modern schools, particularly for those children whose current interests and purposes coincide with those of the school and the currently imposed curriculum. In democratic schools, however, no such coincidence is necessary, and neither are tedious efforts to pry open disinterested pupils. Instead, the democratic school itself is a set of resources available to children for employment in their current interests and purposes.

In the language of educators, alignment with children's purposes is achieved partly through "integrated curriculum," in contrast to the usual discrete curriculum (which is *also* practiced in democratic schools when students choose it).

In a discrete curriculum, segments of time are devoted to exclusive study of subject matter that is not ordinarily encountered in isolation; for example, spelling lessons from 9:10 to 9:35 and arithmetic from 9:40 to 10:05. Of course, spelling and arithmetic are important skills for most people, because those skills are demanded in everyday life. The point is that in everyday life outside of school, spelling and arithmetic do not usually appear by themselves. They are aspects of a great many everyday experiences — using a social media website, buying food — but spelling and arithmetic are built into those experiences, integrated with them, not isolated as separate subjects.

In an integrated curriculum, students encounter spelling and arithmetic (and a host of other subjects) as part of other activities — typically, activities that are inherently valued by students. Cooking and construction projects, for example, might require spelling, arithmetic, and other skills. Publishing a yearbook or blog might require many more.

In short, integrated curriculum presents much of the same basic knowledge as standard curriculum, plus more, but does not dis-integrate real-life activities into individual subject components for isolated study. The primary benefits of integrated curriculum, when combined with student self-direction, are that it more deeply engages student interest, resulting in dramatically greater learning efficiency, and also respects children's autonomy and self-determination.

Integrated curriculum is only part of the picture. Alignment with students' interests is primarily achieved in democratic schools simply through student choice and self-direction, whether the subject of study is embedded in integrated activities or isolated for out-of-context study. Algebra, for example, is less commonly encountered in integrated activities. Nevertheless, students who choose to study algebra in democratic schools pursue their studies with the same self-motivation that might be applied to integrated activities, such as cooking and construction projects. The essential insight is that, in democratic schools, both kinds of studies — integrated and discrete — are driven by intrinsic motivation, a subject we will examine more closely later.

Homework is also better aligned with children's interests, a big improvement for many families. Democratic schools eliminate the expectation that parents will enforce the demands of school upon their children, in the form of homework. Since homework in democratic schools serves the student's own purposes, there is no need for parental enforcement. The student has taken on the assignment by choice. Even if the student fails to complete the assignment, the school imposes no burden on parents and the parent-child relationship. The matter is between the student and the teacher, or between the student and those who might be disappointed by the student's neglect of an assignment. For example, a foreign language learning group may be let down when its members neglect to bring resources, memorize vocabulary, or otherwise do as they agreed, because the group's progress toward fluent conversation in the language is impeded, and the class becomes less satisfying.

In traditional and modern schools, the demands of homework can unduly intrude on family life, driving a wedge between some parents and their children. This source of tension simply vanishes in democratic schools. Families who have experienced chronic homework stress, and subsequent elimination of it in democratic schools, report lasting transformation of their children, their parent-child relationship, and the role of school in their lives. They discover new harmony and rhythm in the family-child-school triangle: "I got my son back," as parents have put it.

Furthermore, democratic schools are more compatible with changes in family dynamics. The trends are well-known: fewer stay-at-home parents, more single-parent families, ubiquitous computers, social media, access to information, and children's increased purchasing power. For better or worse, these trends contribute to children's earlier demands for independence and engagement in society. No longer expected to be "seen and not heard," children and teens actively participate in family dialogue and decision-making. Not so, in traditional and modern schools, where repression of independence and denial of self-determination often lead to alienation. Enfranchisement, as in democratic schools, is the remedy.

Deep alignment with children's interests transforms school and its role in children's lives. The democratic school is a place of joy and purpose, a place to pursue one's important lifework, a place children regard as their own. It is no wonder that student responsibility and stewardship for their school emerge, and no wonder that students sometimes ask can't we please stay open year-round.

To summarize: alignment with children's interests and aspirations is deliberate, systematic, and constant in democratic schools, not merely occasional and coincidental as it is in traditional and modern schools. Systematic alignment with children's purposes is an essential aspect of integral education, exemplified by democratic schools.

As ten-year-old Jyles said, "I just come here and I live my life."

---

## I Want to Fly

Shaun was 12 years old when he said "I want to fly." He and the External Resources Coordinator brainstormed and set out to place Shaun around airplanes and pilots. Sounds like an airport, they thought, so they called one up on the phone and asked if Shaun could be an intern there, working without pay, doing whatever he could to be useful. No, said the airport. That won't fly.

So they tried another airport — this time a small, privately owned airstrip. Sure, said the owner, let's talk. Shaun went to the airport once a week that first year, and Matt and Andy went along, too. Shaun remembers he swept the floor a lot, and sorted nuts and bolts, and tightened screws one day for six hours straight. Sounds tedious? Not to Shaun: the screws he tightened were on a reconstructed World War II fighter. He loved it.

Matt and Andy stopped going after that school year, but Shaun continued when school started again. He helped assemble an aluminum wing for a Percival Provost airplane. He learned sheet metal working, machining, welding, woodworking, painting, airplane fabric covering, and on and on. Occasionally on weekends — Bingo! — the owner took Shaun flying.

The second summer, Shaun worked at the airport for pay, and the next year, at age 14, he started flying. At 15 he began formal lessons, which he paid for entirely out of his wages. At 16 he was part of a team that won a "Golden Wrench Award" in a national competition among antique airplane restorers.

After Shaun left The Circle School, he went to work at the airport full-time. At 18 years old, he got his student license, and at 19 — ta-da! — Shaun was a licensed airplane pilot. During his last year at the airport, he was the manager of a corporate division of the company that owned the airport.

The story doesn't end there. Shaun worked as a mechanic, an airplane restoration technician, and a private pilot. He earned a bachelor's degree in Professional Aeronautics (Embry-Riddle Aeronautical University) and numerous industry ratings. Recently, with the backing of investors, Shaun opened a flight school and maintenance shop. For Shaun, the sky's the limit.

---

## The Moral of Shaun's Story

Shaun's story is fun to tell and inspiring to hear. But what if his interest had ended after a month? Or after that first year? What if he had never taken lessons and never gotten his pilot's license? What if he had later pursued microbiology instead of aviation? Would Shaun's airport internship then have been a failure? And what about Andy and Matt? Was the enterprise just a waste of time for them?

For every story like Shaun's — a passionate interest, pursued as far as the chase can go — there are thousands of stories of interests developed less deeply, and then apparently dropped, or developed just as deeply but without the drama or outward visibility of aviation.

Those thousands of untold stories weave the fabric of life in democratic schools. There's the girl who dissected a cow eyeball, and found that she didn't like it. There's the boy who played with a guitar for a couple of months — never to become a rock star. There's the child who wandered in and helped build the new workbench in the Art Room, exploring an interest in screwdrivers for a few minutes.

And then there's Matt, who tagged along with Shaun. Turns out that Matt learned about tool-and-die work during that internship, and enjoyed it. Would you believe that today he's a professional tool-and-die maker? He's not, but you found it believable, didn't you? The point is that no matter what Matt is doing today, he experienced genuine interest, developed it to his own satisfaction, detected that he was through with that interest for the time being, and redirected his attention to other pursuits, having been expanded by his knowledge of tool-and-die making. It was an experience of self-direction, concentration, acquisition of knowledge about technology, and about himself.

So the moral of Shaun's delightful story is not that kids should pursue their interests because it might lead to a career, or even a lifelong interest. The moral is that the joy is in the pursuit, and the education is deep: new knowledge and skills, learning about resources and how to learn, and love of the chase.

## Bliss It Isn't

The point is *not* that children are always happy in democratic schools. In addition to its many joys, life presents substantial burdens, challenges, pains, and disappointments. Democratic schools do not attempt to shield children from these, but rather to provide a relatively safe place in which to experience them, with significant freedom to navigate by inner lights and outer helpers.

We cannot guarantee happiness for every child, but we *can* provide ample opportunity for its pursuit. Democratic schools are the scaled-down world in which students practice life. Through years of practice, children and teens increasingly realize personal potentials, while seeking satisfaction in self-chosen domains of activity, knowledge, and skill; and develop increasingly fulfilling ways of participating in culture, community, and society. Sometimes the pursuit brings the happiness of pleasure, sometimes the happiness of achievement, sometimes disappointment, often the fulfilling satisfaction of authentic effort, and always learning. Can the striving itself be bliss?

Observers have noted that democratic schools tend to be more demanding of effort than other schools. The structure and culture of democratic schools create obstacles that do not exist in other kinds of schools — challenges to children to deal with real-world problems.

Field trips, for example, illustrate both sides of the freedom-and-challenge equation. Students are free to initiate field trips of all kinds: an hour's walk along the creek, lunch at the pizza place, an all-day bus trip for

40 to a distant city zoo, an overnight backpacking trek, or even a 10-day cultural adventure in Denmark. Spectacular possibilities. Imagine the effort required to make such excursions happen, and imagine students of all ages bearing substantial responsibility for it — planning, fundraising, recruiting staff participation and other adult helpers, permission slips, emergency contact information, compliance with the Field Trip Policy, mileage reimbursement for drivers, paperwork before and after, and so on. In standard schools, it's the adults who think up the field trips and then do the planning and preparation, usually before any child has even expressed an interest. Not so in democratic schools, where students think it up and make it happen, with staff participating and supporting — but crucially, not ensuring that it actually happens. The Denmark trip happened after two years of more-than-weekly meetings, fundraising sales of lunches prepared by the group, and detailed planning of itinerary and logistics.

Democratic governance creates other challenges, too, such as daunting judicial proceedings around rule infractions and public debate over controversial issues such as regulation of skateboarding, viewing of online material, and how to spend school funds.

Importantly, the challenging demands encountered by students in democratic schools are *not* designed as educational devices. Systems, policies, and procedures are put in place by the school's democratic governance to help ensure safety, order, and access to community resources; in short, to manage the school efficiently and effectively. There is no attempt to sneak in a hidden curriculum. Life provides an endless stream of learning.

Perhaps the fundamental challenge presented to children in democratic schools is the challenge of self-responsibility in community. In contrast, modern schooling affords children only superficial experience of self-responsibility and community. Many young people are isolated from personally meaningful life challenge until after graduation from college — or middle age. Some leave school without much sense of purpose, self-awareness, and life management — barriers to effective adulthood and self-actualization.

In democratic schools, children experience the challenge of self-responsibility in community continuously from an early age. In a manner of speaking, this is the curriculum of democratic schools, practiced daily by every student. Such experience is essential to personal fulfillment and satisfying engagement in society, and is thus at the heart of education — struggle, bliss, and all.

---

## *Arnie's First Paper*

Arnie enrolled when he was four years old and stayed through all his school years. He was always curious, busy, and socially engaged, but never did much writing. Shortly into his first semester at college, a class assignment required him to write a paper — something he had never done. So after class, he went up to the professor, told him he'd never written a paper and asked for suggestions. I imagine that professor must have been startled by two things about Arnie. He must have wondered how did this guy get into my college class without ever having written a paper! And here he is, admitting to it as though it's no big deal!

The professor suggested he visit the Student Writing Center for help. Oh, said Arnie, he didn't know that was available, but great, that's what he'd do. And that's what he did. Arnie probably struggled through that first paper, perhaps pulling an all-nighter to get it done, but he did it.

Two aspects of Arnie's first college paper adventure stand out to me as typical of democratic school graduates. First, when Arnie encountered a challenge, he approached it matter-of-factly, using the resources before him. That's what he'd been doing for 15 years of democratic schooling, preschool through high school. Second, whatever difficulties he faced, he just wrote the paper. He did the hard work he had to do in order to get to the goal he was after. It was his life, his choice, his to own. That's typical of our graduates. No excuses, no blame, no shame, no special pleading. Just do it.

The postscript is beside the point, but it's fun to tell. Arnie continued on, probably writing many more papers, and earned his degree. A few years later, I learned that Arnie then went on to law school, took the bar exam, and passed on his first try.

---

## Human Development and Democratic Schooling

Growing children create and explore a series of worldviews, each the essence of a stage of development. In time, each way of seeing the world gives way to another more expansive perspective.

Like a dessert parfait (and like contemporary society, too), the age-mixed democratic school is layered with worldviews. The young child is immersed in innocence, imagination, and family. In mid-childhood comes a concrete worldview, finding identity in hierarchy, authority, rules, and roles. Adolescence brings self-consciousness, individualism, independence, and shifting focus from family to peers. Teens come to value reason, ideals, and sometimes pluralism, inclusion, and global conscience. With each stage, the enduring traits and values of earlier stages remain, now in the service of enlarged awareness facing new challenges.

Each stage also typically brings expanded mental and intellectual capacity. For example, young children tend to have only a vague sense of time and tend to blend memories with imagination. Later this "magical" thinking gives way to literal understandings and "operational" thinking — the mental capacity to plan a sequence of actions. Typically around adolescence and beyond, preteens and teens further develop abstract thinking ("formal operational"): capacities to consider themes, principles, ideas, and ideals — a mental revolution enabling idealism, principled living, and social activism.

In addition to *stages* of development, science discloses *lines* of development or *multiple intelligences*: social, emotional, introspective, intellectual, spiritual, linguistic, logical-mathematical, spatial, physical-kinesthetic, aesthetic, musical, and so on. Generally, development proceeds more or less independently from line to line, with some prerequisites. For example, empathy (viewed as a line of development) depends on emotional capacity to experience a variety of emotional states and cognitive capacity to figure out another person's emotional state — what it must feel like to be in their situation. Relative maturity across lines of development varies over time, perhaps with a spurt of growth in one line while another languishes. For example, it is not uncommon for a child's intellectual maturity to seem out of balance with their emotional or social maturity.

Complicating the developmental picture further are wide-ranging individual differences in children's interests, talents, hopes, fears, personality, energy level, preferred learning styles, and so on. Complicating the picture still further, development is not linear or constant, having its twists and turns, setbacks, regressions, repressions, dissociations, and mystifying leaps. In spite of broad patterns, human development is a messy affair, sprawling across a vast mindscape of possibility. Each person grows uniquely and unpredictably, nudged to novelty in endless mixing of cultural, environmental, and personal factors.

Democratic schooling accommodates the messiness, uniqueness, and unpredictability. Given the opportunity, children's nature is to actively engage the process: build a worldview, explore its possibilities, discover limitations, upgrade to a new one. The driving force is children's inborn impulse: to learn, to grow, to leap to higher orders of thinking, to join in community, to create and transcend self. Speaking poetically, this is the essence and delight of nature seeking infinity embodied in a child.

Each step brings expanded capacity for personal fulfillment and engagement in the world. Democratic schools confer neither status nor stigma on any particular stage or line. Earlier stages are not treated as deficiencies to be corrected or pathologies in need of therapy, and childhood is not hurried as a race to college. Instead, children experience the self-satisfying fullness of each stage, and may therefore be less likely to leave developmental gaps and repressions to resurface in life crisis, years or decades later.

---

Democratic schooling is thus a better fit at three levels: society, school, and child. First, children live and learn in a school world that is more like the "real" world. Second, the school teaches more effectively by applying a multitude of *learning methods,* eliminating *social classes,* and blending *daily functions.* And third, the school enables each child to more fully follow and develop their unique self and life path.

## And Finally There's This

I've laid out a case for democratic schooling. I have pointed out the mismatch of autocratic schools in democratic society; historical trends towards greater autonomy and self-determination, shifting from top-down control to bottom-up self-organization; sociocultural and techno-economic changes; increased understanding of how children learn and grow; and harmonizing alignments of democratic schooling.

Still it feels incomplete without the piece that most compels me: the spirit and sparkle of children practicing life as free agents in human community. I know nothing more hopeful, delighting, and endlessly surprising.

Children's radiant freshness, inventive mischief, crushing disappoint-ments, and exuberant joys are boundless. In community with children, I imagine I will live forever.

I'm not alone in this experience of palpable infinity. I hear it in the sto-ries and see it in the eyes of colleagues and parents in democratic schools. Daily we witness children's self-powered growth made visible. Often loud and chaotic, too.

Without the support of formal research, I find that children's joy of life is strongly associated with character and intelligence. By joy of life, I mean soul-satisfying fulfillment in adventures of discovery, mastery of knowledge, struggle with personally meaningful challenge, deep meeting of minds and hearts, and many kinds of failure and success. I find that education at its best is indistinguishable from hearty life.

Crucially, we see in our graduates what we cherish in ourselves, our friends, and our heroes. They are decent people: ethical, trustworthy, tolerant, humane, and just. They are curious, self-aware, down-to-earth, intelligent, and bright-eyed alert. They are open, creative, active, and adaptable. In short, they live well and we like to be with them.

## Democratic Schools:
## A Better Fit for Society, School, and Child

| SOCIETY | Freedom Responsibility Democracy Community | Democratic schools echo the "real world" in *structure*, *culture*, and *governance*. Young adults emerge fluent in active citizenship, self-responsibility, and the making of culture and community. |
|---|---|---|
| SCHOOL | Learning methods | *Traditional, modern, integral:* all modes and methods are practiced in democratic schools, freely matched to individual needs and purposes. |
| | Social classes | *Students, faculty, administrators:* one community. All are subject to school laws and civil authority. All are empowered citizens. |
| | Daily functions | *Learning, teaching, administration:* all persons participate in all functions. |

| | | |
|---|---|---|
| **CHILD** | **Alignment with children's aims and interests** | Children freely choose and direct their own activity, engaging school resources as needed. Self-direction respects personal autonomy, activates intrinsic motivation. "I just come here and live my life." |
| | **Alignment with children's development** | Each child is one-of-a-kind and in constant flux, a swirling mix of interests, abilities, motivations, and personality. Self-directed education connects kids to the where, when, and how of what they'll learn best. |

Chapter 5:

# Seven Ideas

S o far, I have introduced democratic schooling generally, described
The Circle School in particular, and outlined its founding principles.
I reviewed the historical trends leading to democratic schooling, laid out
its integral features, and made the case that it's a better fit in contemporary society. Now I want to clarify, elaborate, and summarize a few ideas
mentioned or alluded to elsewhere:

- Democratic schooling in a nutshell
- Community — less obvious, more important?
- Intrinsic motivation and autonomy
- Optimal challenge
- Embodied cognition and deep learning
- Coercive curriculum harms children
- Practicing life

## Democratic Schooling in a Nutshell

Conventional education is exhausted and ripe for renewal, its effectiveness undermined by two of its most basic principles: *coercive curriculum*
and *one-size-fits-all.* The system depends on teachers coaxing or coerc-
ing students to achieve specific mandatory curricular objectives in a
prescribed sequence at prescribed grade levels. The problem is not the
teachers, but rather a system that runs counter to human nature. *Coercive
curriculum* undermines learning because human beings naturally resist

coercion and control, preferring autonomy. And *one-size-fits-all* really fits only a few, because human beings come in infinite variety.

Self-directed democratic schooling overcomes both limitations by *aligning school with the larger world*. The democratic school is like a scaled-down version of that world, complete with its own executive, legislative, and judicial functions of government; with relative safety, order, and access to resources; with civil rights, free enterprise, personal responsibility, and equal voice in governance; with fellowship, community, and opportunity; and yes, with burdens, disappointments, and conflict.

Like adults in the world beyond school, students practice *agency in community*: self-determination driven by interest, shaped by culture, and constrained by society. Students are citizens in a self-governed community. As long as they abide by the duly voted laws of the school, including civic duties such as chores and jury duty, they choose for themselves what to do each day, for how long, and with whom. Self-directed democratic schooling thus educates children for life, cultivating *personal fulfillment* and *engagement in society*.

## Community: Less Obvious, More Important?

Visitors easily see the *agency* part of *agency in community*. Walk in the front door and student self-determination — expression of agency — is soon apparent, and especially striking because it is so different from standard schooling. It's easy to see students choosing to play Red Rover in the backyard, or build a city in Minecraft, or bake brownies, or play cards with friends. Less obvious is the other half of the equation: *community*. But in a world tilting towards narcissism, nihilism, and alienation, community may be the more crucial element.

First, let's distinguish three meanings of the word. Sometimes I say "community" to refer to the web of person-to-person connections and informal interactions — bonds of belonging. Sometimes I mean the warm feeling of fellowship surrounding that web. In the phrase *agency in community*, I mean both the web and its warmth, and also "society," the "exterior" of community, its institutions: systems, structures, customs, and protocols; such as Lawbook, judicial processes, chore sign-up, bus time bell, shoe bucket, rag bin, sales table, social scripts, and on and on. The educating power of community emanates from all three meanings.

Community tends to socialize people to societal norms, such as by mitigating raw impulses and curbing antisocial behaviors. But there's more to community than its civilizing influence and its practical training in life skills. Immersion in community is a primal state, with roots as deep as humanity itself. Bonding first with mother, then belonging in family, tribe, and beyond, is an existential need and a fulfilling condition. Satisfying the need involves physical proximity, shared experience, and immersion in a social web. Ideally it also involves trust, emotional intimacy, and ready help.

Community dampens narcissism by drawing self-focus outward, by providing social feedback, and by presenting human examples to follow. Community undermines nihilism and alienation through meaningful interpersonal relationships, social belonging, demands of civic duty, and the inclusiveness of collective self-governance. Absence of community is surely a root cause of today's political antagonism, resurging tribalism, and violence born of alienation.

Democratic schooling tends to foster strong, supportive community, bound by trust in its institutions and shared responsibility. The effects are profound and enduring, particularly in shaping character, social proficiency, appropriate trust, friendship, self-awareness, and civic awareness.

## Intrinsic Motivation and Autonomy

The principle that intrinsic motivation enhances learning is obvious, so it's no surprise that it has been clearly, dramatically, and repeatedly demonstrated in research. Of course, this isn't news to educators, who have known it since the first time a teacher awakened a sleeping student. Democratic schools tap the power of intrinsic motivation by aligning the school program with students' interests.

Intrinsic motivation is what leads a person to do something for its own sake, for personal satisfaction or other inherent value, rather than to earn a reward or avoid a punishment. Personal interest ignites intrinsic motivation. When we are interested in a subject and explore it because of our interest, we learn quickly and deeply, and retain what we have learned.

A primary aim of today's modern teaching is to arouse student interest in a handful of designated areas of knowledge, and then lead students through a sequence of preselected learning objectives that essentially make up the curriculum. Modern education recognizes the great power of personal interest — an essential insight and advance over traditional education — and attempts to engage that power on command.

But suppose instead of first choosing subjects and then arousing student interest, we reverse the order. Arousing interest where it does not arise spontaneously is hard work. Just ask any teacher. So let's *follow* interest instead of trying to *lead* it. This is precisely what democratic schools do.

Autonomy is freedom from external control. The power of autonomy to increase motivation has been clearly and repeatedly demonstrated in research; it's common knowledge. Children choosing their own activities learn more quickly, deeply, and enduringly, with greater personal satisfaction. Respect for personal autonomy is built into democratic schooling, helping to align school with children's individual interests.

Beyond the positive educational value of personal interest and autonomy, educators have come to understand the *negative* value of all of the following, which are known to *reduce* children's motivation: punishment, most kinds of rewards, grades, testing, other imposed evaluation, involuntary competition, surveillance, threats, imposed performance goals, and other controlling tactics. Even praise, when perceived as a controlling tactic, reduces intrinsic motivation.

Decades of research long ago established a commonsense truth: we learn best what we choose to explore out of personal interest. Unfortunately, traditional and modern schools are unable to fully engage the power of children's individual interests and autonomy. Instead, most continue to operate on the unrealistic hope that teachers will evoke and synchronize their students' interest in prescribed subjects. Common sense and science agree that life doesn't work that way.

## Optimal Challenge: Children Reaching Higher

Children, like the young of all species, strive to grow up. By powerful impulse of nature — call it innate wisdom — children strive to grow to adulthood, to take their place as members of adult society. Their striving arises by nature, need not be implanted or externally activated, and is obviously necessary for survival of the species.

The principle of "optimal challenge" helps to explain how children act on their inborn drive to grow. Optimal challenge refers to selection of appropriately difficult tasks, not too easy and not too hard.

From birth, children readily select appropriately challenging tasks, and pursue them with intense focus and persistent effort. Watch an infant or toddler at work, perhaps making sounds, moving objects, crawling, standing, or mounting a stairway. Children are constantly choosing new tasks to master — habit by nature, necessary for survival, and an example of innate wisdom.

The tendency for children to find optimal challenges does not end in infancy. Given sufficient freedom and resources, children of all ages tend to choose activities that are developmentally just beyond them, but still within reach.

This finding is important to education. In teacher-directed schooling, one of the chief challenges for the teacher is to select activities matched to students' abilities and readiness. The teacher's task is complicated by the need to select activities not for one student but for an entire classroom of students, and to do so not once but over and over again. Even the most talented teachers cannot reasonably be expected to succeed at this, day after day.

Selecting tasks that are too easy ("under-choosing") leads to boredom. Selecting tasks that are too hard ("over-choosing") leads to avoidance of challenge, for fear of failure. But these are minor costs, compared to the cost that is certain to be incurred in any case, even if the teacher always chooses optimally. The greater cost is the undermining of children's ability, willingness, and confidence to choose for themselves. This is epic tragedy: systematic repression of children's vital drive to seek challenge — which is nature's basic mechanism for realization of greatest potential.

A program of preselected challenges, a standard curriculum, trains children to depend on the teacher, undermining their own developing independence and boldness in the world. How much more effective and less costly for children to be guided by their built-in challenge-finder, as they are in democratic schools.

## Embodied Cognition and Deep Learning

It's easy to get carried away with the idea that body and mind are separate. Creation stories have humankind beginning with a Creator breathing spirit into matter. Ancient Greeks declared that the mind (or soul) is housed in the physical body. Later, Descartes stayed up all night and then said "I think therefore I am," thus identifying his "I" as mind not body, and reinforcing the idea of the physical body as a container, with noble mind striving for dominion over animal body. Philosophers have since egged us on with talk of Cartesian duality and the "hard problem" of how body and mind relate. *Star Trek*'s Mr. Spock put the icing on the Cartesian cake, ostensibly demonstrating how effective mind could be when untainted by feelings.

But Spock was a writer's fantasy. The duality of body-mind and the trinity of body-mind-spirit are useful ideas representing important truths and inspiration. In the everyday flesh and blood of you and me, though, mind is embedded in body — embodied. Mind is not simply contained in the brain, but permeates body, representing a stream of inputs, a system of systems, a process of processes happening throughout. Cognition, intelligence, and wisdom emerge from our apprehension, comprehension, and assimilation of all of it. The physical body is not merely infrastructure for supporting a mind ("a brain on legs"), but rather the two are interpenetrating, mutually pervasive, forming an integral whole person. Emotion and intuition are part of that whole, too, characterized as body, mind, heart, or spirit, as you wish. In any case, it is our whole self that lives and learns.

"Embodied cognition" and "deep learning" are currently hot ideas in the branch of artificial intelligence (AI) called machine learning. After decades of slow progress and few breakthroughs, AI research has begun to harness higher orders of learning. The idea of deep learning, which is inspired by human neural networks, is to give a general learning algorithm access to data (typically "Big Data") and let the machine's artificial intelligence explore and discover for itself whatever there is to be discovered. For example, instead of programming into a computer the rules of a particular game, there are now AIs that can observe a game being played and discover the rules for itself. Literally, the computer watches a video game being played, or attempts to play it, perhaps millions of times, and eventually learns to play, sometimes with greater-than-human skill.

An amusing example of AI deep learning made news in 2012. Google's AI watched millions of YouTube videos and spontaneously began to recognize cats. Nothing in its programming made any reference to cats or anticipated what the AI would learn. The programmers were surprised.

The central idea of deep learning in AI is, in a sense, that we aren't smart enough to tell the computer exactly what to learn and how to make meaningful connections. Better, then, to immerse the AI in a domain and give it free range to discover patterns, rules, principles, and connections for itself — giving it a capacity for a sort of originality, a capacity to surprise us, a capacity to discover new things in new ways.

Perhaps the AI is approximating aspects of human learning: long observation, inductive reasoning, trial and error, feedback and practice. We see this sort of deep learning every day at school. Children engage with their older friends and figure out the rules of a game — or the social rules of conversation and humor, or how School Meeting operates, or how to be an adult. Every day they surprise us.

I think robust general intelligence is grounded in and emerges from "whole" or "inclusive" experience — embodied cognition and deep learning, embracing a totality of data, impressions, and contexts: physical, intellectual, emotional, social, and spiritual. Certainly, each of us, from birth, is given access to the Big Data that floods through our senses to deep learning algorithms programmed by nature.

Like earlier attempts at AI, conventional schooling tends to program children with specific knowledge and skills, instead of creating conditions for original discovery and individual development. And like those earlier AIs, "programmed" children are limited by what the programmers thought to include, and less able to discover, originate, and surprise.

Later, in Part Three, we will look more closely at how children's autonomy in democratic schools — agency in community — helps to build higher thinking that is grounded in the world, and mindful of context in time, space, matter, nature, self, society, and community.

## Coercive Curriculum Harms Children

A standard curriculum is purported to represent knowledge that every child needs to learn, typically in a prescribed sequence at prescribed grade levels. This kind of standard curriculum is imposed on children in virtually all traditional and modern schools, even the most progressive among them. The curriculum is typically determined by specialists, administered by schools, and "delivered" by teachers in classrooms. The flow is top-down, and children are at the very bottom, required to comply.

In other words, the idea is to compel children for 12 years to proceed through a uniform sequence of learning steps that will lead them from kindergarten to college, and then on to economic prosperity and fulfilling life. Many have questioned whether this is possible, wise, or ethical. In my view it is none of those, but that's not my point here.

My point is to consider the side effects. Even if you believe a standard curriculum is necessary, helpful, or effective, consider that its imposition has unwanted effects, too. For example, if you worry that children might not be exposed to certain important subjects, and you find that standard curriculum relieves your worry, then weigh the benefits of that subject exposure against the harms. Specifically, consider the following harmful effects of a standard curriculum as applied in traditional and modern schools today.

## Displaces Opportunities

People learn best what they are interested in. Given the opportunity, children's curiosity drives them from one adventure to the next, like stepping stones through life. A standard curriculum stops this natural progression in its tracks, diverting students from the knowledge and skills they are most ready and eager to learn. Result: the best opportunities for learning and growth are displaced by whatever happens to be the next learning objective in the curriculum.

## Promotes Shallow Learning

Compelled to attend to something less interesting or uninteresting, children's learning tends to be shallow and fleeting. Sometimes a child's interest coincides with the current curricular objective, and sometimes teachers stir some children's interest, perhaps leading to effective learning in those cases. But these are exceptions, not the usual condition.

## Turns Kids Off to Formal Learning and Academic Studies

We human beings, by nature, come to dislike what we are forced to do. Standard curriculum, as usually applied, tends to turn kids off not only to the subject matter at hand but also to textbooks, instructional materials, teachers, classrooms, academics, and scholarship. The natural appeals of academics, learning, and mastery are diminished.

## Undermines Self-awareness and Introspective Skills

When children are not allowed to follow their interests, year after year, the message is clear: their interests don't matter. It's not just their interests. Food and physical activity are typically restricted to scheduled times, rather than responding to individual needs and preferences. Because their own rich and varied interior life is disregarded, children tend to lose their ability to see it, to be aware of their own thoughts, feelings, needs, and hopes. Development of healthy self-awareness is systematically undermined.

## Deadens Initiative, Fosters Passivity and Dependence

When children don't practice self-direction, when their lives are mostly directed by adults, they tend to become dependent on others to tell them what to do. It's a loss of personal agency and a deadening of initiative. They become less able to function in the world independently.

## Disempowers and Alienates

A degree of control over one's own life is a basic human need. The relentless demands of a standard curriculum dominate the school day, robbing children of self-determination. The result tends to be apathy, alienation, and a sense that others control my life.

## Normalizes Coercion

Most of us want to live in a non-coercive society, free to pursue life, liberty, and happiness. Oddly, though, conventional schools do not exemplify this universal value. Students are compelled to complete assignments and activities in service to a system they didn't choose. From a child's perspective, school looks more like a rigidly controlled dictatorship, demonstrating that it's okay to manipulate and coerce, clearing the way for pecking orders and bullying. Coercion is made normal and acceptable.

## Teaches a Dangerous Myth

Along with promises of future success and incessant daily demands, standard curriculum conveys a dangerous message: Do as you're told and all will be well. Alas, it isn't so.

In summary, standard curriculum degrades the quality of children's lives, even for those children who thrive in it. For those who do not, it tends to induce fear, alienation, and unhealthy stress. Weigh the benefits against the harms. Standard curriculum is a net loss to children, not necessary to achieve the aims of education, and less effective than democratic schooling. Self-selected, self-directed learning is deeper and more enduring, appropriately challenging, and personally satisfying.

## Practicing Life

In wholesome growth, children become progressively less dependent on their parents and others, ultimately functioning as independent adult members of society. From the extreme dependence of infancy to the relative independence of adulthood, the essence of the child's journey is growth of personal capacity for interacting in the world.

Democratic schools support children's growing independence by immersing them in experience of the world and the society in which they are growing. By shaping the school as a microcosm of the larger world beyond school, students enjoy an ideal laboratory in which to practice being members of society, independent of family.

Given freedom to explore and practice among people and resources, children naturally engage opportunities and challenges that stretch their limits, over and over again. Children's natural striving leads them to experiment and innovate with their own behaviors and ideas about the world, finding individual ways of being effective, and discovering increasingly effective understandings of the world.

Buzzing with children practicing life, liberty, and pursuit of happiness, the democratic school is a microcosm of 21st-century society. The school's structure, governance, culture, resources, and practices reflect and ground children in the realities of the world they inherit.

### Seven Ideas in Support of Democratic Schooling

| | |
|---|---|
| **In a nutshell** | Conventional education is undermined by its *coercive curriculum* and *one-size-fits-all* methods. Democratic schooling overcomes both limitations by *aligning school with society*. Students are citizens in a scaled-down version of the world beyond school, practicing *agency in community*. |

| Community | The prominent visibility of student self-determination in democratic schools diverts attention from the profound educating power of community, particularly in shaping character, social skill, and awareness of self and others. |
|---|---|
| Intrinsic motivation | Intrinsic motivation is what leads a person to do something for its own sake, for personal satisfaction, rather than to earn a reward or avoid a punishment. Intrinsic motivation dramatically enhances learning speed, depth, and retention. Personal autonomy (freedom from external control) and personal interest ignite intrinsic motivation. Democratic schools tap the learning power of intrinsic motivation. |
| Optimal challenge | From birth, children choose to engage appropriate challenges: activities and tasks that are developmentally just beyond them but still within reach. Fixed curriculum and teacher-directed schooling tend to repress this built-in challenge-finder by removing task-selection freedom and decision-making responsibility from children. Democratic schooling is founded on children's self-direction, tapping the power of optimal challenge. |
| Embodied cognition | Despite Descartes, Mr. Spock, and philosophers' trouble with the mind-body "hard problem," children and AI demonstrate the effectiveness of deep learning. Democratic schooling cultivates capacities for discovery, originality, and surprise. |
| Harms of coerced curriculum | Displaces better learning opportunities; leads to shallow learning; turns kids off to academics and formal study; undermines self-awareness and introspection; deadens initiative; fosters passivity and dependence; disempowers and alienates; normalizes coercion; teaches a dangerous myth. |
| Practicing life | Bringing children into society's fold as productive members is a fundamental aim of education. From the extreme dependence of early childhood to the relative independence of young adulthood, democratic schools support children as they practice life in the world apart from family. Democratic schools' structure, culture, and governance reflect and ground children in the realities of the larger world. |

# Part Three:
# Thinking about Thinking

One late spring Saturday, at the school's annual gala, I was in conversation with two parents, each having a student who had enrolled the previous fall. I started telling them about recent visits at school from a professor of education. I said to these two dads, "A university scholar noticed that Circle School students tend be skillful in critical thinking…." I was mid-sentence, planning to say "and he's wondering why" and then ask what they thought. But they both broke into loud laughter. One said "Duh!" and the other said "Well, yeah!" They each went on to tell stories about being startled by their kids' expanded use of reasoned arguments and ability to pierce assumptions. They both remarked appreciatively that their parent-child relationship had shifted because of it, in satisfying ways. I never got the chance to ask them why and how it happened.

Like many observers, both of these dads had come to believe that something about students' experience in democratic schools stimulates critical thinking. Without curriculum and teachers' constant pressure, what might it be? How do students develop critical thinking in democratic schools? Why might critical thinking develop more frequently or deeply in democratic schools than elsewhere?

I'll address those questions in the second part of this section, with a draft theory about development of cognition and critical thinking in democratic schools. First, I'll set some cultural context and describe some teaching-learning structures commonly seen in democratic schools.

Chapter 6:

# How and What Do They Learn?

HOW AND WHAT DO CHILDREN LEARN in democratic schools? I'll
answer generally and specifically. First, I'll place education in the
context of contemporary society and outline the expanded scope of
learning in democratic schooling. Next, I'll review conventional teaching-learning patterns that also occur in democratic schools. Then, I'll
mention democratic schooling's decoupling of learning from credentials.
And last, I'll specifically describe a dozen or so learning methods, modes,
and mechanisms that distinguish democratic schools from standard
schools. Oh, and I'll toss in a few stories of life at school as they relate to
these topics.

## Worldviews, Culture Wars, Concerts, and Railroads

Contemporary society is layered with worldviews that have developed his-
torically. Three dominate in the public sphere today: traditional, modern,
and postmodern. Broadly, each represents a distinct constellation of values, ideals, and policy preferences. Although each is built on its historical
predecessor, and therefore shares some foundation, each layer also rejects
some of what came before. The resulting conflicts in public policy debate
are commonly described as culture wars.

Education is an important cultural frontier on which conflicting values
jostle for dominance. Traditional, modern, and postmodern worldviews
each assert exclusive demands on curriculum and methods in schooling.
Each seeks to banish the other two from public policy.

The integral perspective, which is itself a worldview, seeks to accommodate the various layers of personal and cultural development. Democratic schooling does so partly by functioning as a venue rather than a predetermined program. Think of the relation between a concert hall and genres of music. Just as the concert hall can host any genre of music, the democratic school hosts any genre of education. Teaching-learning patterns take on forms that are variously characteristic of traditional and modern education. For example, methods originating in Montessori, Waldorf, and Reggio-Emilia education are easily applied in democratic schools when indicated by the subject matter and preferences of the participants. Democratic schools are eclectic not only in teaching-learning methods but in content, too. With no prescribed "genre" of curriculum, the subjects of study are unlimited, just as a concert hall can host performances of any kind of music.

A metaphor of knowledge as territory further illustrates the inclusive and divergent character of democratic schooling. Think of conventional schooling as a railroad system: train tracks are the curriculum, railroad cars are the classrooms, and conductors are the teachers. As passengers, children are railroaded to preselected destinations (curricular objectives) and limited to the stops and scenery (lesson plans) along the way.

In contrast, think of democratic schooling as open territory (unlimited curriculum) marked by boundaries (rules for safety and order), within which students explore the landscape and develop pathfinding skills for an unmapped future. Train tracks, destinations, and railroad cars are optional, because explorers go anywhere within the boundaries, by any mode of travel.

Stretching the metaphor a bit further, notice the passive role of the railroad passenger, observing the landscape speeding by, in contrast to the active explorer traversing the terrain more directly and fully engaged: guided by needs, interest, companions, and whimsy; drawn by fascination; lingering in awe; resting at waypoints; hurrying on. Same territory, different experience. One is training, the other pathfinding.

In spite of broad accommodation, democratic schools disappoint all three dominant worldviews by not allowing any one of them to impose on everyone its favored curriculum or teaching-learning methods. In both matters — content and method — democratic schools push the choice down the conventional hierarchy to the lowest level: the student.

Thus, among the three dominant worldviews, democratic schools accommodate all and satisfy none. Democratic schools represent not compromise among worldviews but coexistence and unsought synthesis.

Notice that all kinds of conventional schools agree on the principles of coercive curriculum and adult-directed methods. The details are contested, but not the railroading structure itself. If we merely sought political compromise, we would retain the railroading structure and simply offer multiple curricula: several railroad lines to choose from. Instead, democratic schooling provides access to all of the old destinations and adult-directed methods, and adds a multitude of new destinations and modes of travel, by way of open curriculum and open methodology.

## Expanding the Scope of Education in School

Open curriculum and open teaching-learning methodology partly describe the greater scope of democratic schools in contrast to conventional schools. But there's more. Democratic schooling expands the scope of education in three other ways, too.

First, where modern and postmodern schooling aim for cognitive development (instead of mere knowledge acquisition), democratic schooling broadens the scope to include all lines of development: intellectual, interpersonal, introspective, emotional, musical, kinesthetic, logical-mathematical, and other kinds of intelligence.

Second, where much of conventional schooling involves objective study, much of democratic schooling involves immersive experience. This important expansion will become evident in the specifics of teaching-learning methods to be discussed, and then I'll say more about it again in discussion of deep play, cognition, and critical thinking.

Third, where conventional school students are isolated from school governance and administration, democratic school students are actively engaged, making it an integral dimension of education. More about this later, too.

In summary, democratic schooling expands the scope of education in school by more fully incorporating and integrating:

- Open curriculum: a broader range of knowledge and experience
- Open teaching-learning methodology: more ways to explore
- Multiple intelligences: all lines of development

- Multi-perspective experience: objective and immersive
- School governance and administration as part of the program.

Together these features enable old and new modes and mechanisms of learning.

## Old Ways

Most teaching-learning modes and structures that are available in conventional schools are also practiced in democratic schools, such as the following.

## Classes

It's the usual picture: students in a room with an instructor leading the way and providing the expertise. Classes are typically initiated by students rather than offered routinely by the school. No student is required to attend classes, although a consistent attendance expectation and other conditions might be negotiated among teacher and students. In some years, there are many classes, in others only a few, and in some democratic schools, classes occur only rarely. Some students take classes often, others take only a few throughout years of enrollment, and some alumni report they never did. In a typical school year, only a small fraction of students devote significant time to traditional classes. The culture bestows neither status nor stigma on participation in classes.

Classes come about in a variety of ways. A student may approach a staff member and ask to set up regular meetings to study something — perhaps reading, math, biology, Spanish, or college entry exam preparation. A student may get an idea and recruit a friend or a few friends, and approach a staff member to lead it. A student (or staff member in some schools) who wants to lead a group in, say, yoga or martial arts might put a sign-up sheet on the bulletin board, inviting all who are interested.

---

### *Making Things Go Boom*

They called it a physics class, and the staff member involved was, indeed, a former high school physics teacher. Their express purpose was to make things pop, boom, and explode in cool ways. They had to work around school safety rules, including one that forbids open flame. Under the auspices of the Science

Corporation, they proposed and received School Meeting's standing permission to use a Bunsen burner under carefully controlled circumstances for some of their work.

The Bunsen burner provided the drama in at least one project. They extracted hydrogen gas from water and gathered it in a plastic gallon jug. Then, outdoors, they threaded a long rope through the handle of the jug. Holding the rope taut from a safe distance, they dangled the gallon jug lower and lower over the Bunsen burner until the flame burned through the jug and — BOOM! — the hydrogen gas exploded. It made a very satisfying boom and turned the jug into nothing but tiny shards of plastic except for the circular rim intact.

One of their projects was to build a potato cannon — also called a tennis ball launcher, but "potato cannon" sounds cooler. At their request, the Library Committee secured three books to inform their design. Traditionally, potato cannons are powered by electric ignition of a cloud of a certain aerosol product inside a chamber, expelling the potato at high speed. But that propulsion method would violate safety rules at school, so they designed a device using compressed air instead. The engineering calculations had to account for pressure, chamber size, barrel length, launch velocity, and more. They tested the device by launching wet rags at first, but later found that potatoes and apples were more satisfying, especially when thoroughly obliterated on impact with a suitable backstop. Boom.

---

## Internships

Sometimes, older students work or study in an off-campus arrangement with a business or other organization. For example, Circle School students have interned at a comic book store, magazine editorial office, community theater, antique car restorer, automotive repair business, aviary, gymnastics school, tool and die company, window replacement company, and airport. This week, Stefi is writing a proposal, at the invitation of a large hotel chain nearby, for an internship in their Human Resources department. Sometimes an internship is a way of delving into something new, and sometimes it's pursuit of a passionate interest. Either way, it's also a step into the adult world beyond school. The External Resources Coordinator, an elected official, assists students in making the arrangements.

## Independent Study

Often a student will pursue concentrated study of a subject or skill of interest on their own over a period of days, weeks, months, or years. The subject could be a traditional academic subject, studied out of a standard textbook, or something for which there would be no relevant textbook or instructional material. A designated teacher may be involved, either regularly in planned meetings or occasionally when the student gets stuck or is ready for more.

Most independent study isn't called by that name or even noticed as such, I suppose because it just happens and the distinction from other activities would have little meaning in democratic schools. Nevertheless, it is a common mode of learning and it resembles the "independent study" of conventional schooling.

---

## *Angela's Speed Painting YouTube Channel*

This year, 15-year-old Angela is devoting hours each day to digital "speed painting." Using digital drawing software and a tablet, she first imagines and sketches a real or fantasy creature, character, or scene. Slowly, meticulously she adds outlines, details, color, shading, highlights, backgrounds, and flourishes. Typically, she says, it takes her "a few hours" to complete a work. I saw one that took her 10 hours. Throughout the entire creative and technical effort, video recording software captures everything she does on her tablet screen, showing how each artistic step is performed. When the work is complete, Angela speeds up the video so that her hours-long session is reduced to about five minutes. The 10-hour production was speeded up to display in less than eight minutes. Viewing it, the rich, colorful, fantastical image emerges from nothing as you watch. She then adds a music track, or sometimes a voice-over to narrate the process. Finally, she uploads the finished audio-video production to her YouTube channel, where it is available to the public and especially to her hundreds of subscribers, who are entertained for a few minutes or learn to draw with Angela's help.

---

## One-on-one Tutoring

One-on-one tutoring is common, either on a regular schedule or spontaneously. Sometimes both parties are students. The subject might be physics, tree-climbing, reading, dance, guitar, geology, word processing,

Minecraft, cartography, cooking, and so on without limit. The arrangement may be negotiated explicitly or develop informally without remark.

## Off-campus Classes

At The Circle School, older students have taken classes at nearby colleges (Franklin & Marshall College, Dickinson University, Harrisburg Area Community College, and others), typically to get a taste of college or pursue a specialized interest — Latin, in one case, economics in another, for example. The school's elected External Resources Coordinator works with qualified students to develop such arrangements.

---

### *Latin? Really?*

We have no Latin teacher, but Tori wanted to learn it. So she and the External Resources Coordinator approached the admissions office at nearby Dickinson University. They were skeptical about a 14-year-old in a college Latin class, but said okay if the Classical Studies Department agreed. The reluctant professor asked her why she wanted Latin. Tori explained that she had read translated works in English, but now wanted to read them in the original language. She told him exactly what she wanted to read, some of which happened to be in the professor's syllabus anyway. Impressed, he admitted her and she attended. Turns out she was the enthusiastic student who always came to class prepared, raised her hand, and had the answers. She got an A, and the professor said Send Me More Kids Like Her! Tori later attended and graduated from St. John's College, a program based on the Great Books, beginning with ancient classics. Tori had already read some of those, in Latin.

---

## Integral Learning Patterns Enabled by Democratic Schooling

In conventional schooling driven by age-synchronized curriculum, lessons and classes are the primary modes of teaching-learning. The curriculum-oriented approach deconstructs and dis-integrates knowledge and experience, then separates and sorts the fragments by subject, arranges them in sequence from simple to complex, packages them in lessons, and "delivers" them to students in classes, isolated from the original context and experience. Personally, I find this method of study to be a fine way to acquire knowledge, among many other fine ways. For me, it is especially useful after I've encountered a subject and I want to delve deeper, systematically, especially in conceptual and theoretical knowledge. It's not so good if I want to learn to make pancakes.

The curriculum-classroom approach is built around measured units of instruction as a proxy for knowledge and transcripts as proof of accumulated instruction. This is the common basis for awarding credentials such as a college degree — a third-party certification to assure others that you have at least studied (if not mastered) a domain.

The need for formal credentials may weed out incapable practitioners in various professions, and may help to maximize the monetary income of practitioners, by limiting competition. These are commonly seen as socially valued important functions of credentials. But should primary and secondary schooling be so intent on credentials and vocational aims? I don't think so, especially when credentialing interferes with learning, growth, fulfilling life, and engagement in community.

I regret that the word "learning" has come to be narrowly associated with the curriculum-classroom approach and the credentialing function of academic credits. Learning is so much bigger than that. Democratic schools decouple learning from credentialing and expand its scope beyond academic subjects.

After touring the school and seeing students busily and happily engaged in many kinds of activities, newcomers sometimes ask "But when do the children learn?" The question flusters me, because, in my experience, busy and happy usually indicates learning and growth. The question implies that learning is an observable activity rather than an internal process. The classic picture of learning-as-an-activity is a classroom with attentive children listening to instruction from a teacher, in order to acquire certain knowledge. To be sure, that happens in democratic schools, but typically makes up only a small fraction of activity, and is valued by the school no more or less than many other activities. A touring observer might see students engaged that way, but might not, and certainly not a majority of students at any given moment.

Sometimes the question is less about the form of the activity and more about the content, implying that learning in school should be about academic subjects but not about making pancakes, friends, and campaign speeches. Democratic schools reject this presumption and envision a broader scope: life!

"But when do the children learn?" A satisfying answer entails two principles about democratic schools. First, essential teaching-learning patterns are integrated in school life, in contrast to the overt visibility of a teacher directing a classroom of students. Children learn by living their lives in the ordered society and active community of the democratic school and self-directing to acquire the knowledge and skills they need and want. Second, democratic schools do not limit the scope of valued learning to the standard curriculum.

If you're having trouble with these ideas as a framework for school, try this. Instead of a school, imagine a nicely equipped community center where people gather each day and engage in three overlapping categories of activity: pursuit of personal interests, duties that are required of all members, and administration of the community center. This could be a good starting point for understanding a democratic school.

---

## Too Busy for Math

At home one weekend, Jancey's beloved Aunt Joy was visiting from out of town. Eager to learn how to borrow and carry in multi-digit addition and subtraction, Jancey asked Aunt Joy to give her some practice problems. Sitting at the dining room table, Aunt Joy wrote out a problem and passed the paper to Jancey, who worked the problem and then passed the paper back for Aunt Joy to check. After a few rounds of this, Aunt Joy (knowing about Jancey's democratic school) said something like "You know, you could do this at school." Barely looking up from the paper, Jancey replied, "Oh, I'm way too busy at school to do math!"

Aunt Joy was surprised — Isn't That What School Is For? — but I know just what Jancey meant. At school, she was constantly organizing and doing things with other people, deeply involved in many activities. Among other projects, she founded the Philanthropy Corporation, the purpose of which was to raise money to grant to other corporations for their own purposes. Worksheets and other drill-and-practice would have been a waste of her precious time at school. But she needed to add and subtract reliably, probably to count up all that money they raised. Working at home was just good time management.

---

So, one more time, when do the children learn? All the time: deliberately or incidentally; seeking it out or stumbling onto it; pulled into it by a friend or pushed into it by the demands of community, society, and school government. Sometimes it's plainly visible study such as classes, and often it's between the lines, integrated in life, unremarked, unself-conscious, undocumented, unlabeled, unmeasured — and therefore not suitable for a transcript and a credential, and not always obvious when you walk through the school.

If not teachers-and-classrooms, then what are these patterns of learning in democratic schools? Discussed below, most of them are embedded in meaningful experiential context. In fact, they are so integral and unnoticed that there are no names for these patterns in the school's lexicon. I'm giving them names here simply to identify distinct modes, methods, and practices that we see every day.

## Systemic or Meta-message Learning

The very structure and governance of the democratic school convey meaning and messages to students that help accomplish society's basic educational aims. I call this "systemic" because it is the student's experience of the system itself that is significant. To adapt Marshall McLuhan's nugget about media, we could say "the system is the message."

Of course, every school system, by its structure and governance, tends to convey values and messages, but the messages of democratic schooling are in greater alignment with the values and needs of today's students, society, and post-industrial economy. Democratic schools are almost alone today in systemically communicating values of democracy, individual initiative and enterprise, free society, community, peaceful co-existence of difference, and personal responsibility.

In contrast, conventional schooling systematically places teachers in the lead, with students following; casts teachers as rule-makers and police; disregards the student's original agenda; limits children to a fixed curriculum, rather than a divergent universe of learning possibility; cultivates homogeneity, rather than flourishing of individual interests and talents; and isolates students from the rights and responsibilities of citizenship in modern democracies. Conventional coercive education tends to convey systemic messages that aggravate the misalignment of school and society, and school and students. The meta-messages of conventional schooling tend to produce resentment, anger, alienation; apathy, passive compliance, lack of initiative; and dependence on others for direction.

By aligning schools with today's ideals of self-determination, personal and global responsibility, and free access to knowledge, democratic schooling applies the power of systemic meta-messages to achieve basic educational aims.

## Self-service Systems

Students are empowered and challenged by many self-service systems, a practice that is ideally suited to self-directed education: available to all as needed or wanted, without requiring adult permission or supervision. Such systems include room reservations, Judicial Committee (JC) write-ups, chore sign-up, extra-pay chore sign-up, field trip plans, checking out library books, voting, buying stuff, selling stuff, signing out the iPads and laptops, and access to many other tangible resources related to science, art, cooking, music, games, sports, computers, and so on. Some require training before first use — typically a few minutes — and most can be used independently, with assistance available as needed.

For example, anyone can reserve a room for one-time or repeated use for any safe, legal purpose they wish. The process is simple enough for our youngest children to use, and many do, for parties, gymnastics, organized contests, art projects, group games, meetings, and whatever else they dream up. If it's a one-time reservation, you go get a room reservation form from the rack in the back hall, fill it out, and hang it up on the door of the room at least an hour before the reservation is to begin. If it's a repeating reservation, you submit the form to the Aesthetics Committee. They compare it to a master schedule to avoid conflicting reservations and consider the fit between the room and the intended use.

For most students, especially the youngest, the power to take over a room for their own purposes, without even asking an adult, is thrilling and inspiring. Ditto for the power to go into the Science Room any time you please, take out a microscope, use it to examine the dead bug you just found, and then put the microscope away. Or go to the Art Room and do finger painting with a friend, without seeking permission or assistance. Of course, you can get help, but you don't have to. To be able to do something significant entirely on your own — that's a big deal for most young children.

## *The Screen Gene*

Shortly before he enrolled, 4-year-old Jibran and his parents visited the school. After touring the campus, we returned to the Conference Room. I asked Jibran what he had noticed as we walked around, and what he might like to do when he came to school. Without hesitation, he said "the iPads." Had he ever used one, I asked. No, he had not. But, like many 4-year-olds, every day he sees his parents and others fiddle with their tablets and laptops and phones. Screens, it must have seemed to Jibran, hold the secrets of life. He wanted in.

Sure enough, on the morning of the first day of school, Jibran made a bee-line for the Library. He knew he couldn't touch the iPads until he was trained and certified by a Library Committee representative. He sought and received the brief training right away, which included the procedure for signing out an iPad and signing it back in, and turning it on and off, but did not include use of any of the apps. When an iPad soon became available for his first live use, Jibran came to me and asked, "Jim, will you help me sign out the iPad?" He could write his name, with effort, but wanted my help writing the date and time and other details. I did what he told me, step by step, because I wasn't certified and didn't know what was required. He did. He thanked me, took the iPad, sat on the floor, and turned it on. I knew he couldn't read, so I waited, expecting him to ask me to read what was on the screen. He didn't. He touched an icon and waited to see what happened. I said nothing but waited, and then waited some more. He never asked for help. After 15 minutes of watching in fascination and irrelevance, I went back to what I was doing.

The next day, and for weeks thereafter, he would come get me once or twice a day, asking me again to help him sign out an iPad. Each time the routine was the same, and never did he ask for my help with the iPad itself. I peeked in on him several times, and each time he was immersed in an app, using the controls appropriately and deftly. Sometimes I watched as Jibran and two other non-readers sprawled on the floor together, chattering about the action on the iPad and advising one another. By then they knew exactly what they were doing, but I'll never know how.

The big deal of self-service is not merely the satisfaction of using the resource or engaging in the activity. It's the exercise of agency and autonomy, the freedom from adult direction, the capacity to make real things happen in the world, and a growing sense of self-efficacy. It's being a regular person in society, acknowledged as an autonomous being. To achieve this big deal, in each case, you must first learn about the particular resource or activity and society's rules surrounding it. This might be accomplished through certifications (i.e., child-scale credentialing), word of mouth, signs posted nearby, observation of others, or even trial and error.

Pervasive in democratic schooling, self-service systems are a powerful method by which learning occurs in four C dimensions: *content* (knowledge and skills), *context* (societal process for orderly shared access), *capacity* (general intelligence), and *confidence* (in self-efficacy and autonomy).

Combined with other methods of self-directed learning, students cultivate the ultimate superpower: to develop additional personal capacities as needed, to become ever more functional through your own intentional efforts. Think of M.C. Escher's *Drawing Hands* image of two hands drawing themselves into existence. The ultimate superpower is self-creation.

## Decision-making

Self-direction demands frequent decision-making. In democratic schools, decision-making is generally more personal, more meaningful, and has greater real-life impact, making its exercise a more powerful educating influence. Later we will examine decision-making closely, and particularly its role in development of cognition and critical thinking.

## Public Process

Democratic school government entails endless public debate according to documented procedures and meeting minutes. With dozens of officials, committees, and corporations, school governance is pervasive and touches the lives of virtually all students every day. Engagement in public process — judicial, executive, and legislative — is among the important influences in every democratic school student's life, fostering at least basic literacy and numeracy, and offering constant opportunities for more.

All students (and staff) are voting members of the School Meeting, which serves as the school's chief executive and legislative body. Some students attend its weekly sessions frequently, others only when something they care about is up for debate or vote. For example, a trio of skateboarding enthusiasts rarely attended but showed up often for months to propose and debate an overhaul of the relevant safety rules.

School Meeting regularly takes up high-impact matters, such as staff hiring and retention, the annual budget, and whether or not to suspend a student following judicial proceedings. Even these weighty matters are decided by majority vote of students and staff together. In these matters, public process is riveting for many students.

In addition to School Meeting, every student gains extensive experience with the school's judicial system, convening every day, all year, prominent and rhythmic like a communal heartbeat. Students of all ages (and staff) serve rotating terms of service, taking testimony, weighing evidence, and making decisions. In judicial service, every student serves as a school official in pursuit of safety, order, fairness, restoration, and justice. Even the youngest students learn much from judicial processes, whether they are bringing a complaint in a squabble with a friend or defending against an allegation of their own wrong-doing.

The point is that making rules and governing school society is everybody's business, conducted openly, and accessible to all students. Public governance, with authority flowing from the governed, adds a new dimension to education, not previously available in schools. Public process invites and demands children's growth.

## School Administration

The Aesthetics Committee chooses how to furnish, decorate, and deploy spaces in the school building. The Library Committee manages the Library. The Network Committee oversees the school's information technology. The Chore Committee, always busy, maintains written descriptions of all chores, trains Chore Checkers, and manages the school's elaborate chore system. The Attendance Clerk tracks individual attendance to be sure of compliance with state law. The Elections Clerk administers elections. Committees, corporations, elected officials, and teams (such as the Office Team and the Facilities Team) — all functions are open to all and vital to smooth running of the school. Participation in school administration involves rich learning, real-world demands, and collaborative engagement.

## Accelerated Culture

The school buzzes incessantly with active minds engaged in self-motivated pursuits, often invested with high energy and intense interpersonal exchanges. Conversation and debate are constant. Lecture and other passive learning is rare. The pace is fast. Even casual observation reveals that the information volume of interpersonal exchanges vastly exceeds that of other kinds of schools. One result of "high bandwidth" is a more nearly frictionless flow of information, knowledge, and skills. That which resides anywhere in the culture is more easily accessible to all.

We find that accelerated or intensified cultural exchange not only effectively transmits knowledge and skills ("horizontal" growth) but also powerfully stimulates emergence of higher orders of cognition and consciousness along many lines of development ("vertical" or stage growth). It may be that vertical growth is stimulated not only by high social bandwidth but also by age-mixing, which we consider next, as near-stage transmission.

---

### *Preoccupied with Vocabulary*

I was in a bathroom at school. There was a knock at the door. Immediately I called out "Occupied." A few seconds later, another knock. Louder I called out "Occupied!" Two seconds later, yet another knock. Louder still, and beginning to suspect a prankster, I called out "OCCUPIED!!!" as I opened the door to leave. Looking up at me, a sincere 5-year-old said sweetly, "What does occupied mean?"

---

By the way, adults play a crucial role in the culture, disproportionately influential, injecting mature knowledge, judgment, and values, particularly reflecting norms of the larger community and knowledge of resources. As models of excellence and maturity, staff members anchor the school culture to wholesome constants.

Accelerated culture, anchored by adults, powerfully stimulates children's learning and growth.

## Near-stage Transmission (Age-mixing)

Developmental psychology illuminates stages and milestones through which human beings generally grow, along numerous lines of development. Jean Piaget famously theorized that normal cognitive development proceeds through at least four major stages: sensorimotor, pre-operational, concrete operational, and formal operational. Today's scholars of human development affirm Piaget's broad finding that there are patterns in children's development but reject ideas of rigid sequence and timing, finding that each child's development proceeds uniquely. Other researchers have discovered general patterns, also with individual variations, in moral development, ego development, worldview, and numerous other lines of development.

As researchers, parents, and educators commonly observe, children's development is stimulated by interaction with other children, particularly children whose development is slightly ahead of their own. Often such stimulation seems to have greater effect than interaction with adults and with children whose developed capacities are further apart.

In democratic schools, self-direction and age-mixing powerfully enable "near-stage transmission" of knowledge, skills, values, and worldview. By mixing children of various developmental stages, and giving them free range to interact with others, democratic schools maximize growth-inducing encounters. Children seem to learn more and more readily from developmental peers and near-peers than from adults.

It may well be that near-stage transmission is the optimal challenge principle at work: perhaps near-stage partners simply present appropriate just-beyond-your-reach challenges with high frequency. It also seems likely that the later-stage partner gains significant benefit from the cross-stage transaction as well; perhaps aiding consolidation of the later stage, and avoiding dissociation from the earlier stage.

Whatever the exact mechanism, democratic schools' age-mixing and self-direction appear to be important elements in near-stage transmission.

## Multiple Lines of Development

I have already mentioned lines of development (multiple intelligences), such as cognitive, moral, logical-mathematical, and linguistic. The important point here is that democratic schools boost multi-line growth.

The combination of accelerated culture, age-mixing, and expanded variety of activity generates more challenges and opportunities to grow along many lines. Those challenges and opportunities are central to the school experience, not limited to extra-curricular activities and special events.

On the other hand, standard schools impede multi-line development in two ways. First, the standard curriculum concentrates on a limited selection of developmental lines, omitting and displacing opportunities to develop other lines. Second, much of the standard curriculum is *studied* rather than *experienced* — something like eating the menu instead of the meal. Not nearly as tasty and nutritious as the real thing.

## Self-balanced Development

In the self-directed program of democratic schools, children sometimes seem to concentrate attention on their "weakest" areas, perhaps the lines of development most out of sync with others. Democratic schools facilitate this self-balancing by enabling activities and interactions that might otherwise be stigmatizing or difficult to arrange. For example, a child of 8 to 10 years old may have the social-emotional skills more typical of a 5- or 6-year-old. In this circumstance, we have often seen the older child become friends and play partners with younger children. The pattern may continue for many months, with the older child fitting in socially very naturally, as though the older child is catching up on something. Completing a win-win bargain, the younger children may experience benefits of interacting with a child of greater cognitive capacity.

Democratic schools better enable children to pursue development that is balanced according to individual needs or toward a generally wholesome or adaptive configuration. I speculate that the optimal challenge principle (in Chapter 5) extends in two dimensions, not only pointing to appropriate degree of difficulty but also pointing to lines of development that are especially ripe for growth.

## Integrated Curriculum

As previously defined and discussed, integrated curriculum is built into democratic schooling. Every day, students practice self-directed learning through "whole" activities that have not been parsed into component subjects for isolated out-of-context study. In contrast, conventional schools practice integrated curriculum for brief periods, if at all, and it remains secondary to study of component subjects isolated from meaningful context.

## Interest Groups

I'm using the term "interest group" to indicate people gathering regularly to pursue an agreed scope, without a designated teacher. It's something like a teacherless class, I suppose, although often there is a knowledgeable staff member participating. Gather some friends and get it going, or put a sign-up sheet on the bulletin board. Anybody can do it. Book discussion groups are a popular example, typically following a pattern of some agreed reading, planned session by session, perhaps a chapter at a time. In recent years, groups have read *Ishmael* and *My Ishmael* (Daniel Quinn), *A People's History of the United States* (Howard Zinn), *To Kill a Mockingbird* (Harper Lee), *Catcher in the Rye* (J.D. Salinger), *Twilight* (Stephenie Meyer), *Animal Farm* (George Orwell), *Live from Death Row* (Mumia Abu-Jamal), and *The Picture of Dorian Gray* (Oscar Wilde). A popular "Racism Discussion Group" began in response to a national news story and continued across two school years, sometimes involving various books and articles, carried by the flow of the group conversation. Other groups have formed around anime, creative writing, critical thinking, martial arts, yoga, and zombies — a to z and more. What would *you* like to do?

## Drag-alongs, Tag-alongs, Stumble-ons, and Happenings

Democratic schooling is a form of self-directed education, but sometimes that term misleads. Emphasizing that the school does not present a schedule of classes for students to choose from, I sometimes tell newcomers that most of what happens at school originates in school government (such as School Meeting), school administration (such as in the business office and Library Committee work), corporation offerings (such as Art and Science), or student initiative. That, too, can be misleading. Assertions about self-direction and student initiative sometimes create the impression that each student is on their own to self-direct and initiate. Developing self-reliance is valued and important, but the on-your-own aspect of self-direction and initiative is balanced (and cultivated and enhanced) by everyday dynamics, such as the following, that do not depend on each student's original ideas and initiative.

*Drag-alongs.* Often a student says to a friend (or two or three or many) something like "Let's go do [whatever]." The friend may resist — disinterested or unexcited — but goes along anyway, venturing into something they would not otherwise think of or choose. The activity has thus originated in student initiative — one student's initiative, affecting the dragged-along parties. The self-directed choice to accompany a friend exposes the less interested or non-initiating student to something that might turn out well (by whatever measure you care to apply).

*Tag-alongs.* Instead of being reluctant and persuaded, a friend hears what's up and asks to go along. The tag-along posture can be ideal for someone who is curious but doesn't want the leadership responsibility that goes along with initiating an action. Furthermore, the casual tag-along can more easily bow out after their curiosity is satisfied but before the episode is concluded.

*Stumble-ons.* At The Circle School, interior doors have glass panels. Cruising around the building, you readily see what's going on. Who knows what you might stumble on, join in, and find useful? Sometimes it's not appropriate to join in, and there is no automatic right to do so, but often everyone is welcome. Art projects, backyard games, and science experiments are examples.

*Happenings.* When the Science Corporation holds its periodic rocket launchings, it draws a crowd. When School Meeting is considering something juicy — like The Hour Of No Rules or a sleepover at school or suspending a student for something sensational — everybody seems to be drawn into the talk, for days or even weeks. Happenings are widely attended or talked-about school-day occasions and currents. Happenings stir the cultural stew in one exciting way or another, awakening some students to new ideas and possibilities.

Some happenings are planned and organized: lip-sync contest, Halloween costume party, talent show, field trips. Anyone can think one up and bring it to life, but sometimes they pop up spontaneously, such as a large-scale Capture the Flag game or rolling a snowball so large it takes ten people to push it to the rim of the big hill, and then over the edge.

Occasionally a deep play scene in the Playroom catches on and draws people in, sometimes spanning days.

Drag-alongs, tag-alongs, stumble-ons, and happenings are serendipitous artifacts of friendship, imagination, people in proximity, flowing culture, access to resources, and time to explore. Democratic schooling creates these conditions.

## Commerce and Entrepreneurship

At The Circle School, there's a long countertop in the Downstairs Kitchen, reserved for displaying merchandise for sale. Anyone can place things there, typically along with a sign identifying the seller, the price, and sometimes a statement that the seller will or will not accept IOUs. To buy something, you seek out the seller and pay them, or sometimes put your money in a collection can beside the goods.

Food items are popular — either store-bought for resale or made at school. Fresh baked items command a premium price, especially if the aroma has filled the school. By the end of the day, the price might be halved. Simon has been selling freeze pops for many years, and other awful sugary items. He knows his customers' habits and thoughtfully stocks their favorite flavors. One year he took in more than $1,000. Last week someone was offering mustaches for sale. Really. (I saw the sign, but I couldn't tell what would actually change hands or happen if you bought one.)

Commerce is mostly free and unregulated, but sometimes School Meeting rules kick in. For example, the rule against exploitation is occasionally invoked when an older entrepreneur sees opportunities arising from younger students' ignorance of merchandise values and gets too greedy. Energy drinks are also affected by a rule — see the story "Debating Energy Drinks."

Jaelin offered digital avatars for sale this year. You tell her what you want, perhaps describing an elaborate vision, or you can give her free artistic rein. She creates the image and delivers it to you, perhaps by email or text. At 50 cents apiece, I thought it was a bargain. Jaelin's work is playful and imaginative.

Chores create an entrepreneurial opening. You can opt out of doing your daily chore by paying the Chore Committee a fee of $2. Every year a few enterprising students put up signs offering to do your chore for a dollar. The buyer saves a dollar that way, so it should be an easy sell. But there's a catch: chore duty is yours personally. If you hire a contractor to do your chore and they neglect to do so, it is you, not the contractor, who will then have to pay a fine the next day ($3) or do extra chores, or get written up and have to go before the Judicial Committee. You've got to trust your chore contractor — or check up on them. Or you can negotiate to get your contractor to indemnify you: your contractor agrees to reimburse you if you pay a fine.

Watching young children figure out IOUs is entertaining. They already understand the concept of selling and buying: you give someone money and you get something good in return. In the classic first encounter with a vendor's offer to take an IOU, the child is amazed and confused: All I have to do is write "IOU," some numbers, and my name, and you'll give me an ice cream sandwich! How cool is that! No amount of explaining seems to burst that bubble of delight. A day or so later, when the vendor tries to get them to pay up, the child has no idea what they are talking about. Why should I give you money? I already gave you the IOU. If the child remembers that much, the vendor just might collect the payment. But sometimes it's too late, the price of an ice cream lost in the dreamy fog of a 4-year-old's yesterdays. Savvy sellers don't take IOUs.

## Avery's Hot Dogs

A few years ago, 10-year-old Avery announced that she would sell hot dogs for lunch every Tuesday. She borrowed money from her mother to buy initial supplies. She also persuaded her mother to drive her to school on Tuesdays, because she couldn't carry on the school bus everything she needed: hot dogs, crock pot to cook them in, buns, and condiments. On arrival at school, she carried everything in from the car — bulging tote bags about as big as she was. She'd get the hot dogs cooking on low heat, and by lunch time they were ready. Some weeks she sold dozens. Remarkably she continued right on through the school year. She paid off the loan quickly and then got rich.

## Play and Deep Play

The importance of play in children's learning is widely acknowledged now, and the lamentable loss of time for play in many children's lives. I'll raise the subject again later, but here are some highlights:

- The impulse to play is natural and universal.
- The value of play is established by research, both from human and animal studies.
- There is no substitute for play. Curriculum-driven activity is rarely as effective in promoting children's making of meaning and often inhibits meaning-making.
- Refrigerator art is not an indication of play (or learning).
- The rich, immersive, creative experience of "deep play" happens when children have plenty of time and space, *in a culture that values play*. (I'll examine deep play later, in discussion of cognitive development.)
- Play and deep play accelerate development along many lines: cognitive-intellectual, social, emotional, physical, verbal, introspective, expressive, empathic, and more.
- Deep play cannot be directed or even guided by adults but rather arises spontaneously from what is meaningful and important to the players (no matter what their ages).
- Deep play is enhanced and richest when embedded in social relationships in secure community with meaningful limits.
- Traditional academic activity tends to cultivate superficial or one-dimensional skills, in contrast to play and deep play, which tend to cultivate complex and multidimensional skills.

## Functional Apprenticeship

Formal apprenticeship in trades is a time-honored tradition and an effective arrangement for transmission of knowledge, skills, values, and customs. In democratic schools, children adopt functional apprenticeship relationships spontaneously, evolving fluidly as proficiency grows and interests shift. Typically without spoken agreement, a "novice" and an "adept" pair up — or small groups form — and pursue a shared interest with passionate devotion. The novices obviously gain the benefit of intrinsically valuable new knowledge and skill in the chosen domain, and the pleasure of deepening excellence. The adepts may benefit in a whole host of ways, such as cultivation of worthy colleagues; refinement of understanding and skill, by teaching it; increased self-esteem; and increased social standing. The domain might be almost anything: reading, cooking, tree-climbing, guitar, role-playing games, physics, tetherball, folk dancing, desktop publishing, pencil sketching, martial arts, or Minecraft....

## *Minecraft*

For years now, kids have been fascinated by Minecraft, and I've been fascinated by their fascination. As a former software developer, I understand the challenge and satisfaction that comes with immersion in a virtual world of your own imagination and creation. So on a chilly February day, I watched Keller, Charlie, Noam, and Gavin as they huddled at the little table in the Downstairs Kitchen, with lots of bustle around them in that high-traffic room.

Keller, age 14, generated a Minecraft world, and the other three (ages 5, 8, and 11) joined the world, each holding their own tablet or other screen device. Together in an unexplored world, each could see the other players on their own screen — or rather the avatars of the others, the on-screen humanoid icons representing the real human participants and their actions.

They continued for more than two hours, during which I observed closely in three sessions totaling about 45 minutes, remaining mostly inconspicuous. There was constant chatter among them. In one session, I timed the silences and found that no silence lasted more than about three seconds. They worked together, not competitively, with active teaching and coaching, even while all four seemed well challenged by what they were doing. Here are some snippets of what I heard:

"Okay, I'll start mining. You start chopping down trees." They need materials to build things.

"Ohhh, this is a nice world." It's a lovely scene of lake and forest. The others pause their action to take a look.

"Why do you have to be invisible?" The 14-year-old explains. I don't understand, but the younger boy seems to.

"Hey, can I attack him? He just hurt me." "Sorry, it was an accident."

I go away and come back 35 minutes later. They are still going at it, having built several structures and working on others. Three more people have joined.

"Keller, how do I log on?" Keller talks the newcomer into the virtual world.

"I found a lava ball!" Others look at his screen, appreciating the find.

"Where's my shield?" "Don't worry, Charlie. I have your stuff in my chest. Tell me when you need it."

"Can I have this house?" Noam is pointing to a house he came upon in the forest. "Is that the one with a spiral staircase?" asks Gavin. Noam adeptly zooms around the house and reports yes, it does have a spiral staircase. I can see it's a nicely furnished cabin. "That's one I built. Yes, you can have it."

"Look where I am! Look at all the water!" Others look and appreciate the lovely view of a lake from a mountaintop. Actually the graphic impression is primitive and rough — a characteristic of Minecraft graphics that some say forces or allows active imaginative effort.

The subject of chatter jumps around among three necessary contexts or levels of mental abstraction: the immersive level of virtual world experience; the self-conscious level of how to control your avatar's actions using the software tools; and the team-aware level of coordinating your actions, real and virtual, to accomplish group goals. (This sort of context-switching seems to be a theme in kids' lives today, online and off, with electronic devices and without. If you think of multitasking as switching among horizontally distinct channels of [physical] activity, then this might be switching among vertically distinct [mental] channels or layers. These Minecrafters are pressed to do both kinds of channel hopping, which I think may represent a frontier in human cognition — a sort of three-dimensional simultaneity in working memory; perhaps a precursor to whole-systems thinking. Call it omni-tasking.)

In the end, Keller abruptly says "Let's go outside now." It's freezing cold out there, but like a school of fish moving in unison, as though Keller simply speaks what their collective mind is converging on, they all shut down their devices, and in less than a minute, they're outdoors. Soon they're back indoors, going around the school saying "Base Tag?" in each room. Everyone knows what that means: a game of Base Tag is about to crystallize in the backyard. It's an invitation to join. As in the Minecraft mission, skill level doesn't matter. All are welcome, and a surprising number join them outdoors on that cold day.

## Once Again, Practicing Life

As I said, the names by which I have identified these various modes, methods, and mechanisms are not in the school's lexicon. We didn't think these up as teaching-learning methods and then find ways to work them into the school because of their educational value. We didn't anticipate these patterns. I'm simply observing and reporting. It is not the school's aim to camouflage a curriculum and sneak predetermined lessons into the program here and there.

Noticed or not, teaching-learning patterns emerge from school society and life together. We design systems and we legislate to address opportunities and challenges of shared space and resources, in a community with a wide range of ages and abilities. When School Meeting debates a new law or a new chore system, there are many values, viewpoints, and constraints at issue — safety, convenience, and economy usually among them — but not usually educational value.

You might think it an educationally fortuitous coincidence that patterns of relevant learning emerge in democratic schools. But it's not coincidence, and that's the point: the school functions as a scaled-down real-world society and community, complete with comparable pressures and challenges, and real-life systems created as real-life community responses. It's kids practicing life, acquiring knowledge and skills that are necessary and helpful in life here and everywhere.

This might be a good time to point out the double meaning of "kids practicing life." You can think of "practice" in its meaning as "rehearsal." But really, democratic schools are more about "practice" as that which a practitioner does. Just as doctors practice medicine, kids practice life.

In democratic schools, children are immersed in a community of diverse perspectives, abilities, and resources. Life presents a steady stream of challenges and examples — opportunities and invitations to borrow and try on new ways of seeing, being, and doing. Keep what works and dump the rest. Build a toolkit of ideas and practices, a modular operating system, adapting and evolving to meet new challenges. This is educational bricolage, the ongoing creation of something new — your self — from what catches your eye nearby, like an inventor in a well-stocked maker space. We are all self-inventors in a maker space world, cribbing incessantly from everywhere and cobbling ourselves together from the best of it. The democratic school is a kids' maker space for the creative bricolage of self-authorship.

## Traditional and Modern Methods in Democratic Schools

| Classes | Traditional teacher-led studies of discrete subjects. |
|---|---|
| Internships | Student works or studies in an off-campus arrangement. |
| Independent study | Focused study of a particular subject without constant involvement of a teacher. |
| One-on-one tutoring | Teacher-student or student-student. |
| Off-campus classes | At nearby colleges. |

## New Methods Enabled by Democratic Schools

| Meta-message learning | The system is the message, conveying values of democracy, community, individual initiative, free enterprise, free society, personal responsibility. |
|---|---|
| Self-service systems | Use a microscope, sign out an iPad, organize a talent show. Kids can do significant things on their own without depending on adults — cultivating ability, confidence, independence, sense of self-efficacy. |
| Decision-making | Self-direction demands frequent decision-making in personally meaningful situations with real-life consequences. |
| Public process | Open government engages all members in the making of culture, community, and public policy. |
| School administration | Join the Office Team, the Library Committee, the Facilities Team, many more. Help run the school. |
| Accelerated culture | High-bandwidth social commerce efficiently transmits knowledge and skills (horizontal growth) and stimulates higher-order thinking (vertical growth to higher stages). |
| Near-stage transmission | Age-mixing and free society foster high-efficiency exchanges between cultural partners at slightly different stages of growth. Both partners gain. |

| Multiple lines of development | Children freely seek and find stimulation along multiple self-selected lines of development — cognitive, moral, ego, logical-mathematical, spatial, empathy, musical, time sense, etc. |
|---|---|
| Self-balancing | Self-direction in a broad range of activities and social possibilities appears to facilitate growth that is balanced across lines of development. |
| Integrated curriculum | Self-selected and self-directed "whole" activities, rather than subjects isolated for out-of-context study, lead to high motivation and retention of learning. |
| Interest groups | A "teacherless class" such as book group, creative writing, critical thinking, anime, racism discussion group, and zombies. Anybody can do it, any time. Gather friends in a drag-along or start with a sign-up sheet on the bulletin board. |
| Drag-alongs, tag-alongs, stumble-ons, and happenings | Dragged by a friend, allowed to go along, notice what's going on, school-wide ripples: serendipitous artifacts of friendship, community, culture, time, and resources. |
| Commerce and entrepreneurship | Free-market, free enterprise. Buyers and sellers of all ages. Perennial favorites are food, art, and services. Make money doing other people's chores for them or sign up and do extra chores for pay. |
| Play and deep play | The impulse is natural and universal. Deep play accelerates development — social, emotional, cognitive, verbal, and more; helps kids make meaning from experience. |
| Functional apprenticeship | A novice and an adept pair up. The novice gains knowledge, skill, and pleasure. The adept deepens mastery, gains a worthy colleague, rises in social standing and self-esteem. |
| Practicing life | Be a regular person in society, treated like nobody knows you're really a kid. Oh, and it's not practice. It's for real. Like doctors practice medicine, kids practice life. Immersed in a community of diverse examples, pick the best and cobble yourself together in the lifelong bricolage of self-authorship. |

Chapter 7:

# Critical Thinking

T HOSE DADS WHO WERE SURPRISED BY THEIR KIDS' newfound
ability to analyze and reason were not alone. I have heard many
times from parents of recently enrolled students about sudden bursts
of growth in vocabulary, maturity, dialogue, reason, and critical thinking. It often takes me by surprise because I have observed the student
in question and I've seen nothing unusual about their engagement
at school. They're just people pursuing their interests in a dynamic
community.

Each person's story is a new one, but I see patterns in how critical
thinking develops in democratic schooling. Here's my thinking about
thinking, grounded in many thousands of hours among children. I esti-
mate that two thousand of those hours have been at my desk in a small
room at school, while young friends talked or played on the floor at my
feet or nearby, sometimes for hours on end — within my sight and hearing but ignoring my presence.

Consider dissonance, cognition, and critical thinking. *Dissonance*,
as I'm using the term here, is an internal experience of disharmony or
incongruity, a tension between things that somehow conflict or do not
fit together — an itch. *Cognition* is the mental process of understanding
or comprehension, which is involved in creating dissonance, and also
resolving it — scratching the itch. *Critical thinking* is a learned practice
of examining and organizing one's own thoughts, aiming to draw conclusions, derive new knowledge, and improve thinking processes.

Critical thinking develops in the presence of three necessary conditions: (1) sufficiently capable cognition, (2) personally meaningful provocations, and (3) a culture of critical thinking. Respectively these represent potential, stimulation, and acculturation. The three can be viewed as a repeating cycle of development, an upward spiral expanding in increments the power of critical thinking. Here's how the three-step cycle works in democratic schools:

First, *cognitive potential*. Students' free agency in community incessantly generates dissonance, requiring frequent, divergent decision-making and creative adaptation. Dissonance, decision-making, and adaptation drive development of increasingly capable cognition.

Second, *stimulation*. Immersion in self-determined activity and community presents personally meaningful existential and situational challenges that cannot be resolved by raw cognition alone. Such challenges are invitations, provocations, and opportunities to acquire new ways of thinking.

Third, *acculturation*. Personal and collective self-determination sustains a culture of self-examination, conscious living, and critical thinking. Rule-making, judicial systems, and school administration are driven by observation, reason, and meritorious argument in collaborative dialogue and formal debate, as in Western democracies generally. Universal participation in such dialogue initiates students in critical thinking every day from an early age, relentlessly.

By these mechanisms, democratic schooling drives the cycle of cognitive development, supplying an endless stream of dissonance and meaningful provocation, keeping up with each student's growing potential, in a culture biased to critical thinking practices.

That's the summary. Now let's unpack it.

## Capable Cognition

Cognition is the mental process of understanding or comprehension, which is the foundation of general intelligence and critical thinking. Cognitive development, the growth of cognition, is often regarded as a fundamental or immediate aim of education. Cognition emerges from a complex mix of mental activity including sensation, attention, perception, experience, memory, introspection, knowledge, thought, imagination, insight, intuition, and internal articulation. Cognition is a mental stew from which we ingest bites of truth. Its inner workings remain obscure, but the importance of cognition is obvious, fundamental, and universally acknowledged.

To one degree or another, cognition enables other lines of development, the various intelligences. For example, mathematical intelligence, in order to reach beyond concrete arithmetic to symbolic algebra, requires cognitive capacity for abstract thinking. Similarly, development of empathy requires cognitive capacity to imaginatively "calculate" the state of another person's mind. (Prerequisites for empathy also include emotional capacity to experience the relevant feelings, cognitive capacity to associate feelings with generalized trigger conditions, and introspective capacity to make feelings available for projection — illustrating the tangle of dependencies across developmental lines.)

## Dissonance

Have you ever played hide-and-seek with a young toddler? When it's their turn to hide, they might stand in plain sight, cover their eyes with their hands, and think nobody can see them. (Yes, this is real and normal.) At that stage of development, the very young child has not yet fully differentiated their own experience from that of other people. In effect, they understand everyone to be seeing what they are seeing, because to them there is only one stream of experience in the world, shared by all. They do not yet account for any perspective other than their own. Psychologists say they have not yet acquired "theory of mind."

At some point, or gradually, they understand that others *do* seem to see them; the game is somehow rigged against them. Maybe the child experiences a preverbal rendition of "Whoa! Freaky! With covered eyes, all was darkness and nothing was seen, but there was seeing anyway! What's up with *that*?" You can conceptualize the cause of confusion in at least two ways: the child's inadequate mental model of the world (failing to account for other minds) or conflicting beliefs (seeing *cannot* happen in darkness, but seeing *happened* in darkness). However you explain it, something doesn't add up, and it doesn't feel right. That's dissonance, an irritation of being, an itch that must be scratched.

Over many repetitions of similarly dissonant circumstances, the young child eventually scratches the itch: "Wait, what? How can there be *not*-seeing and also *seeing* at the same time? Are there two perceiving minds? Is there a *me*-mind and a *you*-mind? Do I see one thing while *you* see another? Holy Sippy Cup! It's all about the pronouns! Who knew?" Obviously the child doesn't think it through in words like this, but the unarticulated insight is nevertheless assimilated in the child's understanding of the world. Cognition becomes more capable.

The new understanding emerges in the child's mind that each person experiences a distinct perspective, a stream of experience all their own. The revised worldview is more powerful, more useful — and sure makes hide-and-seek more fun. Over time, cognition is upgraded with expanded capacity for imagination (to see what someone else is seeing), working memory (to hold the information needed for that imaginative calculation), abstract thinking (to represent other minds), and probably a host of other bug fixes and enhancements. It sets the stage for sympathy, empathy, and compassion. Furthermore, and not incidentally, this is an occasion of growth, an actualization of self, an experience of fulfillment, and a joy of life.

My earliest memory is of a similar experience. I was lying in my crib, eyes closed, nearly awake but not quite. Nearby, just outside the bedroom door, I heard my sister and mother talking softly, one of them wondering if Jimmy (that's me) was awake. I heard sounds of motion and then a voice say no, he's asleep. I wasn't awake enough to get their attention, but apparently awake enough to form a vivid memory of a feeling that I can now describe as a mixture of sudden insight, transforming empowerment, and ecstatic delight. I suppose the insight, though wordless, was something like "They can't hear my thoughts! Only I can hear my thoughts! I have a private interior and a public exterior!" Thus dissonance gave rise to an important insight in self-awareness.

Dissonance is a certain kind of discomfort. Every living creature experiences dissonance, along with a felt need to resolve it. In its most primitive form, biologists call that capacity "irritability," a hallmark of life, enabling reaction to stimuli.

Dissonance is an internal experience, personal and subjective, even though it often arises from external factors. Sometimes you sense the tension — "Something's wrong here" — but cannot identify the exact cause. Whether or not you acknowledge dissonance, and whether or not you identify its origins, dissonance can influence choices and motivate action.

In the hide-and-seek example, dissonance eventually leads to the major cognitive advance called theory of mind. Developmental psychologists have identified scores of other cognitive building blocks. Undoubtedly many more of these modules of cognition remain unidentified. We must each build them for ourselves through experience, dissonance, action, insight, and assimilation. Each incremental advance sets the stage for the next.

There's the crux of it. "Theory of mind" is only one of countless steps on the path of cognition (although it's a big one). Without diminishing the body of knowledge amassed in neurology, developmental psychology, artificial intelligence, and other fields, I believe our understanding is still primitive. We can generalize about broad patterns of cognition and its development, and we can generalize about the dependencies across some capacities, but that's about it. We don't know all or even most of the links in chains of mental growth; we don't even know all or most of the chains themselves, the possible capacities or modules; and we cannot plot or predict the developmental route for any individual person. What we do know is that we each build our mental machinery and write our mental software through our own individual experience. We don't know exactly how or in what order.

The sign-in board at school exposes a common pattern of dissonance in our youngest children. A school rule requires each student (and staff member) to sign in upon arrival at school. You have to write down the time you arrived, and later the time of your departure. If you don't know numbers and time, then you might draw shapes on the sign-in sheet to match the shapes you see on the digital clock nearby. At some level, you are aware that the shapes have meaning to others that you don't understand. That contrast gives rise to irritating dissonance and a subtle compulsion to resolve it. Eventually you will hit upon the cognitive advances to disclose the meaning of numbers generally and time in particular. Others' explanations of time and numbers may help or hurt, like wiggling a tooth when it's ready to come out, or not. Of course, once you understand the meaning of numbers, many more experiences of dissonance lie ahead. Just wait till you get to algebra.

It never ends. We are itchy creatures, we human beings, and each time we scratch an itch to satisfaction, we are drawn to yet a new frontier in our still imperfect understanding of the world and ourselves, leading inevitably to new itches. Life is a whack-a-mole game of itches. Do you love the game?

The important point is this: dissonance drives cognitive development — cultivation of the many coordinated mental activities that contribute to understanding. Life in freedom, responsibility, and a lively, mixed-age community generates an endless stream of dissonance.

## Decision-making

When you come to a fork in the road, you must make a choice. If the choice is meaningful to you, there will be dissonance. In effect you must consider two conflicting beliefs: (1) the left branch is the better path to take, and (2) the right branch is better. If the choice is not important to you — for example, if you don't care where you go — then you will feel the dissonance only mildly. If you care a lot — for example, if you have a particular destination in mind — then the felt dissonance will be relatively greater. Caring counts. If you care about the outcome, the decision is more meaningful and the dissonance more provocative.

Students in all schools face choices and decisions, but in democratic schools, there are important differences: more decisions that are meaningful and more care invested in each. This is easy to see. Democratic school students are self-directed. They choose what they will do, moment by moment, throughout the day, the week, the year. They choose the who, what, when, and where of their lives. Just as adults in the world beyond school, they even choose on what basis they will rest their choice: pleasure, need, duty, honor, whim; going along with a friend's preference; jumping through hoops to reach a desired objective; social conformity; social rebellion; earning a reward; avoiding a penalty. At any time, they can choose something else and change course. The "choice tree" is divergent and relatively unlimited, branching in many directions and extending as far as you care to go.

In contrast, conventional school students face fewer personally meaningful choices, and what choices they have are narrowly limited. Their class schedule or teacher tells them where to be most of the time. The people in each class with them are selected by school officials, and in some classes, they must sit in assigned seats. Activities are usually directed by the teacher. Generally, they cannot decide the who, what, when, and where of their school life. The choices they do have are generally directed choices in which they have little authentic investment or care. Of course, most students become excited about some things some times, and some students become excited about many things often. But even in the best case, most decision-making is flat rather than internally animated — directed rather than self-chosen — and therefore bound to carry less personal meaning and care.

In summary, conventional school students tend to face a decision tree that is more limited and convergent, with low to moderate personal investment. In contrast, democratic school students face a decision tree that is divergent, dynamic, and omni-directional, with greater personal investment. Call it three-dimensional decision-making.

Decision-making requires you to look inward, to introspect; to examine your internal states, weigh values, and rely on or reject selected knowledge and beliefs. You make easy decisions in a flash, barely paying attention. Hard decisions require more of you, perhaps to manipulate ideas, principles, themes, and even your thinking processes — the domain of critical thinking.

Decisions may "fail" because of deficiencies in your decision-making processes. Perhaps there was missing knowledge, false belief, faulty processing, unanticipated events, or misreading of your internal states. No matter what, the failed decisions are fertile ground for cognitive development (and lots more). Failure creates dissonance like nothing else. Perhaps you weighed conflicting values, and in the future, you will weigh them differently — as though an internal voice, consciously or not, says "Oh, now I see that this friendship is more important to me than money." Perhaps you left some important values out of the equation, and in the future, you will know better: "Oops, I didn't think of that." May you fail often and fruitfully.

Decision-making beefs up cognition. In democratic schools, kids get a cognitive development push: the need to make personally meaningful choices constantly and play them out in the real world. Moreover, failure needn't be final and doesn't affect a grade or a report card. Like in the movie *Groundhog Day*, democratic school students get to try over and over, without penalty for the do-over.

## Provocations

Dissonance and self-directed decision-making help to satisfy the first condition for development of critical thinking: sufficiently capable cognition. The second condition is personally meaningful challenge that cannot be resolved by raw cognition alone, and thus provokes higher orders of thinking such as abstraction, generalization, organization, and deductive reasoning. These are intellectual tools that involve cognition attending to itself — thinking about thinking, the domain of critical thinking.

Consider two broad categories of such provocations in democratic schools: first, existential needs built into human nature, as exemplified in Maslow's famous hierarchy of needs; and second, situational challenges arising from interpersonal dynamics, life's vicissitudes, and the civic demands of government, law, and society.

### Existential Needs

From birth, throughout life, we each experience needs that are built into being human. You don't have to seek them out. They just turn up in the ordinary course of your life in nature, community, and society. They are "existential" because they are inherent in human existence.

In the mid-20th century, Abraham Maslow formulated a hierarchy of existential needs, beginning with physical and safety needs such as food and shelter; continuing to needs of belonging, friendship, self-esteem, knowledge, and competence; and culminating in higher needs such as beauty, justice, unity, fulfillment of potential ("self-actualization"), and expanded identity ("self-transcendence"). Unmet lower needs are a barrier, tending to inhibit striving and growth to meet higher needs. As lower needs are met, we are motivated by nature to strive to meet higher needs.

Many other researchers have also found inherent human needs and an inborn drive to meet them. Some see a sequence or hierarchy; others see a more fluid configuration. Self-determination theory identifies three universally innate psychological needs and persistent efforts to meet them: autonomy, relatedness, and competence. Manfred Max-Neef, in his model of "human-scale development," includes nine universal fundamental human needs, across time and cultures: subsistence, protection, affection, understanding, participation, leisure, creation, identity, and freedom.

There is much overlap and similarity across the many studies of human needs. In addition to having some themes in common, they all assert three basic ideas that are self-evident from ordinary experience. First, there are human needs that are universal. Second, our needs go beyond physical survival needs. And third, human beings are instinctively motivated to satisfy those needs.

We are born with these lifelong challenges, and nature impels us to meet them. How does this play out in self-directed democratic schools?

Start with attention. Conscious attention is a primal, sovereign, inalienable function of each person. Focus of attention may be the most basic choice you make, over and over again, innumerable times each day. Along the lines of Maslow's hierarchy of needs, we generally give our attention first to the urgent basics of food, shelter, security, and health. In the absence of urgent basic needs, we shift our attention to a second tier: belonging, intimacy, acceptance, respect, competence, achievement, knowledge, and understanding. With suitable opportunity, our attention moves on to higher needs still: justice, goodness, beauty, order, and unity. Is there an upper limit?

Those higher needs are as instinctive as lower needs, and their satisfaction is equally driven by nature and fulfilling when met. When higher needs are not met, the person may experience such pathologies as apathy, alienation, and anguish.

We are born with existential needs and instinctively driven ability to meet them through attention and growth. In effect, we are born with an internal compass pointing in the general direction of well-being and greater capacity. We don't always read the compass clearly and follow it faithfully, sometimes leading us on apparent digressions from a straight path to self-actualization. But on balance over time, the compass guides us. The cumulative effect is a tendency to strive, thrive, and grow.

In democratic schools, students are immersed in practice of attentional choice and relative freedom to follow their internal compass. Their introspective skills grow: sense the needs, read the compass, focus attention. The journey weaves through the most basic needs to higher needs. The path is unique to each person, with twists, turns, loops, shortcuts, and dead ends. Moment to moment, day to day, year to year, students direct and redirect attention based on needs, urgency, interest, ability, and opportunity. The waves and tides of needs pursued and fulfilled are never still, ebbing and flowing. Over time the high water mark tends to reach higher and higher. Personal capacities grow.

Democratic schools give children and teenagers relatively free rein to experience their inborn impulse to seek and their power to find; to play with their internal compass, ignore it or follow it, again and again. Crucially, the whole existential adventure takes place not in a void, nor in exaggerated freedom, but in a flesh-and-blood community of human beings, with a full array of examples, opportunities, demands, and constraints.

In contrast, conventional schools divert students from this enterprise of self-knowledge and needs fulfillment, substituting instead a static curriculum that purports to present a universally important set of learning objectives in a universally best sequence linked to students' ages. Chronic (mis)direction of children's attention to curricular objectives isolates them from their internal compass and exercise of personal agency.

Nature impels us to seek infinity through satisfaction of humanly insatiable needs. Call it an aesthetic, transcendental, or spiritual imperative, if you like. The relevant principle for education is clear: if we feed, clothe, secure, and love our children, they naturally seek knowledge, understanding, wisdom, and high purpose.

The instinct to sense and follow one's compass is powerful and promising. Its exercise leads not only to personally meaningful challenges that stimulate critical thinking but also to across-the-board development and the ultimate superpower of self-creation. Kids ought to practice it in school, don't you think?

## Situational Challenges

Existential needs come to us by nature. Situational challenges are brought to us by mere human beings, circumstance, and society — respectively, through interpersonal dynamics, life's vicissitudes, and social demands. Situational challenges may be simple or complex, lasting minutes or months, involving one person alone or the entire community, and overlapping or prompting existential challenges.

Following is a list of a hundred or so examples of situational challenges, merely hinting at the myriad situations engaged daily by democratic school students. Even the simplest can be laden with subtlety and complexity when played out in actual experience, especially by someone who is not-quite-capable-but-wants-to-be. Some of these situations would be challenging only for the least developed students; some impossible except for the most developed. All are provocations and invitations to go beyond raw cognition into the realm of critical thinking.

- Sign in on the attendance sheet (find your name, write the time)
- Pick a chore and sign up
- Store your stuff in a way that it won't get messed with or damaged
- Decide the who, what, and where of your next move, or plan your day
- Make an appointment; keep an appointment
- Figure out when it's chore time
- Know how to do your chore; how to use a vacuum cleaner
- Do your chore and get it checked
- Learn to play Capture the Flag, or Pickle, or Tribes
- Recruit and organize people for a backyard game
- Pick fair teams
- Make rules to accommodate variety of player ability
- Get injured and get help
- Become a Medical Responder and give first aid
- What to do when you get mud on the floor and nobody sees you do it
- Write somebody up for leaving a mess or breaking something
- Look up the rule number you think someone broke
- Go to Judicial Committee and tell your side of the story
- Figure out how to get in on extra chores for pay
- Sign up for extra chores, do one, and get paid
- Figure out why nickels are bigger than dimes but worth less
- Count money and buy freeze pops from Simon
- Open the darned freeze pop without squirting all over, or get help
- Sell something you made in the Art Room or brought from home
- Design a sign to sell something on the for-sale counter
- Set a selling price that's not too low and not too high
- Understand IOUs and why it isn't buying something for nothing
- Understand IOUs and why you might not get paid back

- Collect a debt from someone you view as less powerful
- Collect a debt from someone you view as more powerful
- Measure brownie ingredients by tablespoon and cup, without knowing fractions
- Double the recipe
- Use a screwdriver for the first time, to help build a new table in the Art Room
- Get certified to use kitchen dishes
- Get certified to use paints in the Art Room
- Get certified to use magnets or microscopes in the Science Room
- Find the field trip sign-up on the bulletin board, and add your name
- Organize a group pizza order
- Find out what's on the agenda for the next session of School Meeting
- Check the schedule to see when you are on Judicial Committee
- Dissect an old computer or a cow eyeball with the Science Corporation
- Get certified to go on field trips, or to plan field trips
- Master your impulses, especially the ones that get you in trouble
- What to do when you find a dollar on the floor
- How to get out of boredom
- How to deal with frustration, irritation, over-stimulation
- How to talk and listen to a frustrated friend or a young child
- What to do when a friend suggests something you don't want to do
- What to do when a friend does something damaging or unsafe
- What to do when a friend takes advantage of you
- What to do when you take advantage of a friend
- How to break out of ongoing patterns of unwanted social dynamics
- Conflict with a friend
- Reconcile with a friend
- Taking sides when two friends are in conflict
- Making peace when two friends are in conflict
- Win an argument
- Understand another's good point
- Amend your beliefs
- Share clean-up of a group mess
- Persuade others to do their share
- Arrange a math class, or a Spanish class, or a book discussion group
- Collaborate on the class content, format, and schedule

- Do the work you agreed to, for the class you arranged
- Recognize when you've had enough of the class, and end it
- Prepare to take college entry exams
- Give and receive signals of romantic interest
- Know the rules that are important to you, and why
- Know when it's important to follow the rules
- Break the rules when a larger principle is at stake
- Find out how to get a rule changed
- Rally support for your cause
- Write, make, and argue a motion at School Meeting
- Get a rule changed, or live through a failed attempt
- How to be cool among peers
- How to be true to self among peers
- Relation to cultural expectations
- Relation to parental expectations
- Relation to school staff members
- Recognize your own self-expectations
- Develop self-image
- Find styles of dress and expression that work for you
- Know your own aspirations, fears, talents, weaknesses

- Make a room reservation
- Run for election (to any of a couple dozen offices)
- Plan and give a campaign speech to persuade voters
- Be part of the vote tallying team
- Learn how to be Elections Clerk
- Fulfill the duties of the office
- Be the treasurer of the Art Corporation
- Devise time-management techniques to meet deadlines and get stuff done
- Receive and assimilate praise
- Receive and assimilate criticism
- Receive angry criticism week after week, because of continued neglect
- Pursue a serious interest
- Organize a lip-sync contest, party, theatrical production, field trip
- Plan and go on a backpacking trip
- Arrange an externship in a business or organization of interest
- Determine your readiness to graduate and move on
- Find a college that suits you
- Reflect yourself and your aspirations in college applications

Some of these situational challenges are specific to democratic schools, and some can happen to a certain degree in other kinds of schools. Other schools undoubtedly generate other kinds of situational challenges, too. But notice four defining differences about democratic school challenges:

*Authenticity.* These situations are not contrived or assigned as part of a curriculum. They emerge in "real life." They are thus likely to be more personal, meaningful, and provocative. Immediate, authentic challenges such as these have greater power to educate, actualize, and fulfill than the artifice of predetermined lesson plans. It's self-powered education.

*Centrality.* Although some of these situations may occur in conventional schools, they are often unsanctioned and outside the scope of the curriculum — for example, in hallways, recess, cafeteria, locker rooms, and extra-curriculars. In contrast, democratic schools place this lifework at the center of education: valued and validated, rather than sneaked in or devalued as peripheral, incidental, and irrelevant.

*Breadth.* In conventional schools, the range of challenges tends to be limited by the predetermined and finite learning objectives of the curriculum, making many of the listed situations unlikely or impossible. In democratic schools, without predetermined curriculum, the situational possibilities are unlimited.

*Motivation.* In conventional schools, students' self-direction and choice are severely limited by imposed classes and close monitoring. Human beings are naturally less motivated when their actions are dictated and surveilled; engagement and learning tend to be shallow. In democratic schools, situational challenges tend to involve substantial elements of choice and self-direction, resulting in greater motivation and deeper learning.

Although situational challenges occur in schools of all kinds, these four crucial differences amplify their power to educate in democratic schools.

## Culture of Critical Thinking

Dissonance and decision-making sharpen cognition. Existential needs and situational challenges stretch the mind beyond the limits of raw cognition, calling for higher orders of thinking. Basic cognition alone will not meet the challenges. More power of thought is required for personal and collective self-examination and satisfying resolution. Critical thinking helps. If cognition gets us bites of truth, critical thinking gets us gulps.

Critical thinking is a learned discipline of intellectual techniques and practices for organizing, analyzing, and expressing the products of cognition. Unlike basic cognition, critical thinking seems largely dependent on culture for transmission to new initiates. Given the intellectual demands of today's technology and complex society, cultural transmission of critical thinking seems more important than ever. To learn it, you need to see it in action, try it out, find it useful, and refine it over time through practice in problem-solving and dialogue with adept critical thinkers.

In democratic schools, there is a pervasive cultural commitment to reason, the presenting face of critical thinking. Principled living, such as democratic society, necessarily favors it. The bias to reason is rooted in the formality and structure of democratic principles such as public governance, rule of law, civic duty, civil rights, and collective responsibility. You can see it everywhere in democratic schools, not only among the adults, or the teenagers and adults. Even in the Playroom, filled with young children, I hear dialogue and arguments based on critical reasoning — or beginners' imitations anyway. Often the imitations are, well, reasonable.

It's not an obsession with critical thinking. It's not usually intense, nor eggheady, and critical thinking is not the baseline mode of discourse in casual conversation. But it is always present and surfaces quickly when conversation turns to principle, public policy, rules, fairness, science, gaming, planning, and many other matters that conversation often turns to.

Perhaps the cultural value of critical thinking at school is partly a reflection of contemporary culture. As a society, we tend to adore reason. We accept it as the final arbiter of truth in science, law, and public policy. We tend to apply it to justify or prove things that aren't really subject to reason at all. And for better or worse, some people are devoted to reason as the governing principle of personal life, too.

Perhaps democratic schools appear to promote critical thinking not because of anything special about democratic schooling but rather because conventional schools actively undermine and suppress it. There is merit to this argument. In spite of teachers' best efforts and commitment to critical thinking, conventional schooling works against it. Perhaps you have heard the humorous cartoon words of a teacher in front of a classroom, something like this: "I expect you all to be independent, innovative, critical thinkers who do exactly as I say!" The point is that conventional school systems were designed (long ago) with conformity and passive compliance in mind, but those values are incompatible with originality, innovation, and critical thinking. Thus, when it comes to critical thinking, conventional schooling tends to make democratic schools look good.

In addition to pass-through of values from the larger culture, and regardless of the comparative subversion of critical thinking in conventional schools, certain democratic school features affirmatively cultivate critical thinking and make it visible. Judicial systems are foremost among them, nicely illustrated by Mickey.

## Mickey's Cookie and Critical Thinking

Mickey was new to The Circle School. In his old school, the 13-year-old made mischief — lots of mischief — and he was well accustomed to the summary judgment of the principal. No due process there. Mickey thought he and authority were natural enemies. So he was very pleased to learn during his admissions visit that The Circle School has no principal, head-of-school, or anything like that. I told him he has as much authority in this school as anyone else, including the adults. But of course, he had no context for understanding what that meant.

Mickey was also pleased to learn that when he got in trouble, as he assumed he would, he could argue his own defense before the Judicial Committee (JC), composed of four students and one staff member. If, despite his best arguments, they charged him with breaking a rule anyway, he could plead Not Guilty and then, within four school days, argue his defense before a jury. This got his attention. Mickey smiled and decided to enroll.

His first opportunity came up very early on. He ate an Oreo cookie in the Library, violating a rule about where it's okay to eat and where it's not. Called to JC, he readily admitted eating the cookie, and also agreed with witnesses who said they had told him not to eat the cookie in the Library, but he did so anyway. He and the JC discussed why the rule forbids food and eating in the Library — having to do with messes, ants, and mice. After that, Mickey said oh, well, he had actually put the entire cookie in his mouth, so there was no possibility of crumbs, and he shouldn't be charged with breaking the rule. Good thinking, I suppose, but not persuasive and maybe not honest.

The JC charged Mickey with breaking the rule. As is common with new students, they gave him a warning instead of sentencing him, and then asked for his plea. "Not guilty," said Mickey, and so the case went to trial with stakes of principle and pride but not punishment.

Mickey worked hard on his defense for the next couple of days, including significant research. In a packed courtroom, addressing the six jurors (five students and one staff member), he laid out his case. Food, he said, is an edible substance with nutritional value, and he read a dictionary definition to back him up. Then he called attention to the nutritional label on the Oreo package. There is some nutritional value in an Oreo cookie, he said, but not much. However, by his calculation, if a person ate less than half a cookie, they would ingest less than 1% of the government-recommended Daily Value of every nutrient on the label. Furthermore, percentages less than 1% are shown as 0%. With a charming grin, Mickey then testified that he had taken only one bite, amounting to less than a third of the cookie. That meant he had consumed less than 1% of the Daily Value of every nutrient, which translates to 0%. Thus, having no nutritional value, it wasn't food after all, and he had not violated the rule. The defense rested its case.

The jury was, shall we say, confused. In our system, jurors have an opportunity to question witnesses. My favorite moment in Mickey's trial was when the youngest juror, 5-year-old Leo, penetrated the fog and went right to the heart of the matter with his incredulous question for Mickey: "You ate a cookie in the Library???"

The prosecution neglected to note the discrepancy in Mickey's testimony: to the JC, he testified he ate the whole cookie; in trial, he testified he ate only a small bite. It didn't matter. The jury took only a few minutes to find Mickey guilty. As Leo's question aptly highlighted, the case was as black and white as an Oreo cookie.

---

Mickey's trial is an interesting case study of critical thinking in development. Mickey was enthralled with his growing grasp of the mental world of ideas, principles, logic, and the power of argumentation. This is typical around adolescence, sometimes leading to idealism, principled lifestyle choices, and adolescent agony around self-conscious creation of a social persona. Mickey's logic was also typical in its Swiss cheese gaps and squirrely leaps. His defense failed to persuade the jury, but was a genuine show of spirit and a critical thinking circus for all to see.

The social repercussions of Mickey's case are interesting, too, and offer insight about the culture. Socially the case hurt Mickey, for reasons that speak of student empowerment in democratic schools. In Mickey's old school, confronting The System might have made him a hero. Win or lose, it might have been hailed as a symbolic blow for freedom, a sign of spirit in the face of oppression. In his democratic school, however, it just seemed clueless and disingenuous, not heroic or even principled. Students of all ages rejected his cat-and-mouse approach to authority. Of course, it can be thrilling when someone escapes through a loophole, but the thrill is diminished if it's your own good purposes that have been evaded. And that's the crux of the social repercussion: Mickey wasn't fighting The System; he was fighting all of us, including himself. In School Meeting, we had crafted a law together as best we could to address a practical problem, and he seemed to disrespect that effort. Mickey didn't get that he is The System, along with the rest of us. I hope Mickey is someday elected as JC Chair, among the most trusted and challenging offices in school government. Recalling Pogo the comic strip character, I imagine some part of Mickey eventually saying to himself, "We have met the enemy, and he is us."

## Judicial Committee As Critical Thinking Culture Builder

Existential needs and situational challenges, such as the hundred examples already listed, create natural needs for critical thinking and the creative problem-solving it enables. Splashy events such as Mickey's trial (above) and the Hour Of No Rules (below) engage the entire school in thought-provoking examination of ideas. These events put critical thinking on display in the manipulation and presentation of ideas: organization, analysis, conceptualization, interpretation, structure of arguments, fallacies of logic, rhetorical pitfalls, intellectual gymnastics, respectful criticism, effective rebuttal, and so on.

This same sort of examination and dialogue occurs daily in the Judicial Committee, and everyone participates in turn. JC is a prime venue in which critical thinking is learned and practiced, because it is needed in order to perform JC's functions. In particular, JC is ideal as a critical thinking incubator partly because of three constant conditions.

First, JC is expected to adjudicate every case, so the pressure to think and work effectively is heightened. JC members cannot decline to serve, and the JC cannot simply decline to do its job.

Second, JC is a small, mixed-age group. At The Circle School, each day's JC includes a young child, a middle child, an elected Scribe (usually a teen), an elected JC Chair (usually an older teen), and a staff member. Typically, the JC represents a wide range of critical thinking skills. Everyone involved is likely to be stretched by dialogue that is beyond their easy comprehension, and also stretched to make themselves understood by others.

Third, JC always, necessarily, examines situations after events have occurred. Unlike ordinary immersive experience, after-the-fact examination requires imagination, reflection, abstract thought, organization, analysis, and articulation. The story does not unfold in a stream of direct experience, and cannot remain unarticulated. It must be recreated in imagination, assembled from pieces of testimony and evidence, and put into words. Like a jigsaw puzzle, it must present a coherent picture. Sometimes the 4-year-olds fall asleep.

The special conditions of JC — pressure to resolve, mixed-skill task group, and after-the-fact analysis — make it a nearly ideal environment for cultivation of critical thinking. JC is designed as a practical system of enforcement and justice, and is not intended or regarded as the perfect device for teaching, learning, and practicing critical thinking. Nevertheless, it is exactly that.

Of course, JC engages more than its five members and two runners. In every case, JC calls witnesses — sometimes one, sometimes 20. Each is questioned, contributing to the story, partaking in the examination, and unavoidably being initiated in critical thinking culture.

Without regard to the content of cases — the alleged facts and infractions — here are a few generic kinds of challenges that are part of every student's regular experience in JC. Each creates needs and opportunities for critical thinking in reflective examination of recently past events:

- As a witness or defendant, answer JC questions about past events
- Organize facts and events as a story

- Separate your blended memories of multiple events
- Differentiate between external/objective and internal/ subjective
- Determine what details are relevant
- Support or contradict another witness
- Support or contradict your friend and co-defendant
- Figure out your relation to JC and truth/honesty/ self-disclosure
- Understand what you are supposed to do as a JC member
- Strain your brain just to follow the proceedings
- Learn how to investigate a case
- What to ask witnesses, and what not to ask
- How to ask open-ended questions, rather than yes/no; and why
- How to treat witnesses who are scared or dishonest or angry
- When to interview witnesses together, and when individually
- Understand influences behind actions
- Get to the underlying reasons and motivations
- Understand developmental differences
- Deal with uncertainty and more uncertainty and again uncertainty
- Keep an open mind, even when you can't stand the defendant
- Examine principles and values
- Understand the fuzzy line between fact and interpretation
- Collaborate to develop findings, charges, and sentences
- Deal with diversity of values and heated disagreement
- As a JC Scribe, compose objective findings while still listening
- As a JC Scribe, receive, assimilate, and act on criticism of your work
- As JC Chair, manage high emotion and six people talking at once
- Balance justice and compassion
- Understand mitigating factors
- When to withhold charges even though a rule was violated
- Understand rule of law, impartiality, due process, defendants' rights

- Attend to restitution, restoration, atonement; or find it unworthy
- Balance the needs of individual and community

Critical thinking comes into sharp focus as the JC composes its findings — a succinct statement of the facts as determined by the group. The statement aims to be "just the facts" without interpretation or judgment (which may come later). Sometimes the Scribe composes findings on the fly, and the JC simply votes to adopt, but sometimes it takes longer to agree on findings than it took to examine witnesses and evidence. Sometimes witnesses are called back to flesh out details or resolve discrepancies. Often defendants are engaged with the JC in crafting findings that satisfy all parties as to accuracy, fairness, and completeness.

How much judicial experience do students encounter? It varies a lot from year to year and from school to school. This year at The Circle School, with about 75 students, the Judicial Committee heard about 900 cases and recorded approximately 1,300 charges in approximately 700 of those cases. The rest were investigated and closed without charges or dropped without investigation. The point is that every student is regularly engaged with the JC as a witness, defendant, or member.

In addition to time spent in JC sessions, each of the 900 cases began with someone writing up a complaint. Sometimes that's quick — perhaps two minutes — but can take 20 minutes or more, depending on the writing ability of the complainant and the complexity of the story. The complainant must also identify at least one rule in the Lawbook (by number) that is alleged to have been broken.

By the way, the number of cases heard this year was unusually high because the numbers of young students and new students were unusually high. New students bring special challenges, especially young teens coming from conventional schooling. At the other extreme, some years might have only half the number of JC cases.

Young children, empowered by the true recourse of JC and typically motivated by a strong sense of fairness, are prolific writers of complaints even though it takes them longer to write each one. Many of them recruit the help of older students and staff members to fill out the complaint form. For young children, the need to reflect on and recount events coherently in a complaint is a significant challenge in itself, and a precursor to or example of critical thinking. The need to identify a rule that has been broken can be a project and discussion all by itself. A copy of the Lawbook is kept in the Playroom, where you can often hear the empowered threat: "If you don't stop, I'll write you up!"

JC is a strong and central builder of the school's culture of critical thinking. Collaborative governance of the school is another.

## The Hour Of No Rules

Five minutes before the Hour Of No Rules, I saw Cord and Zach sneaking out of the Conference Room lavatory. It was Zach who had proposed to suspend the rules for an hour, and brought it to a vote with mischief behind his charming grin. And Cord — well, Cord is our homegrown chest-thumping outlaw wild man, with epic experience as a defendant in the school's judicial system. So I knew something was up and I should pay attention.

They tried to block my way as I approached the lavatory to see what they were doing. I was surprised to find everything looking normal. I opened the closet and still nothing looked ransacked or primed for trouble, so I had to ask: "What Are You Up To?"

They shushed me and motioned for me to follow them away, not wanting to draw attention to the lavatory. Then they quietly explained. They were acting as officials of the Games Corporation, which is responsible for the board games and the system for signing them in and out. They were moving the games from their usual place and hiding them in the lavatory closet to protect them from Disorder during the Hour Of No Rules.

Got that? This was Anarchists protecting the Establishment, and Establishmentarians relishing Anarchy. You might think it was foxes guarding the henhouse, but these were sincere foxes, acting lawfully in accord with an action duly adopted, in secret, by the Games Corporation. Their written Minutes are specific that this would be a "secret operation." I felt the exhilaration of their adventure, and their pride in duty served.

Our Lawbook has about 200 laws, all adopted by majority vote of students and staff together, following public notice and parliamentary debate. That doesn't count hundreds more provisions relating to committees, corporations; certifications, job descriptions, and so on, also adopted in democratic process.

Altogether the book runs to 238 pages just now. Some laws go back 20 years or more, but every week, School Meeting debates legislative proposals to adopt, amend, or repeal rules.

The Hour Of No Rules wasn't anarchy. Mostly we just suspended enforcement of laws about "victimless crimes." Rules about property damage and boundaries remained in force. We also designated one room as a "safe zone" in which all rules still applied as usual. The safe zone was barely used, and entirely empty about halfway through the hour.

Cord and Zach had brought their skateboards to school, and Jonathan his low-slung silvery scooter. They placed orange safety cones in doorways and stationed guards to avoid accidents — precautions they thought of on their own. Then they zoomed down the hallway and into the Library, again and again. It was deliciously scandalous and gleefully outlaw, a fitting climax to the long effort leading up to the occasion.

School Meeting's vote to conduct the Hour Of No Rules followed four weeks of lively discussion, including hours of formal debate on the floor of School Meeting. We also spun off a large committee to comb the Lawbook for rules that can be thrown out permanently.

How did the Hour Of No Rules come about, and why? Was there a particular objectionable rule or perceived injustice? Was the mood more rebellious than usual? My take is no, this arose from playfulness in a moment of calm security. Sometimes there are waves of dissatisfaction with a rule or situation, but not in this case. The school culture was humming along with people generally living their lives busily engaged socially and in personally fulfilling pursuits. The judicial system was functioning well. The busy buzz of life in dependable community makes a sturdy foundation for bold adventure.

"Throw out the rules" is always in the air — a healthy thing, I think — a naturally recurring idea wafting through the culture from time to time. This time the air was still and thus more sensitive to such breezes. I think it was like the butterfly's wings in Asia stirring the air to a tornado in Kansas. Playful musing in a secure culture empowered imaginations to launch bigger thoughts and chains of action.

Throwing out the rules is such a sensational idea on the surface that we may not notice deeper meaning. Adults, teens, and children of all ages engaged together for weeks in analytical examination of the proposal. What will happen? How will people behave? What cool things can I do? What should I be afraid of?

Why do we have that rule? Which rules are really important? Do we need any rules at all? Why?

Although we discussed many hypotheticals, the talk was riveting precisely because it wasn't hypothetical. We all knew we were a simple vote away from making it happen. The meeting room was packed. The talk was starkly real and earnest. This was life, not lesson.

Deeper still was the Hour itself. Analysis and discussion are one way to critically examine our beliefs and values. Acting them out is quite another. I think children, more than adults, engage in self-examination and self-authorship through action. Especially through deep play, children explore, adopt, and revise their values, beliefs, and ways of making meaning from the world. For many children, I expect the Hour will last a lifetime.

By the way, Cord is 12 years old and Zach is 13. Proudly they said I could use their real names, and maybe I did. They take their official duties seriously. They love freedom and they love responsibility, sometimes both at the same time and hard to tell apart. They know community, and skateboarding in the Library, and they walked like a tightrope the sublime connecting thread.

## Other Cultural Influences

As the Hour Of No Rules illustrates, critical thinking is not limited to JC. Every week, School Meeting critically examines legislative proposals and administrative actions. School Meeting also reviews JC cases weekly, sometimes overriding JC because the findings don't support the charges, or because the sentence is deemed too harsh, too light, or impractical.

Corporations and committees also take up many matters that call for problem-solving and critical thinking, such as creating and maintaining standards and procedures for certifications to use certain equipment or engage in certain activities.

Field trips — more than 50 of them this year — also contribute significantly to the culture of critical thinking. Field trips always have a student sponsor with a staff co-sponsor. Ambitious field trips are planned in a group, sometimes over months or occasionally a year or two. Like JC, field trip planning involves reflective thinking because it is not about the present. Where JC demands higher-order thinking because it involves after-the-fact examination, field trip planning demands higher-order thinking because it involves before-the-fact examination. Field trip planners must consider what-ifs and contingencies. Many field trips this year have been planned by young students with little help from staff (although at least one staff member goes with each field trip).

Finally, human examples of critical thinking in action are a powerful cultural influence and template for others to embrace or reject. In this sense, the school is a living library and laboratory. Staff members are a special class of human example, typically living examined and principled lives in community with students over long periods. Studying how to be an adult is constant "curriculum" here, especially among the teenagers, but even the younger kids. Maturation to adulthood is a primal drive, and it is certainly evident here. Staff members represent a distinctly important kind of example for children, and are typically adept at critical thinking.

## Deep Play and Critical Thinking

My desk at school is in a tiny room. The space between the front of my desk and the door to the hallway is often fully occupied by a few children and their things. Sometimes they have dozens of props, occasionally hundreds of tiny pieces or creatures. They are oblivious to my presence at my desk except when I need to enter or exit — a delicate process of stepping over and squeezing through the door that can open only a few inches without knocking down a village, space station, forest, zoo, cemetery, horse stable, restaurant, or child. But we cheerfully accommodate one another. Occasionally their accommodation of my coming and going makes me part of whatever fantasy plot is unfolding — "Then the alien came through the fortress wall...."

What we call deep play is a form of children's intense exploration of the world in several dimensions: interior and exterior; natural, social, cultural, personal, physical. Sensing the presence of important meaning that has not yet surfaced in conscious awareness, children employ imagination like a magnifying glass to discover and study something new; to assimilate it; to "incorporate" it — literally to make it part of their corpus, their extent.

Deep play is neither pleasure-seeking nor zoned-out stress relief. It is earnest instinctual work with the adaptive aim of maturation to adulthood. Unscripted, flowing, and free of adult direction, deep play is usually pursued with intensity, sometimes playful, sometimes serious, and sometimes lasts for hours at a stretch. Sometimes the basic story or structure of a deep play adventure continues from day to day or even week to week.

---

## *Playroom Restaurant*

I remember a deep play saga that unfolded in the Playroom continuously for most of a week, involving dozens of players throughout each day. The props were handmade for the purpose, or improvised from wooden blocks and other readily available items. The setup was unmistakable at a glance: a restaurant.

Patrons sat at the tables, some with menus, some with meals; some in casual street dress, some fancied up in dress-up clothes. Servers carried dishes and food, some recognizable only because the maker thoughtfully labeled the cardboard prop with its identity written in crayon — perhaps "Salad." Near the door was a cashier's station, complete with toy cash register and paper money. In the corner, a dishwasher labored, wearing an apron and looking suitably overworked. And of course, the cooks were always busy.

Interactions never stopped: patrons ordered, servers wrote up tabs, diners chatted, workers called out instructions, fussy patrons complained, tip-hungry servers indulged them, cooks grumbled. Patrons arrived, dined, paid, and left, some of them there to be fed, and some to feed the fantasy and please the players.

As in a TV series, you could see simple vignettes, episodes with plots, and ongoing themes and threads. Some players worked their own shtick, refining it or stuck in it. The youngest were wide-eye delighted to be so thoroughly indulged by so many big kids and staff. Subgroups, subplots, and side-currents appeared to be deep play within deep play. All were immersed in worlds of their own creation.

---

We see deep play daily in democratic schools — sometimes solitary, more often in groups, in a great variety of settings, involving mostly young and middle children, but also sometimes teens. Deep play is a familiar constant at school, with no noticeable difference over decades in its frequency, intensity, and purposefulness. Deep play often involves verbalizing aloud, sometimes in assumed characters and voices, but its greatest effects may be in nonverbal apprehensions and insights.

Deep play may be a precursor or early version of critical thinking. At the very least, deep play solidifies the base of cognition on which critical thinking is founded. Both deep play and critical thinking examine and operate on internal experience. Both tend to assimilate and organize experience, and produce insights. Both generate meaning of a higher order than their inputs. Both can be iterative (repeating with variation), and both can be recursive (outcomes of one round feeding into the next). Both can change course spontaneously to pursue interesting new directions.

The defining difference between deep play and critical thinking may be the perspective taken. In critical thinking, you examine your own thoughts as though from an outside perspective. This requires a degree of abstraction (as in all formal operational thinking). You adopt the viewpoint of an observer of your own thinking, as if you are the quality control inspector in a factory. Imagine wearing a white lab coat, holding a clipboard, and watching the assembly line go by. The assembly line is your stream of thought passing before you and subject to your review for approval, rejection, and revision.

In contrast, deep play is immersive. You aren't *watching* the assembly line; you *feel* it. You *enact* it. You *are* it. In imagination, you create a stream of experience and feel the experience as though it were external reality. What a great way to try new things and see how they play out, in many iterations and variations, if you like. Seeded with thoughts, memories, fears and fancies, you play out the simulations, carried by story to possible worlds in havens of mind.

Deep play is *subjective*. You are the first-person subject of your internal experience, immersed and living in it. You are *subject* to it and *subject* of it: playing out memories, thoughts, fears, and hopes in felt experience. Critical thinking is *objective*. Standing back, in third-person, you observe units of internal experience as *objects*: organizing and manipulating to make meaning, follow deductions, discover principles and themes, and perhaps evolve revised beliefs in the process.

Like critical thinking, immersive deep play requires a degree of abstraction. Creating a stream of experience in imagination is essentially the same as inventing a fictional character and adopting it as your own identity. You see through that character's eyes, think their thoughts, and feel their feelings. I suppose it piggybacks on the ability acquired in early childhood to take another's perspective — the foundation of empathy. I suppose deep play not only piggybacks on but also *cultivates* perspective taking and empathy. I suppose deep play, perspective taking, empathy, and critical thinking are all mutually reinforcing and overlapping.

Unlike critical thinking, which is understood in terms of reason and intellect, deep play is assimilated more poetically as felt meaning — like dream, symbol, and myth. Learnings of deep play are absorbed without the articulation of critical thinking. Deep play is visceral. Critical thinking is intellectual. Both expand intelligence and extend the reach of understanding.

Children's knowing is often deeper and more nuanced than their vocabulary and their ability to verbalize. Hence the more intellectual modes of critical thinking are less available or effective for children, and the more visceral modes of deep play serve instead. Deep play congeals experience into visceral clusters of meaning. Words crystallize clusters of meaning into intellectual units of communication. "Use your words" is the classic admonition to connect the visceral to the intellectual. If you can make meaning from the visceral, and tag the meaning with words, then you enable satisfying communication of internal experience. If your knowing is nuanced and your vocabulary spare, deep play helps you use your words.

Deep play helps kids find and fashion meaning from internal experience. Without meaning, words are hollow placeholders in scripts insisted by adults, and the internal experience is trapped without expression, perhaps a lost opportunity, a missing link in a chain of growth, or eventually a troubling repression. With fullest felt meaning, authentic communication quenches an existential thirst for meeting others' minds and hearts. Deep play illuminates meaning, increases self-awareness, and enables authentic dialogue: elements of creative, fulfilling life.

Sometimes I see in children the frustration I remember from my own childhood: not being able to communicate absolutely, to bridge the gap and fully meet another's mind. As a child, I craved the ability to convey in one mental heave the full state and content of my mind, enabling truly satisfying dialogue and approach to unity. Until we learn to mind-meld, though, I suppose I'll have to use my words.

Deep play and critical thinking are alike in their potential for discovery of meaning, insight, order, beauty, and fulfillment. Everybody needs that.

I believe deep play has always been a fundamental feature of child-hood, on which critical thinking is founded. When compulsory schooling arrived with its micromanagement of children's time by adults, some opportunity for deep play disappeared. In recent decades, as children's lives outside of school have also become increasingly adult-directed in planned activity, many children have little opportunity for deep play. To be responsive to basic human needs and shifting societal needs, I wish schools would make more space for deep play, as democratic schools do.

The essential points are that deep play assimilates experience, develops introspection, cultivates perspective taking, enhances communication, and fosters critical thinking. Children's capacity for deep play is inborn and adaptive, contributing to personal fulfillment and societal engagement.

## With and Without Words

When you see a family photo from your childhood, you immediately experience personal meaning without conscious reasoning. Thoughts and words may follow, but first you are aware of meaning in a wordless way. When you see a beautiful sunset, you grasp ineffable meaning. Insights that arrive whole in an instant can take thousands of words to convey, or can be entirely beyond words. Your experience of meaning does not depend on finding words or conscious reasoning. Some meaning you think through and express in words, but much of meaning passes through your experience without expression.

Meaning is immediate, nonverbal, internal experience but can be ren-dered in transmissible form. Through the alchemy of language, meaning is articulated with words. Railroad trains and human backbones are also said to be articulated: wholes constructed from segments that are jointed together. Just so, meaning is articulated as words strung together in sen-tences like beads on a necklace.

In effect, meaning is digitized by words. Words are to meaning what pixels are to an image: dots to be connected by the receiving mind to con-struct a coherent impression of a whole that cannot itself be conveyed directly. (Right there, by the way, is the unbridgeable gap between minds. Meaning is first approximated in words — articulated — then transmitted in written or spoken speech, and then created anew in the receiving mind, following the words like guideposts on a path to meaning. But the fullness of the original flow and context are not transmitted, and no two minds are alike, thus introducing miscommunication like errors in genetic replication, to be lamented or celebrated depending on your outlook and the particulars of the mutation.)

Here's the point. Meaning is made and assimilated *with* and *without* words. Deep play tends to be immersed in wordlessly felt meaning, occasionally rising to a self-observing perspective, perhaps to narrate the story in words — articulated meaning — before submerging for more. In contrast, critical thinking tends to dwell in the observing perspective of analysis, occasionally diving down into wordless meaning unseen from above, perhaps returning to the objective stance dripping with insight begging for words. *Both* deep play and critical thinking engage *both* worded and wordless meaning-making. Does the difference between deep play and critical thinking hang simply in the balance between felt and articulated meaning?

Deep play and critical thinking both engage the creative spark of spontaneity and the analytic eye of observation. Deep play generates clusters of meaning, potential objects of analysis that sometimes rise to the surface of reasoned awareness as crystallized knowledge. Critical thinking playfully examines its own reasoned articulations to feel and absorb wordless meaning of a higher order, which then calls for further articulation, perhaps in progressive distillation to essence, to higher truth. Thus deep play and critical thinking each bring out the best in the other, spinning in delight like partners in dance.

## Critical Thinking in Perspective

Children's free agency in community allows nature and culture to mix and merge for satisfying growth of mind. Instead of the brute force approach of conventional schooling, democratic schooling channels natural forces to drive development, including deep play and critical thinking, in a nifty sort of educational jujitsu.

Finally, let's put critical thinking in perspective. First of all, critical thinking is a common *outcome* of democratic schooling but not a *design goal* and certainly not a curricular aim. Democratic schooling doesn't start from a commitment to teach critical thinking. The systems and practices of democratic schooling are not pedagogical devices but simply what they appear to be: our best efforts to manage our school and community together. Rather than an educational aim, critical thinking is a valued capacity that emerges when children freely pursue personal fulfillment engaged in dynamic society.

Critical thinking is also not the ultimate in human capacity, nor even in intellect. I highlight it here because it is much discussed and holds exalted status in the world of education. It is not the pinnacle of intellectual achievement, nor the only way to seek truth. It's not the pinnacle of anything really — just an important intellectual toolset and a branch or stepping stone on a continuing adventure of mind. Higher faculties await, perhaps extending comprehension into realms beyond reason, and able to ingest ever greater gulps of truth.

---

## What's Big and Gray, Fits in a Briefcase, and Provokes Critical Thinking?

Gavin (5 years old): What's in your briefcase, Jim?

Jim (adult, with a straight face): An elephant.

Gavin (with wrinkled brow and concern in his voice): There's an elephant in your briefcase, Jim?

Jim (with straight face and matter-of-fact tone): Yes, Gavin. It's gray and it has a long trunk.

Gavin's eyes are riveted on the closed briefcase. He thinks for a very long time.

Gavin (intensely): I don't think an elephant will fit in your briefcase, Jim.

Jim: Why not?

Gavin (after very long pause, unsure): An elephant is too big.

More rounds, more long pauses as Gavin thinks.

Gavin (smiling, almost conclusively): You don't really have an elephant in your briefcase, Jim.

Jim (smiling, as if busted by Gavin): Let's look.

Gavin is visibly anxious while we open the briefcase. He seems relieved not to find an elephant, and bursts out laughing.

---

# Part Four:
# In Practice

Now we get down to details about selected aspects of the program. What does self-directed democratic schooling look like, day to day? I'll begin with some jargon. Then we'll walk through the school together so you can see a typical day, and I'll show you the bulletin board and room reservations. Then I'll describe school government, with lots of examples and details to flesh it out. I'll tell you about our chore system, as an example of how School Meeting addresses a big need that affects everybody. I'll finish up with safety and college.

Keep in mind that each democratic school is an independent community. Each discovers its own favored ways of dealing with things. I'm going to tell you about The Circle School's ways, which are not quite what you will see when you walk into another school.

Really, by the time you read this, The Circle School's ways will have changed a bit, too. Every day is different. Every year brings new challenges for the community, and new ways of dealing with old challenges. Restless, we change our minds. Life is one itch after another.

Chapter 8:

# Jargon

## School Meeting

GOVERNS THE SCHOOL as both chief executive and also legislature. Includes all students and staff (but not parents). Manages day-to-day school operations, school officials, and committees. Oversees corporations. Drafts the school's annual budget, manages income and expenses, hires and fires staff. Oversees the Judicial Committee and hears appeals from judicial processes. Meets weekly (mostly optional attendance). Runs by formal parliamentary procedure (*Robert's Rules of Order*) and majority vote.

## Ends We Seek

Formal statement of a dozen fundamental ideals of the school that are embedded in the school's bylaws (and listed in Chapter 2). Binding on School Meeting and the Board of Trustees, something like a Bill of Rights. Can be amended only with formal consent of the broad school community: students, staff, parents, alumni, alumni parents, and trustees. Example: "All members of the daily school program — students and staff — enjoy equal rights of voice and vote in matters of governance and the common good."

## School Meeting Committees

Agencies of school government created and managed by School Meeting and authorized to act on its behalf in specified ways. Examples of committees: Admissions, Aesthetics, Chores, Field Trip, Fundraising, Library,

Computer Network, Social, Public Relations. Most committees comprise students and staff; some include parents, alumni, trustees, and others.

## School Meeting Officials

Agents of School Meeting, elected or appointed, and authorized to act on its behalf. Examples of School Meeting officials: Chair, Secretary, Elections Clerk, Admissions Director, Business Manager, Bus Supervisor, Chore Checkers, Chore Supervisor, Development Officer, External Resources Coordinator, Facilities Manager, Legal Affairs Officer, Library Clerk, Medical Officer, Medical Responders, Judicial Committee Chair, Judicial Committee Scribe. All students and staff are eligible to run for election or appointment to all positions. Some have always been filled by staff, some always by students, some both. Sometimes "Assistant" positions are created to enable service by the semi-qualified.

## Corporations

Pseudo-private organizations of students and staff, chartered by School Meeting to manage specialized equipment, space, and activities. Examples: Art Corporation, Cooking Corporation, Games Corporation, Gardening Corporation, Music Corporation, Science Corporation, Skate Park Corporation, Sports Corporation. Making their respective domains available to all students and staff, corporations develop and administer certification procedures for personal safety and to ensure proper use of equipment and supplies. Each corporation has its own bylaws and officers. Some fundraise to support activities.

## Certification

Formal demonstration of knowledge and ability, required by corporations and committees for safety and protection of equipment. Examples in the Science Room: Basic/Blue certification for use of basic equipment, such as Legos, Geomags, and beakers; Primary/Green for intermediate equipment, such as microscopes, electricity, tuning forks, and molecular models; Advanced/Red for equipment that is delicate, expensive, or hazardous, such as advanced microscopes, digital balance, multimeters, strobe light, big gyroscope, super-strong magnets, and glassware; and Special for items requiring special training, such as cryogenics, dissection, robotics, soldering, and chemicals. Examples in the Cooking Kitchen: blender, coffee maker, griddle, mixer, and stove.

## Lawbook

Official repository of current laws — about 200 of them, all adopted by majority vote of School Meeting. The Lawbook continues from year to year, with new or amended legislation under consideration virtually every week by School Meeting. By the rule-of-law principle, if it's not in the Lawbook, it's not illegal. Seekers of loopholes are common and clever; occasionally successful.

## Judicial Committee (JC)

Investigates and processes allegations of law violations, hundreds per year. All students and staff take turns serving. Meeting every day, the JC interviews witnesses, examines evidence, composes written findings, presses charges when warranted (every day), and prosecutes cases at trial when a defendant pleads "not guilty."

## Board of Trustees

Preserves the school's democratic structure, long-term assets, and students' civil liberties. Authorizes annual budget drafted by School Meeting. Sets broad business standards of prudence and ethics. Seven members; four elected each year, one each by School Meeting, Board of Trustees, alumni, and the school community (i.e., students, staff, parents, alumni, alumni parents, and trustees).

Chapter 9:

# A Typical Day?

IT'S A HARD QUESTION TO ANSWER. "What's a typical day?" Sigh. I usually start with, "Well, every day is different. There's no such thing as a typical person and no such thing as a typical day." While I say this, my mind is flooded with the many things that happen at school. Sometimes I just rattle off a few common scenes and a few unusual scenes and leave it at that. But if we are at school on a school day, I say let's just walk around and see what's happening. So that's what I'll do now. Come along.

## Walking Tour

First, a word about the building. Obviously, every democratic school is different in its campus and buildings. I suppose our building is typical — there's that word — with about a dozen rooms of various sizes. We have no rooms that look like a regular classroom; no desks in rows. And don't be fooled by the room names; every room is used for many purposes. Okay, let's walk through the building. Here's what we see, probably the same sort of thing you'd see in any democratic school:

- In the Library, a 5-year-old boy is signing out one of the iPads, a 15-year-old girl sits in a comfy chair with a laptop and earbuds (because Library sound levels can be no more than a whisper), a 17-year-old boy reads a book in the corner, two students and a staff member are processing new books to be shelved.
- In the Sunspace, four boys, 8 to 14 years old, are on three computers, all running Minecraft in the same world, in a joint

project to build a town, complete with furnished houses. Their chatter is nonstop.

- In the Cooking Kitchen, a 12-year-old boy is putting something in the oven; looks like a pan of brownies. No aroma yet, but it will fill the building, and then people will sniff it out and come see if they can beg or buy a brownie.

- In the Publishing Room, we see a math class with three students, a staff member, and numbers on the whiteboard. There's a "Reserved" sign on the door, indicating three times per week. We won't go in, but you can look in, because all of our room doors have transparent tempered glass panels (contributing to literal and social transparency, and also minimizing needless door opening when looking for someone or something).

- In tiny Room 2F, two girls are in side-by-side chairs, bent over their phones and talking to one another. We look but don't go in. My desk is in there, and some bookshelves — the Library collection is spread around the school, all computerized and with Dewey Decimal Classification.

- The Conference Room is empty even though it's a cozy comfy room, but there's stuff on the table (for which someone might get written up for leaving a mess). When not in use for a conference, it's restricted to absolute silence and no group activity, even in silence. The sign on the door flips between "Conference" and "Silent."

- In the Playroom, eight 4- to 8-year-olds, boys and girls, are more or less engaged together. Two of them say hi, but since we have no little kids with us, they mostly ignore us. Some are wearing dress-up clothes and improvising a scene with deliberate drama, including voices and accents. Some are arranging wooden blocks to be part of the scene, some darting over to the little table where they have placed their lunchboxes and water (because in the Playroom you can only have food at the table, and the only drink allowed there is water).

- On the landing at the top of the back hall stairs, three 11-year-old girls are seated on the floor. The one in the middle holds a tablet computer. All three are looking at it and talking quietly.

- At the bottom of the back hall stairs, an older teenager (the elected JC Facilitator) rearranges the JC documents on the bulletin board, and a young child is looking for her shoes in the shoe bucket.
- Outdoors, eight students of all sizes are playing Base Tag. One runs past us and says hi.
- Outdoors, two boys and one girl are shooting basketball.
- In the Music Studio, a 16-year-old boy is engineering a CD of his electric piano compositions.
- In the Parlor, two teenage girls and one teenage boy are playing a board game, and one teenage girl is reading a book. They greet us and look ready to answer our questions. What do you want to ask?
- In the Science Room, three young students, one middle student, and one staff member, all wearing goggles, are huddled around the table, dissecting something. They tell us excitedly they have just been certified by the Science Corporation for that activity.
- In the Coat Room, there's a massive mess of shoes and coats and papers and lunch boxes that aren't supposed to be there because you're supposed to put them on the lunch shelves. Oh, and it looks like someone spilled glitter. Argh. Seeing it, I'd like to make a law against glitter, but I don't think it would get the majority vote needed to pass. Democracy sometimes glitters, but it's messy.
- In the Art Room, two teenage girls are making elaborate digital designs on a tablet and a laptop, with a younger girl hovering, talking. Two youngish students are finger-painting at the end of the large table. Ann, a staff member, is sitting at her desk, talking with a student beside her about a field trip to the grocery store. At my request, one of the teenagers explains the Art Corporation's system for certifying. Everyone can use stuff on the shelves with a picture of a parrot, but for everything else, you get certified in progressive stages: Beaver, Giraffe, Whale. Some things require special training, like airbrush and wood-burning; those are marked with a unicorn.

- In the Downstairs Kitchen, four older students are sitting at the booth table, talking and hanging out together, getting too loud. Another student is heating something up in the microwave, and two others are sitting at the little table, writing a complaint for JC. On the for-sale counter, there's a plate of cookies (50 cents apiece), packaged snacks, and some small toy cars.
- In the front office, staff member Ellen is sitting in her usual place at the helm, talking with two students sitting nearby. Two other students — members of the Office Team — have just arrived to pick up and distribute today's mail. There's an older teenage girl sitting at the other desk, practicing for the college entry math test (SAT).
- In Room 1A, JC is happening. An older teenager is the (elected) Chairperson, a young teen is the (elected) Scribe. There are two other younger student JC members, one staff member, two runners (to go get witnesses when the Chair tells them), two student witnesses being interviewed (one obviously quite distraught, probably going to get charged with something), and several students just observing.
- On the back porch, three boys are hanging out and laughing loudly, watching another boy on his skateboard. If they get any louder, the JC Chair will have to tell them to keep quiet and stop disturbing the JC.

What do you think? Is that what you expected? What was interesting to you? On another day, or the same day at a different time, you might see very different scenes — perhaps 30 students outdoors and nobody in the Playroom. You might see a jam-packed session of School Meeting, a crying child clutching an ice pack to a knee, a cluster of students receiving a delivery of Chinese food at the front door, a group of five students and a staff member leaving campus on a "walking field trip" to the nearby creek, the Facilities Manager repairing a broken chair with the students who broke it. If we had walked through around 2:45, we probably would have heard vacuum cleaners all over and squeezed past a dozen people in various places, hurrying around and doing their chores — which have to be done and checked (by an elected Chore Checker) by 3:00.

Here are a few things we didn't see but might have — one-time and occasional events, some of which are related to running the school and the rest thought up, initiated, and organized by students:

- Halloween costume party
- Mad Hatter Tea Party
- Soccer game with 15 players from 8 years old to 18 (and me, if I weren't with you)
- Fall Festival
- Animal Ear Workshop (making, yes, animal ears to wear)
- Planned and staged "wedding" in the Playroom
- Gymnastics on the mats in Room 1A
- Birthday party with pizza for the entire school
- "Party in the Pit" (variety show, mostly musical performances)
- Red Cross First Aid & CPR training
- Vote tallying team at work, after semi-annual elections
- Science Corporation Take-Apart event
- Art Corporation meeting to develop certification procedures
- Chore Committee meeting to plan permanent chores
- Field trip meeting, planning a cross-country trip a year in advance
- Social Committee meeting, planning an evening bowling event
- Trial, complete with judge, jury, prosecution, defense, and observers

## Bulletin Board

We didn't stop at the main bulletin board, where groups and individuals can post notices and sign-up sheets. Here is some of what's there right now, excerpted:

- Anime Club. Like Drawing? Sign here.
- Wanna be on a podcast? See Lily J.
- Join Now / *Forever Love* the movie [Recruiting a cast, I think.]
- Fridays at 1:00 is Science Corp[oration] / Discover the answers to your curiosity
- Abby's Art Commissions [$3 to $10]
- Garden Corp[oration] Wednesdays at 9:00 in the Pod Suite

- Join Team Vipers or Join Team Ice Cream [I don't know what it means.]
- NEED Someone TO TALK TO! or even a hug! Then come find Olahna or Nora. [Lots of hearts]
- The winners of the Dance Battle are Noah, Caelyn, James, Caitlyn
- Need a babysitter? Hi! My name is Sadie…
- Library Committee meeting on Fridays at 2:00 in the Library
- You Talk. I Talk. Club. Are you Talkitive [sic] and Wanting to Share your Feelings? And do you love to eat? Then join!!
- Cooking Corp[oration] Tuesday at 10:00. Pursue your culinary passion.
- Literature Analysis Class. Come learn to find symbolism in short stories and poetry!
- *HORROR in the ORPHANAGE.* Movie Premiere. 9:00 Round Room. Written by Maya. 10 Can Only Come! Dahlia as Arieanna… [cast list]
- Art Commissions / See Jaelin / Headshot 50¢ / Full body $1.50 / Feral animals / Anime / Cartoon / Mystical Creation / Anything
- Cheyenne will do your chore for $1 [instead of the $2 opt-out fee]
- LINUS WILL DO YOUR CHORE FOR 85¢ [underselling Cheyenne]
- Facilities Team Job Sheet [for tracking job status and who's doing what]

## Room Reservations

Room reservations provide another glimpse into the school day. One-time reservations can be made by anyone, simply by filling out a form and hanging it on the door of the reserved room, perhaps for a cooking project, private meeting, or birthday party. The Aesthetics Committee coordinates *repeating* reservations — for example, every Monday, Tuesday, and Thursday from 10:00 to 11:00 for a math class; or every Monday from 12:00 to 2:00 for a Pathfinder game with 10 players. The number and nature of room reservations varies from year to year and from school to school. This year there are many more reservations for traditional academic studies than usual, perhaps because there are many new students, and new students sometimes try at first to replicate their old school patterns.

The school keeps no record of room reservations, but here's a list of what I've observed this year on repeating room reservation door signs:

| | | |
|---|---|---|
| Aesthetics Committee | Grammar | Reading & Literature |
| Algebra | History | Rocket Building |
| Art Corporation | Household Chemicals | Science Class |
| Astronomy | Library Committee | Science Corporation |
| Boundaries Committee | Lodging & Routing | Script Writing |
| Chore Committee | Mandarin Chinese | Skate Park Corporation |
| Circuits | Marine Biology | Social Committee |
| Cooking Corporation | Math | Spanish |
| Cool Things Outside | Media Subcommittee | Spelling |
| Critical Thinking | Microscopes | Sports Corporation |
| Dance Planning | Money Subcommittee | Staff Evals Committee |
| Debate Team | Mythology | Take Apart |
| Elections Committee | NRG Trip Planning | Talking about Socialism |
| Equipment Subcommittee | Organic Chemistry | The New Avengers |
| Ethology | Painting | Video Games Corp |
| Food Subcommittee | Pathfinder | World Cultures |
| Français | Playroom Committee | Writing |
| Gardening Corporation | Programming | Yearbook Corporation |
| Geometry | Raffle Ticket Sellers | |

## Daily Schedule

Although there is much variation from day to day, there are dependable structures that tend to shape the school day. The familiar rhythms provide a measure of stability, security, and predictability, always present in the background and quietly reassuring, like breath, that all's well and life goes on:

| | |
|---|---|
| 8:00 | Opening staff member unlocks front door; school's open |
| 8:00 to 8:35 | School buses arrive (about two-thirds of students come by bus) |
| On arrival | Sign in, put your stuff away, sign up for a chore |

| | |
|---|---|
| 9:00 to 11:30 | Tuesdays only: Playroom reserved for public playgroup |
| 10:00 to 12:00 | Wednesdays only: School Meeting |
| 1:00 to 2:30 | Judicial Committee (every day) |
| 1:00 to 3:00 | Chore Time (except for morning chores & special chores) |
| 2:00 | Extra chores for pay (at the sign-in board) |
| 3:00 | Bus Supervisor rings the bell (for those who can't tell time) |
| 3:05 to 3:35 | School buses depart (Chaotic! 10 buses in the first 10 minutes) |
| 3:45 | Outdoors and upstairs close; all must be indoors downstairs |
| 3:55 | "Rope Time;" must be west of the rope strung across the Kitchen |
| 4:00 | School day ends; must be signed out and leaving, or staying for... |
| 4:00 to 5:30 | After-4 Time |

Visitors sometimes ask when is lunch time, and my standard reply is "When do you think?" Some then smile and say oh, it's when you get hungry! Yes, say I, you're getting the idea. It's a lot like life, don't you think?

## What You See and What You Don't

Democratic schools don't show well if you are looking for "learning activities" like what you see in conventional schools. In our walk-through, remember, we saw only one class and there were only three students in it. Some years, there are numerous classes every day, and some years, there are only a few each week. But durable learning happens all the time, between the lines, integrated in life, often invisible, unself-conscious, and unremarked. Kids don't usually arrive in the morning thinking of something they want to *learn.* More often they arrive thinking of something they want to *do.* You learn what you're interested in, often because it's part of doing something. In the process, you learn things like initiative, self-direction, how to be a good friend, what's important to you, how to stay safe, how to make and keep commitments, how to manage your time, how to run your life. If I've learned one thing in 30-some years of doing this, it's that kids who are busy and happy are learning and growing. It's that simple.

You may see some teacher-directed activity here, and you may see some textbook-oriented study — freely chosen by students — but those modes don't predominate as in conventional schools. You *will* see lots of students who look happy, engaged, and self-directed. You'll see lots of hanging out and hear lots of laughter. You'll probably see lots of eating, no matter what time of day you visit. Many little kids have their lunchbox out by 9 o'clock, and then again every hour or two. If it's a cold, rainy day, you might see more reading, art, music, and board games; and some rowdy outdoor play happening indoors (which could get someone written up). If it's a nice day, you'll probably see lots of people outdoors.

What you may see but not recognize are the challenges students are dealing with. (Remember the existential and situational "provocations" in Chapter 7?) You may not see that a group appearing to be "just hanging out" in the Art Room is actually a meeting of the Music Corporation, perhaps simplifying a certification procedure to make it more available to younger students. But hanging out is just as likely to be productive in important ways.

One thing that's typical of all democratic schools is this: What students do at school is limited only by imagination, safety, and the ever-present Lawbook. Students are practicing life in all its dimensions and novelty, in a vibrant community with materials, equipment, and time.

---

## My Worst and Favorite Walk-through Story

As the school's Admissions Director (elected annually), I have walked around the school hundreds of times in the last few years with visiting families. As we set out, I sometimes think to myself of Forrest Gump, whose mama, had she been in my shoes, might have said "A walk through the school is like a box of chocolates. You never know what you're gonna get."

My worst and favorite story of a family walk-through was a setup for disaster from the beginning. The mom and prospective student had already visited and loved the school, but they needed ex-husband dad to like it, too. This visit was with the ex and his new wife. I could tell they were not happy to be here, and they were not inclined to agree with wife #1 on anything. They seemed to relish the opportunity to not-like the school. So there was an edgy tension as we left the Conference Room to do a walk-through tour. As we headed down the hall toward the Library, I could see through the glass door that four teenagers were seated at a round table, perhaps playing cards, but I don't remember. It looked like a great opportunity to engage my visitors in conversation with thoughtful students who could talk about the school. But at the exact instant I opened the door for my guests to enter, we all heard a teenager exclaim loudly, with admirably crisp enunciation, the quintessential four-letter word that begins with *F*. Or as it's colloquially said, he dropped the F-bomb, loud and clear in the Library, our exalted cathedral of quiet scholarship. It was a stunning moment, which so dominated my thoughts for the rest of the visit that I have no other memory of the walk-through. What I do remember, aside from that most vivid moment, is that I never heard from that family again.

The incident was written up for JC, but I don't remember who wrote it up — me or Ian, the lad whose enunciation was so clear. When I was called to JC, I told my story with suitable indignation at those darned teenagers' insensitivity to visitors, and the cost to the school when we behave badly in front of guests. I hadn't had a chance to talk with Ian beforehand, so I heard his story first in JC.

Here's what happened. With the four of them around the table, Ian had his back to the Library door. Andrew sat across the table from Ian, saw me coming, and with all good intentions commented to the group, "Here comes Jim with visitors." Quick-witted Ian, with exquisite timing as the door opened, impishly replied with emphasis on his last word, "Oh, so I probably shouldn't say F – – –!" The JC charged him with Excessive Vulgarity, and I took some comfort in knowing that my teenage friends weren't as insensitive as it first appeared, and sounded.

---

Chapter 10:

# School Government

D EMOCRATIC SCHOOLS ARE SMALL-SCALE DEMOCRACIES, as I've said, but now let's be more precise. In a direct democracy, the majority rules and the rule of the majority is absolute — famously like two wolves and a sheep voting on what's for dinner. That's not what happens in democratic schools. Like Western democratic nations, democratic schools limit the power of the majority, by tradition or by constitution, to protect the minority and individual rights. Elected officials carry out many governing functions. You might argue democratic schools are more like a constitutional republic. Fair enough. Democratic schools are democracies in the same sense that France, Britain, and America are democracies, even though you could also call them a unitary republic, parliamentary monarchy, and federal republic, respectively. All three function as constitutional democracies.

Democratic schools are similar to those democratic nations in broad principles, such as public government, rule of law, and protection of civil liberties. But democratic school governments are not structured as national governments because of obvious differences: schools are much smaller, the "populace" is mostly children, and schools are not sovereign states. For example, the democratic schools I know do not elect an empowered chief executive (like a president), but instead place executive authority in a collective body, commonly called the School Meeting.

The Circle School's government is more or less typical of democratic schools, with much variation in the particular names and functions of government officials and agencies. Here's a table of organization.

## School Meeting

Members: Students and Staff
Officers: Chair, Vice-chair, Secretary, Elections Clerk

### Officials

Admissions Director
Alumni Liaison
Attendance Clerk
Bus Supervisor
Business Manager
Chore Checkers
Chore Supervisor
CMO Manager
Computer Wizard
Development Officer
External Resources
  Coordinator
Facilities Manager
Financial Officer
JC Chairs (4)
JC Facilitator
JC Scribes (4)
Legal Affairs Officer
Library Clerk
Medical Officer
Medical Responders
Registrar
Staff Members
Staffing Coordinator
Tenant Liaison

### Committees

Admissions
Aesthetics
Chores
Computer Network
Elections
Emergency
Field Trip
Fundraising*
Judicial
Library
Pay and Benefits*
Playroom
Public Relations*
Social*
Staff Evaluations
Ad Hoc Committees*
* Open to parents
  and other
  non-members

### Corporations

Art
Cooking
Cool Things Outside
Games
Gardening
Music
NRG (Hikes, camping)
Science
Skate Park
Sports
Video Games
Yearbook

## Elections

Terms of office and election schedules vary from school to school. At The Circle School, elections are held twice a year. A few weeks into the school year, fall elections include all positions: officers, officials, committee chairs, and committee members. Most serve for the rest of the school year and into the beginning of the next school year until elections are held. Judicial Committee officials, however, serve for about half the school year, until winter elections, with those terms extending to the next fall elections.

In between elections, School Meeting fills vacancies and appoints additional committee members from time to time. In some schools, committee membership is open to all members without going through School Meeting. Ad hoc committees are also appointed by School Meeting from time to time, to complete temporary assignments rather than ongoing missions. For example, School Meeting has created ad hoc committees to overhaul the Lawbook, plan and conduct a graduation celebration, arrange for visits to and from other democratic schools, and manage a staff search and hiring process.

Running for election is voluntary for students and sometimes competitive, sometimes including spirited campaigning. School Meeting typically conducts a special session shortly before each election, devoted to campaign speeches. This year, in a first, a 14-year-old delivered a campaign speech in rap ("If you want your findings straight, vote for your mate, Isac, he'll be great…").

Although all members are eligible to run for all offices, some have always been held by staff members, such as Admissions Director, Business Manager, Financial Officer, and Legal Affairs Officer. Occasionally School Meeting creates an assistant position, such as Assistant Facilities Manager or Assistant Medical Officer, to create an opportunity and engage the efforts of a qualified student or staff member who isn't prepared to assume the full responsibility.

## School Meeting

School Meeting performs executive and legislative functions, and oversees the school's judicial functions. Students and staff (but not parents) are all members of School Meeting, each having one vote and equal rights to make proposals and speak in debate.

At The Circle School, regular sessions of School Meeting are held on Wednesdays, 10 am to noon. Sessions usually fill the allotted time and are sometimes extended (by vote) when there is much or urgent business to be done. Some members attend and participate regularly, others sporadically or only when something personally important is up for a vote.

Special sessions are called occasionally as needed, usually by the School Meeting Chair, and rarely by petition of ten members. Special sessions may be called to consider a single topic, such as a recommendation from the Judicial Committee to suspend a student, or to take action on an urgent matter that cannot wait until the next regular session. Special sessions and their subject matter must be announced at least two hours before convening, but are usually announced a day or more in advance.

For regular weekly sessions, an agenda is posted at least a day in advance and typically includes most of the following:

- Standing reports from school officials (many of them students) and standing committees
- Report of all cases completed by the Judicial Committee (subject to review and sometimes overriding action)
- Reports from ad hoc (temporary) committees
- Submission of new or revised training and usage procedures ("certifications") from a corporation or two
- Proposals for a new law, amendment, or repeal ("first readings")
- Continued legislative proposals ("final readings," which can be continued again and again before coming to an up-or-down vote)
- Proposals or continuations of executive actions, such as to appoint a new Chore Checker; conduct a Games Night event; allow a visitor to spend the day; create an ad hoc committee for a short-term assignment; spend money from the discretionary budget; or appoint a newly trained student to the Medical Officer's Responders Team
- Announcements and miscellany, which can include any topic any member wants to discuss

Occasionally the agenda includes high-impact actions related to staff hiring and retention, the annual budget, or suspending or expelling a student following judicial proceedings. Even these weighty matters are decided by majority vote of students and staff together.

Any member can place an item on the agenda, either by posting it on the bulletin board reserved for School Meeting business or by posting a message to the email forum for School Meeting members. The elected School Meeting Secretary compiles and posts the agenda.

School Meeting sessions are chaired by the elected Chairperson, with the Secretary nearby to record actions, report correspondence, and assist the Chair. Business is conducted according to *Robert's Rules of Order* — similar in principle to the parliamentary rules under which formal conventions and legislatures operate. *Robert's* provides for orderly transaction of business and protection of the minority from the majority. Members may speak only when recognized by the Chair, and proposed actions must be presented as motions, sometimes with prescribed wording or characteristics.

*Robert's* is designed to be effective in very large bodies, such as a policy-making convention with hundreds of voting participants, but also allows "informal consideration" of matters. This is a relaxed mode of dialogue — essentially informal conversation — that is well-suited for small groups, such as sessions of School Meeting. At The Circle School, our sessions begin in informal mode and mostly remain informal (except for voting), but the formality of *Robert's* can be imposed at any moment by the Chair or by member request. Formality is typically invoked in high-attendance sessions, heated debates, and when order breaks down.

Although the rules require only a simple majority for most actions, in practice most matters are discussed until the group is mostly in agreement. Whether the topic is bland or controversial, most people want to continue discussion until every point of view has been examined, and accommodated if practical. However, anyone at any time can propose to end discussion and bring the matter to a vote, an action that requires a two-thirds majority under *Robert's Rules* and happens only rarely — not at all this year. Consensus is common, and close votes are rare. A good Chair senses the will of the group and slows things down or keeps things moving procedurally, sometimes by asking something like "Do we have unanimous consent for this [minor or obviously needed] amendment?" or declaring what will happen next, prefixed with the phrase "If there are no objections, we will now...."

Parliamentary procedure can be daunting because, for example, actions must be proposed as precisely worded motions. In practice, though, School Meeting commonly pauses to coach and assist members in wording their proposal or fitting their intentions to parliamentary protocols. Occasionally a parliamentary wizard comes along — someone who has studied the dense text of *Robert's Rules* — and then we are treated to all kinds of parliamentary maneuvers aiming to outfox competing viewpoints or make sure we stick to technically correct procedure. Generally, though, *Robert's* serves to empower, facilitate, and protect, while transacting business with crisp clarity and visibility.

## Executive Function

In its executive role, School Meeting runs the school, like a principal, head-of-school, or executive director. As a collective entity rather than an individual, and meeting only weekly, School Meeting necessarily delegates much authority to its officials and committees. Directly or through its officials and committees, here is some of what School Meeting does:

- Draft the annual operating budget
- Manage operations within the budget
- Manage the school's business, accounting, and bookkeeping
- Maintain the building and grounds
- Manage safety and security
- Hire, fire, and manage staff
- Suspend and expel students
- Conduct after-hours family social events
- Manage public relations, marketing, and fundraising
- Preserve rule of law and student civil liberties
- Comply with local, state, and federal laws and regulations
- Delegate authority and responsibility

Vesting executive authority in a collective chief executive, rather than an individual, directly enfranchises all students and staff in school governance and administration, promoting access, engagement, transparency, trust, and security. Collective executive authority is a feature of all the democratic schools I know. The degree of delegation of authority to officials and committees varies from school to school.

Here's a sampling of executive actions adopted by School Meeting in the last three months, as recorded in Minutes:

- MOTION: To adopt the attached school calendar for next year. ADOPTED
- MOTION: To create an ad hoc committee consisting of Isabella, Ann, Cordelia, and Beth to plan a commencement celebration for graduates Cordelia and Isabella, in collaboration with the Social Committee, to take place on Saturday, June 4, coordinated with the events published in the school calendar for that day. ADOPTED
- MOTION: To allow Science Corporation to raise tadpoles to adulthood. The tadpoles will be kept in the fish tank in the Science Room and will be cared for by the Science Corporation. The tadpoles will come from a local pond and will be released back to that pond when they are grown. ADOPTED [This required School Meeting permission because it would otherwise violate a rule about animals at school.]
- MOTION: To invite a group of up to 12 students and adults from Fairhaven School (Upper Marlboro, MD) to visit on Monday, April 11, or another date approved by the Staffing Coordinator. The visit will be planned and supervised by the ad hoc Democratic Schools Get-Together Committee, with background checks and paperwork subject to approval of the Legal Affairs Officer. ADOPTED
- MOTION: To impeach Kari G. as a chore checker. ADOPTED
- MOTION: To requisition one desktop computer (approximate value $900) through the Act 195/90/35 lending program. The computer will be cared for by the Network Committee. The requisition will be processed by the Library Clerk during the ordering window using the online Act requisition system. ADOPTED
- MOTION: Following JD's review of the local rental market, to increase rents as follows: Bonnymead Ave house and Elder Rd house — increase by $25 per month (from $995 and $960 to $1020 and $985, respectively; comparables range from $1250

to $1500); and Oakleigh Ave apartment — increase by $10
from $595/month to $605/month (comparables range from
$720 to $800). ADOPTED [The school owns adjoining properties, rented out but held for future expansion of the campus.]

- MOTION: To approve as a Special Field Trip an outdoor
  sleepover at school, on a date in April to be approved by the
  Business Manager to prevent conflicts with other school events,
  and reported to School Meeting at least two weeks before the
  sleepover, to include the following people who are working
  to go on the NRG's Great American Eclipse trip: [list of 10
  members]. This event shall be exempt from Field Trip Policy
  paragraph numbers 9 (Field Trip Approvals) and 13 (Staff
  attendance outside of scheduled work hours). The group will
  abide by the written guidelines which follow, to ensure safety,
  order, and sensitivity to neighbors. JC consequences shall
  be suspended when school is not open during the sleepover.
  Guidelines are as follows: [list of guidelines]. ADOPTED [This
  sleepover is a practice event, to test camping gear in preparation
  for a 10-day cross-country field trip to take place 16 months
  later, allowing time for fundraising and other practice events.]
- MOTION: To conduct a Games Night at school on Friday,
  March 4, from 5:00pm to 8:00pm, with food to be sold by the
  NRG Corporation. The event will be organized and managed
  by the Social Committee. ADOPTED
- MOTION: To appoint Lexi to the office of Judicial Committee
  Chair. ADOPTED [Interim appointment to fill a vacancy
  between elections]
- MOTION: To elect Klayton E. to serve as a Responder on the
  Medical Officer's Response Team in accordance with section
  8277.19. [This follows Klayton's Red Cross certifications, appren-
  ticeship, and endorsement by the Medical Officer.] ADOPTED

## Legislative Function

In its legislative function, acting by majority vote, the School Meeting
adopts laws and policies. These are officially recorded in publicly posted
minutes and made part of the Lawbook, which continues to evolve week

by week from year to year. The Circle School's Lawbook today comprises 214 laws and 45 pages, governing safety, order, personal rights, and many other matters. Nobody knows all the laws, or even most of them. Next week, something will change — a new law, perhaps, or more likely an amendment to an existing law. (See Appendix A, Management Manual Table of Contents.)

Laws and amendments are proposed by students and staff members at any time by placing a motion on School Meeting's agenda. Legislative proposals undergo readings at two (or more) sessions prior to a vote. Laws are constantly being proposed, debated, referred to committees, adopted, amended, and repealed. Typically, a couple of laws are in play in any given week.

Later we will discuss the Lawbook and laws. For now, though, here are a few legislative motions adopted recently by School Meeting, as recorded in Minutes. Most include a brief statement of rationale — why we are adopting this rule — in addition to the legislative text itself:

- MOTION: In order to prevent damage and injury, and keep snow out of the building, to (a) create a new rule: "4853.45 (No projectiles through windows) You may not throw objects into or out of the building through open windows or doorways." and (b) amend rule 4874.18 to replace the word "etc." with "or any windows or doors" and to change the short name to "The snowball rule." ADOPTED [As with almost all rules, it's fair to assume this one was not created out of the blue, but in response to real events.]
- MOTION: To amend 5625.07 (Videotaping by visitors only with SM permission) so that it includes not just videotaping but other forms of recording, too, to read as follows: 5625.07 (Recordings by visitors only with permission) Visitors during the school day may not take pictures and may not make video or audio recordings, except with advance permission of the School Meeting. ADOPTED
- MOTION: In order to comply with insurance company requirements (for Employment Practices Liability Insurance), to adopt the following Whistleblower Policy: It is the policy and intent of The Circle School to observe high standards of ethics,

and to comply with all applicable laws and regulations. This policy is intended to encourage and enable employees, staff, students, volunteers, and trustees to raise concerns so that the school can address and correct inappropriate conduct and actions.... [Minutes include the full text of this lengthy policy] ADOPTED

- MOTION: To amend 1206.02 (Sign in/sign out, and departure waiting areas) to insert a sentence, after the first sentence, that reads, "The Attendance Clerk may levy a 50-cent fine for each failure to sign in or out on the attendance sheet, to be paid to the Attendance Clerk within two school days." ADOPTED
- MOTION: To reduce obnoxious odors, to create new rule 4847.07 (Odors from personal care products), to read "Strongly smelling personal care products with odors that spread rapidly through the air, such as nail polish remover and Axe, may be sprayed or applied only in well-ventilated areas." ADOPTED

## Corporations

*Officials* and *committees* are agencies of school government, acting in their respective areas on behalf of School Meeting and with its authority. Some manage particular line items in the budget, having authority to spend the budgeted amount.

*Corporations* are something else. At The Circle School, corporations are semi-private, nonprofit, nongovernmental organizations of students and staff, chartered by School Meeting to manage designated equipment, space, and activities. Each corporation has its own bylaws, officers, directors, treasury, and procedures. Corporations choose their own directors — typically open to anyone who is interested — and officers are chosen by directors. School Meeting does not elect or appoint corporation officials, and does not directly control corporation operations, but can withdraw its charter if the corporation performs unsatisfactorily.

In effect, each corporation holds a concession granted by School Meeting. The corporation gains special access and rights to their own domain of interest, in return for making that domain available, safe, and orderly for all students and staff. In practice, it is viewed not as a concession but more as a privilege, a valued responsibility and authority, and an opportunity to pursue something you love to do.

Corporations may not charge fees for their service or for access to their space and equipment but may conduct fundraising — such as selling prepared lunches to students and staff — and use their funds to advance their mission. Corporations occasionally ask School Meeting for funds, typically matching their own fundraising for a particular project. For example, School Meeting matched the Music Corporation's fundraised $350 to buy a digital keyboard.

The school holds corporation funds on deposit, like a bank, and disburses those funds only as directed by the corporations. For legal and financial reporting purposes, the school and its accounting firm treat the corporations as unincorporated nonprofit foundations that are not required to organize formally and not required to submit annual financial returns to the federal government because their annual receipts fall below the IRS reporting threshold.

Most democratic schools have corporations or the equivalent (such as "cooperatives"), but define them in different ways.

## Certifications

Each corporation manages some combination of equipment, space, and activity. The Art Corporation, for example, manages the Art Room and lots of equipment and materials. Before you use certain things for the first time, you get "certified" by a corporation official who teaches you their rules and procedures. In the Art Room, if you have no certifications, you can use anything on the shelves labeled with a picture of a Parrot: paper, scissors, markers, crayons, old magazines for making collages. But if you want to use supplies on the Beaver shelves — pencils, tape, staples, ribbon, yarn, simple beads, and more — you must first undergo training by a designated certifier. Beaver certification takes only a few minutes, after which your name is added to the posted list and you may then use the Beaver supplies whenever you wish.

Giraffe certification, with Beaver as a prerequisite, involves still more training: beads (different from Beaver beads), crayon melter, drawing supplies, fabric, glitter, glue gun, paint supplies, paper rolls, poster board, rubber cement, Sculpey, sewing supplies, sewing tools, rubber stamps, tempera paint, yarn, and lots of instruction in how to clean things and put them away.

Whale certification, with Giraffe as a prerequisite, involves much more still, from paints and plaster to stone carving tools. You get the idea. And then there are Unicorn certifications that are specific to certain pieces of equipment, such as the laminator and X-Acto knives.

Each corporation develops its own ways of keeping people and property safe and orderly through training and certification. In the Science Room, it's color-coded certifications for Basic, Primary, Advanced, and Special. In the Cooking Kitchen, it's each piece of equipment.

---

## Uncapped Glue

About 17 years ago, the Art Corporation got sloppy. Supplies weren't replenished. Equipment wasn't maintained. Certifiers weren't available. Tools were misplaced. Paint brushes weren't cleaned properly. People complained. School Meeting issued edicts. Alas, to no avail. The Art Corporation had dried up like an uncapped bottle of glue. School Meeting ordered removal of all equipment and supplies from the Art Room, to be stored in the basement! Outrageous! But nobody stepped forward to take responsibility, and so that was that. No more art! That was the year Amy Z. was gone — off to another school. She came back the following year, and oh she was mad to find that her precious Art Room had been trashed and stashed. Amy set to work to make it right. She recruited others, revived the Art Corporation, came up with plans and promises, and persuaded School Meeting to give them another go. They rescued their stuff from the basement, brought the Art Room back to life, and imbued the whole enterprise with energy and discipline. With its huge project table, its walls covered with art, and thanks to Amy, the Art Room still today remains a lively center of culture, creation, and community.

---

## Staff

What do staff members do? Here's what the staff employment agreement says (among much more):

> Staff members are collectively responsible, under School
> Meeting's supervision and with other School Meeting members,
> for management of the school and the daily program. In addition

to this general responsibility, each staff member assumes a variety of formal and informal duties, functions, and responsibilities that are not enumerated here and may or may not be elaborated in job descriptions or the Management Manual.

Staff members also "participate in the life of the school beyond the daily school program, such as after-hours social events, fundraising events, and committee meetings." Looking at it from another perspective, here's what The Circle School's website says to prospective job seekers:

> Staff members at The Circle School act as dependable stewards of the school; facilitate student access to resources; exemplify mature practice of personal fulfillment and societal engagement; and anchor school culture to values of interpersonal respect and trust in the natural impulse toward personal growth.
>
> Staff participate in the school's democratic governance, including executive, legislative, and judicial processes, and do not unilaterally establish or enforce rules. Being a successful staff person at The Circle School requires an ability to honor the choices of others even when those choices are not those you would make, and an ability to trust in the school's peer-based judicial system to adequately resolve rule infractions. Staff people at The Circle School are available as facilitators and friends as students pursue their own interests.

Each staff member assumes a unique combination of formal responsibilities, informal responsibilities, and functional roles. The mix may change from time to time and year to year, especially when there is staff turnover, but some offices tend to be filled by the same staff member for many years.

Formal responsibilities are associated with offices to which the staff member is elected. The powers and duties of all offices are enumerated in the Management Manual. All members of School Meeting are eligible to run for election to any offices, but some offices have always been held by staff members. Much as in any small organization, informal responsibilities and functional roles emerge dynamically as needs and abilities coincide.

Every successful staff member develops a niche over time, finding a configuration of roles that fit their skill sets and interests, and contribute to effective business and thriving community.

## Hiring

In most democratic schools, the School Meeting or equivalent governing body makes hiring decisions, but the pre-hiring process varies from school to school and from time to time. Because the final decision is by vote of students and staff members, every process is likely to include significant candidate visitation at school to get to know the many decision-makers. The Circle School conducts committee screening of candidates, and then School Meeting invites a few finalist candidates to come spend up to three days at school.

Retention of staff also varies much from school to school. Most of the democratic schools I know hold annual staff elections, or a yes/no vote for each staff candidate (including returning staff members), typically in the spring for the coming fall. In some schools, the results directly determine hiring for the next school year, sometimes producing surprising changes. In others, the results of voting simply inform School Meeting debate as a staffing configuration is negotiated and voted in one or more sessions of School Meeting. Sometimes the process is contentious and stressful for staff whose jobs are on the line.

The Circle School's staff retention practices are more traditional. Staff are hired by School Meeting with a general expectation that employment will continue indefinitely, although either School Meeting or the employee may terminate employment with reasonable advance notice. School Meeting also enters into employment agreements with staff, for terms of one to five years. Contract renewal is subject to debate and vote of School Meeting following evaluations by survey or polling of School Meeting members.

Regardless of hiring and retention practices, and regardless of employment contracts, all staff members are entirely and unconditionally subject to School Meeting laws and judicial processes. Our School Meeting has never expelled a staff member — terminating employment because of infractions of its laws — but it could happen.

At The Circle School, staff openings develop only occasionally — intervals averaging around three or four years — and typically have drawn large numbers of applicants in spite of modest pay. At this writing, staff compensation is roughly comparable to independent schools of similar size, which is roughly half to two-thirds the compensation of teachers in nearby public schools, and roughly three-fourths of local median income.

## But What Do Staff Really Do?

What's a typical day for a staff member? There's that word "typical" again. No such thing. Beth is often in committee and corporation meetings; or teaching math or reading; or learning a foreign language with *other* learners; or training a student to do a chore; or at her desk in the Playroom, where her mere presence is sometimes a lighthouse of calm adultitude illuminating a stormy sea. When I told her what I wrote here, she said what I expected: that this doesn't begin to convey the variety and richness of her days. JD's day is likely to be as busy and varied and thoroughly student-engaged, but more often in the Science Room or the workshop, or working with a student Medical Responder, or doing facilities maintenance with students. Ann is likely to be in the Art Room or the Cooking Kitchen or the Library. Ellen might be in a dance planning meeting or anchored in the office and busy with phone calls, email, bookkeeping, newsletter creation, special projects, and front-door reception and gatekeeping, but interacting dozens of times a day with students, often immersed in a stream of friendly chatter and minor emergencies. Jim — that's me — might be in the Conference Room with a visiting family or trying to concentrate on budget drafting until someone needs a shoe tied, or Jibran wants to sign out an iPad, or Evie wants help signing up for a chore; or helping Stefi prepare for her college entry math exam; or in our daily Critical Thinking Discussion Group; or playing soccer in the yard.

But again, what do staff *really* do? Listen, talk, teach, learn, play, write, work, comfort, argue, reflect, watch, stand back, intervene, and listen some more. We are there in community with children, living our own lives and our own passion for democratic schooling, and thus serving as examples of adulthood for kids to study and be in community with.

I think we all find our days busy, sometimes hectic, filled with student interactions, relentlessly real, and deeply satisfying. Democratic school staffing requires a lot of personal energy but often leaves us energized. Exhausted and energized. No, that doesn't feel like a paradox.

## Come Take a Picture

About once a week, a student comes to me and says, "Jim, will you take a picture of...?" It might be a floor-to-ceiling block tower in the Playroom, a fabulous dress-up clothes ensemble, a teenager's serious artwork, or an elaborate fort outdoors with decorated interiors after two days' work. Usually it's a group production.

Sometimes it's performance art, like six kids forming a human pyramid. Yesterday it was five young girls staging a play after an hour's planning and rehearsal. A few weeks ago, it was young teen boys doing flips on mats. A while ago, it was four teen girls doing back bridges in a line. After much practice and many attempts to align and synchronize, they held their back bridges while a smaller child crawled through their human tunnel.

Often, I don't say a word. I just grab my camera and silently photograph the scene. My silence reflects my own aim not to break the dynamic of their group, still bristling with creative charge. Typically, the mood is joyfully serious in proportion to the magnitude of the achievement.

The interesting thing is that whatever purpose is served, it's complete when the picture is captured. Afterwards it's forgotten. They almost never come to me later asking to see the picture or what I'm going to do with it. They may later be pleased if the picture appears in a yearbook, slideshow, or other production, but that seems incidental.

What's happening here? Why do they come get me? They aren't looking for approval or praise — which anyway would tend to shift the focus from their meaning to mine. I think if that's what I offered, they'd stop inviting me. Of course, the picture-taking ritual marks completion, brings closure, and etches the moment into the world — helpful functions, I'm sure, but there's more.

I think it's also about validation: knowing that your thoughts, feelings, and accomplishments are understood and accepted — the fiber of belonging and community. We validate others when we understand and accept what is meaningful to them in the moment. Validation seems most powerful when it stands alone, when it is not accompanied by agreement, disagreement, approval, disapproval, praise, criticism, advice, suggestions, or anything else that involves evaluation.

Don't get me wrong. Evaluation and feedback are often vitally important to the giver or receiver. I am not suggesting we should withhold judgment and validate everything and everyone. I am suggesting that when kids find joy in creating, that's a good time to look on in awe, and witness the spirit and sparkle of the moment.

---

## Management Manual

The Management Manual is our comprehensive collection of rules and regulations governing life at school. By the principle of rule of law, the school is governed by what's in the Manual, not by arbitrary decisions of government officials or the adults who are staff members. Nobody can make up rules on their own, but anybody can propose rules, and that — plus a majority of yes votes in School Meeting — is how rules and regulations make their way into the Manual.

The Manual currently runs to about 240 pages. Here's what's in it:

- The Lawbook, comprising about 200 laws in 45 pages
- Procedures and protocols related to sessions of School Meeting (not including rules of parliamentary procedure, for which we rely on *Robert's Rules of Order*)
- Procedures and protocols of the Judicial Committee (under headings such as Investigation, Fact Finding, Indictment, Arraignment, Sentencing, Recording & Reporting, Trials, Appeals)
- Job descriptions for 26 elected officers and officials
- Committee charters for 14 standing committees, each an agency of school government (describing functions, membership, meetings, powers, and duties)
- Corporation charters and the certifications administered by each
- Staff-related procedures and policies

Appendix A reproduces the full table of contents to the Management Manual.

## Laws

Laws can be long or short, general or detailed, casually or meticulously worded, and occasionally somewhat goofy. Laws have been initiated and championed successfully by students of all ages, including very young students, and by staff members. Some laws are adopted without contest, but most undergo significant debate, and some are adopted only after months of debate, amendments, committee referrals, and re-introductions. For example, the law requiring check-out of library books was adopted without contest, but the lengthy and detailed sexual harassment law took months of committee work and political consensus-building. Some proposals, of course, are defeated. Some have been adopted with a sunset clause, causing the law to expire if not renewed. Occasionally a law is adopted after a clever perpetrator invents a brand-new way to offend the community, not previously outlawed — perhaps getting away with it, or perhaps being prosecuted under an umbrella law. Sometimes a visiting alumnus proudly checks the Lawbook to see if "their" law is still on the books — the one School Meeting adopted because they were the first offender.

Perhaps not surprisingly, highly debated laws, and those that are adopted after months of arduous amendment, are typically those that receive greatest compliance. The community's intense consensus-building efforts seem to reverberate for years in the form of well-anchored, self-sustaining cultural values.

Law #2056.06 is typical of our simplest and shortest laws: "Yelling, screaming, and shouting are prohibited indoors." Here are two more short ones: "Stealing is prohibited." and "It is illegal to throw food indoors." Here are a few more (with the "short title" in parentheses):

2411.25 (No throwing things out of bounds): Do not throw or place things outside campus boundaries.

2417.08 (Calling "after" on computers): If you've been on a general use computer for 30 minutes or more within the last hour, and someone calls after you, you must yield the computer immediately, provided that you may take a few minutes to finish what you're doing. If you call "after" on a computer, you don't have to stay by the computer to keep your place, but you do have to come back before that person is finished or else the next person in line gets that computer. Computer users may take brief bathroom breaks without jeopardizing their computer.

2419.05 (Damager must pay for repair or replacement): The person or persons responsible for causing damage to school property shall repair or replace the damaged property, or pay for repair or replacement, at the option of the Facilities Manager.

2427.09 (Door opening — no excessive force): It is prohibited to open any door with excessive force. Excessive force is such that could cause injury to a person standing on the other side of the door.

2479.18 (Water containers must be empty indoors): Water guns, water balloons, bottles, tubs, and any other object being used to hold water to squirt, dump, toss, or otherwise propel water through the air are to be completely empty of water at any time they are in the building.

2479.41 (Ask before watering a person!): No one is allowed to throw or squirt water at a person who doesn't want water to be thrown at them. You must ask permission first.

There are lots of food rules about where you may and may not eat, where you can store it, and so on. Some of the food rules are about ordering take-out food for delivery to the school, for example, this one, intended to eliminate the burden on office staff to go find the person who placed an order:

2853.02 (Food delivery acceptance/payment): Any person who orders food to be delivered to the school must be at the front door to accept the food and pay the delivery person when he or she arrives. Persons ordering food shall not provide the school's phone number to the restaurant without prior permission from the Office Committee.

When a popular local restaurant refused to deliver any longer because their drivers weren't getting tipped, School Meeting adopted this one:

2853.05 (Paying for food): If you order food for delivery to school, you must pay the full amount plus a tip of at least 15% or $2.00, whichever is greater.

To the relief of many, the restaurant then resumed deliveries. Helpfully, someone put on the bulletin board a chart showing how much you must tip, based on the amount of the order. Here's another rule that was adopted reactively; in this case, after someone invented a new way to get hurt:

4853.28 (Quick movement/blindfolding games prohibited): Games involving both quick movement and full or partial blind-folding are prohibited.

But when the danger is great enough, laws are adopted before some-one demonstrates the need:

4859.72 (Stay away from utility wires in trees): When climbing a tree, you must remain at least ten feet from utility wires and cables.

## *Debating Energy Drinks*

This year our School Meeting adopted a rule about energy drinks, after a new, oblivious teenager cheerfully sold to a 9-year-old an energy drink with a warning label containing the word "death" and other scary ideas. There was much debate in School Meeting about the role of government, the need to regulate, and the school's stated standard of safety as that of a "prudent parent."

School Meeting sometimes decides issues based on generally accepted standards in the world beyond school. In this situation, School Meeting learned (partly from research conducted during debate, with websites projected up on the wall for all to see) that three influential organizations recommend against children's consumption of energy drinks: the American Academy of Pediatrics, the American Medical Association, and even the American Beverage Association.

After the topic was introduced one week, it took three more weekly sessions of School Meeting to amend the proposed rule into its final form. Then, as with most debated and amended legislation, the final vote was delayed (by procedural vote) one more week for reflection and then adopted without much opposition: "You may not consume or possess energy drinks at school, except those that you personally have brought from home." The idea was to place the matter of kids and energy drinks back in the family sphere.

The 9-year-old, by the way, took one sip, made a disgusted face, and drank no more. He deemed it a waste of money, but others might say he bought valuable knowledge through (distasteful) experience.

The energy drinks rule reflects community standards. Another democratic school might decline to rule against energy drinks, or might outlaw them altogether. We find much variation among the schools in calibration of community standards of all kinds.

Here's a rule to reduce litter, or at least nab the perpetrator later. Like some other rules, this one was proposed after someone got tired of cleaning up other people's anonymous messes:

3653.29 Paper airplane makers must write their names on the airplanes they make.

Some rules are long or complex or both. The rule called "Scooters, Skates, Skateboard, & Bike Rules" fills more than a page. "Excessive vulgarity prohibited" lists seven factors that turn "vulgarity" into "excessive vulgarity" — for example, "unwilling observers are subjected to it" or "it occurs in a public or high-traffic area." Other lengthy rules include "Off-Campus Lunchtime Privileges," "Sexual speech and behavior," "Verbal assault prohibited," "Sexual harassment prohibited," and "Video games, Rated and Unrated."

---

## Is It Still My Fort Tomorrow?

At School Meeting tomorrow, we'll hear a motion to amend the current rules about WIPs (Works In Progress) to allow for WIPs to be kept on forts outdoors overnight. In other words, to establish some form of property rights — the right of a fort-builder to maintain possession of their creation from day to day. WIPs are currently allowed only on indoor projects, so yesterday's fort can be hard to reclaim today.

Forts are big business. Whether part of high-drama epic fantasy or low-key domestic fantasy, they occupy hours — even days — and are often as impressive in their construction as they are varied. But they are vulnerable.

During a "war" (usually waged through stick fights regulated by rule #4885.08), whether between factions of a Medieval Times scenario or between wolves and hunters, forts are given some respect — but may also become a target. Destroying a fort that's under active construction could be written up as disruption of activity. (#4415.04: *No one may knowingly disrupt people's activities [...] so long as said activities are legal and within the rules of the school.*) But a fort left unattended for a few hours is largely unprotected legally. In 30 years, School Meeting has never established a rule that would allow a person or group to retain the rights to their creation overnight.

I don't know what will happen at School Meeting today (or next week, when we'll likely vote on the proposal), but I do know that thinking about the history of forts at school made me a bit nostalgic for the forts and stick fights I've seen over the past thirty years.

*— From a blog post by alumna and staff member Julia James ('98)*

Update: A week later, School Meeting voted to amend existing rule #3692.43 to add an exception at the end of the last sentence for forts: "WIP projects outside don't require a WIP sign, but the projects may not be left overnight, *except that fort WIPs with a sign can be kept overnight.*" As often happens, much discussion and debate resulted in an amendment of just a few words.

---

## Enforcement and Empowerment

Law enforcement and the judicial system are prominent in the daily program and central to the school experience. Hundreds of laws govern life at school. On most days, several people — students and staff — submit written allegations of lawbreaking, called "write-ups" or "complaints."

One of our most commonly violated laws is the mess rule (#3653.09): "Before going on to something else, clean up your previous activity. Littering or leaving messes is not allowed anywhere in the school or on the school grounds."

Although *all* persons — staff *and* students — are expected to enforce laws, *no* person acting alone is empowered to determine guilt and issue sentences. Findings of fact and determination of guilt are accomplished only through due process played out in the school's judicial system.

Individual responsibility for enforcement of rules is a cornerstone of the school, enabling safety and freedom for all. Students practice great freedom at The Circle School and are expected to practice corresponding responsibility, not only for self but for the general welfare, too. Mostly this expectation is fulfilled, but not always. Sometimes friends agree not to write one another up, and sometimes that has led to charges of corrupting judicial processes or jeopardizing the well-being of the school. Sometimes

new students are reluctant or determined never to write judicial complaints, because they don't want to get anyone in trouble — perhaps
thinking it unkind to do so, or perhaps because they identify more with
defendants than enforcers. Newcomers, especially teens who have been
in conventional schools, may take some time to fully understand the idea
of individual responsibility for community welfare. Having been essentially powerless in their previous school experience, they understandably
hesitate to trust and buy in to the school culture and community norms.

Two factors in particular may account for widespread positive regard
for shared enforcement responsibility and the judicial system. First is the
legal empowerment of students. Imagine a five-year-old who perceives
that she has been wronged by an older child. Without fear of reprisal
(partly because reprisals are just not tolerated and everybody knows
that), she writes up the older student, and hours later she tells her story
to a panel of five JC members, including older students and a grown-up.
They listen intently to her, perhaps making notes, and they take her complaint seriously. Then they receive testimony from the other student and
witnesses, and investigate in other ways as appropriate. Whatever the
outcome, the five-year-old has received a full and fair hearing and usually knows it. Furthermore, and just as important, she knows that she,
too, will sometimes sit on the other side of the table hearing cases, and
she, too, will be called upon to make real-life decisions about fairness
and justice. Both experiences — having fair and true recourse when
wronged, and personal service as a judge — build deep trust in our judicial system.

The meta-message available to children from judicial experience is
clear: "I am treated with the same respect and rights as every other person. I am just as worthy and responsible as every other person for making
this happen. I am a full member of this society. I have authority and ability
to shape my world."

The second factor that accounts for widespread willing cooperation is
the "deal" offered by the school to students: You receive freedom, safety,
order, resources, and an equal share in government, in exchange for compliance with laws (that you help to adopt) and shared responsibility for
their enforcement. Properly understood, this offer is instantly embraced
by almost every person of school age that we have ever met. Properly

understood, it is exactly the same sort of social contract that most adults enjoy and appreciate in free nations.

As it plays out in practice, it is not really a contract at all, because the "cost" is realized as additional benefit. Children welcome both *sides* of the "deal." Children not only eagerly exercise personal liberty, they also delight in and benefit from the profound experience of being in authority, as all students are, in democratic schools. The responsibility side of the equation is every bit as appealing to children as the freedom side.

Some observers have commented that the school is a great big civics lesson. In a manner of speaking, maybe so, but without the artifice and scripted nature of a lesson. Students experience the school as life, not lesson.

## How Do You Spell "Sex Videos"?

Ten students were in the small Publishing Room. Isaiah and Gage, 7-year-olds, sat at a computer at one end of the room. Drew, 16, newly enrolled a few weeks earlier and already elected Computer Wizard, was on the floor fixing one of the school's broken computers. Seven girls, ages 6 to 10, sat around a table. Gage, 7, turned to Drew and asked "How do you spell 'sex videos'?" Drew refused to spell "sex" for them but helpfully called out the spelling of "videos." The boys typed it in, pressed Enter, giggled nervously, and quickly closed the screen, having seen thumbnail images of nudity. A few minutes later, they asked Drew for help again. Drew refused — "No, you shouldn't be doing that" — so Gage left the room and came back with a 9-year-old who helpfully typed "YouTube" for them, beside the word "sex" that the boys had already typed into the search window, and then the 9-year-old left the room. Again the boys pressed Enter, giggled, and shut it down. At about that moment, a 13-year-old entered the room, saw what was happening, stopped it, and wrote it up for JC.

The Judicial Committee investigated and charged the two 7-year-olds for violating community norms of decency regarding sexual expression (Section 2023.16) and also for "jeopardizing the well-being of the school" (2000.12). They were banned from all computer use for a few weeks. The 9-year-old who assisted them and neglected to stop them was charged with a rule that creates an "individual obligation to promote the school welfare" (2000.08) and was also banned from computer use for a while. Drew was charged with the same rule but was sentenced more harshly, in light of his age, proximity, and opportunity to intervene. All seven of the nearby girls were also charged for failing in that duty because they were well situated to see what was happening and put a stop to it but did not. They were all banned from computer use for a day. All defendants pled "guilty," and all said they were treated fairly.

---

## Judicial Committee

Every democratic school has a Judicial Committee or function, by whatever name, and everybody takes turns serving — everybody, meaning youngest students to oldest and staff members. The number of JC members, the officials, and the procedures vary from school to school, but in every school, JC is central to daily life — like the school's heartbeat.

Anybody can write up a complaint for the JC to hear — an allegation of rule-breaking. A complaint is only an allegation and may or may not be borne out in investigation. Every complaint must identify at least one rule (by number) that the complaint writer alleges has been broken. If the rule number box on the complaint form is left blank, the JC is permitted to drop the complaint without investigation, although if the allegation is deemed serious, the investigation will proceed anyway.

Young children especially find great empowerment in writing up their friends — or more often simply threatening: "If you don't give that back to me, I'll write you up!" Threats of write-up far outnumber actual write-ups. Complaints can be nitpicking, naïve, mundane, or serious. Here is a sampling of actual recent complaints (names changed but misspellings retained):

- The Peaople in the Sunspace were swearing [which breaks a rule in some circumstances, but not others].
- Rudy left orange peels on the round table in the Playroom. I have a photo.
- Shayla sprayed me in the eyes with spray cleaner.
- I was drawing a picture in the Art Room. Tyson took it from me and showed it to Billie. Billie got mad and started punching and kicking me. [Written by Billie's little brother.]
- Brenner has not yet paid his $20 damage fee, which was due by winter break.
- Allie poked me with a protractor three times.

- Casey toock my shoo.
- Kristen and Connor were riding on Noah's hoverboard in the upstairs Kitchen.

JC meets every day, often for the full 90 minutes allotted. When a backlog develops, there may be two daily sessions of JC for days or weeks, and sometimes a special JC is formed to pursue a lengthy investigation.

At the prescribed meeting time, the JC Chair and JC Scribe, who are both elected officials (usually students), are supposed to have everything set up and ready to go. Sometimes the JC Chair has walked around the school to find and remind those who are scheduled to serve that day, but that is not an official duty. (If you don't show up on time, you can be cited by the rest of the JC and sentenced.) The Chair has retrieved the day's complaint forms from the box and, ideally, read through them. The Scribe has the laptop computer set up, with the judicial records database open and ready to record minutes.

In addition to the five JC members — four students and one staff member — there are two "runners" and two alternates. The runners' job is to go and summon witnesses as needed by the JC. When summoned by a runner, you must stop what you are doing and go immediately or face contempt charges. Failure to cooperate with the JC is regarded as a very serious infraction, likely to lead quickly to suspension if repeated. JC is our only mechanism for enforcing the rules, so cooperation is imperative.

There are also two alternates scheduled every day, who are called on to serve when a regular JC member steps down (i.e., recusal) because of personal involvement (as a witness or defendant) or other strong personal interest in the case. Rarely, an alternate might be called to serve in place of a very young child when an investigation necessitates extensive, explicit consideration of matters that would commonly be considered experientially inappropriate for young children. This latter situation can be controversial, as it involves political and moral philosophy, paternalism, diverse sensibilities, and public relations.

Sessions of JC are generally open for observation by any and all students and staff. The idea is to favor open, transparent justice and easy access to public proceedings. Observing JC is a good way to learn its subtleties, perhaps in preparation for running for election as JC Chair. Every year we have a few "JC groupies" — perhaps with an interest in law or justice, or with a vigilante spirit, or for entertainment. Observing JC also tends to keep one up on current social conflicts and shifting patterns of social dynamics. It is also an endlessly fascinating study of human psychology, particularly how people see themselves and others in relation to events, how they behave when their actions are called into question, and how investigators' own expectations and biases shape the process.

A JC can vote to close the room to observers during investigation and deliberation (but not arraignment and sentencing) if it finds reason to do so. In that event, the JC must state its reason in writing and report it to the next session of School Meeting. Closing JC is a rare event, perhaps happening a couple of times per year. An investigation might be closed, for example, to avoid spreading a particularly damaging rumor about a person or when a lengthy investigation is likely to be compromised by early witnesses colluding with later witnesses.

JC sessions can be fast-moving and chaotic or agonizingly slow and tedious. It's not uncommon for a case to involve a dozen witnesses, and sometimes dozens. Runners and witnesses are coming and going, sometimes interviewed in groups. Often the Chair struggles to keep order as two JC members are trying to question a witness at the same time, while several witnesses and observers are also talking, sometimes with high emotions and high stakes. A visiting university researcher, after observing a session, described it as "a lot of boring detail punctuated by high drama." Sounds about right to me.

The JC process includes the following structured steps, as laid out in the Management Manual: triage, investigation, findings, charges, arraignment, sentencing, recording, and reporting.

## Triage

When all members are present, the Chair reads aloud the day's complaints. At the beginning of a school year, the load is usually light — sometimes no complaints for several days running. By late January, with more people staying indoors, the load gets heavy. This year we took on a surge of new students mid- to late-winter, and now we have set a new backlog record: 33 complaints awaiting investigation. Time for double JC sessions. After hearing a read-through of pending complaints, the JC then decides together in what order to investigate the complaints, perhaps choosing the most serious allegations first, or selecting a cluster of complaints about one person, or selecting a cluster of complaints involving one witness. Often, complaints involving the youngest students are selected first, because their memories tend to fade sooner, or several memories are blended into a new confabulation that will confound the investigation.

## Investigation

When a complaint is selected, the committee quickly determines what witnesses to summon for testimony, sometimes all at once, sometimes one at a time, sometimes in a definite sequence based on the anticipated quality or completeness of the testimony. JC members sit on three sides of a rectangular table, with the Chairperson in the middle of a long side and the Scribe at one end. Witnesses sit on the long side opposite the JC members. Witnesses are questioned by JC members, sometimes primarily by the Chair. If the Chair is new or young or flustered, then other members, especially the serving staff member, will take the lead. Some who give testimony as accused perpetrators are starkly honest: "Yes, I did that." Many are evasive: "I don't remember." Of course, some, even among the sweetest-looking little darlings, are just flat-out lying. Sometimes the JC can tell the difference and sometimes improperly jumps to conclusions because the person's reputation precedes them. But still the JC must gather sufficient evidence to justify a charge or else close the case without charges. In some democratic schools, prospective defendants can plead the Fifth Amendment and refuse to testify. Witnesses are dismissed when JC members run out of questions. Investigations sometimes include examination of photos and occasionally physical evidence — for example, a broken object or a photo of a mess. Occasionally the JC visits the site of the alleged crime to examine evidence or even to recreate the event.

## Findings and Charges

When the JC is satisfied they have come close enough to relevant truth — a fair approximation is often the best we can do — they compose a brief statement of findings. Ideally the Scribe has drafted findings along the way and reads the draft aloud. Ideally the findings include facts but not interpretations, characterizations, and speculation. In simple cases, the findings are immediately adopted by quick vote. Sometimes, though, it's a laborious process to craft words that will capture the essential story and include all the elements necessary to establish an infraction. Sometimes witnesses are recalled. Often the prospective defendants participate in refining the findings. Sometimes a defendant asks to include an acknowledged fact that tends to mitigate the defendant's culpability or justify their actions. "She took my shoe and that's why I sprayed her with the spray bottle. Put that in the findings." Maybe they will both get in trouble. Findings are finalized only by majority vote of the JC. In most cases, the findings are adopted unanimously.

The JC examines its findings, once adopted, to determine if rules have been broken, and if so, then the JC may charge one or more defendants. Findings must support charges by stating a set of facts that constitute a violation. For example, a finding that "Evie left her lunch spread out on the kitchen table for an hour while she was in the Playroom" would support a charge of leaving a mess. A finding that "Evie left a mess" would be inadequate because it is too vague — more an interpretation than a set of facts.

Usually the JC knows when it begins an investigation what charges are possible or likely, if only because the complaint form requires that the complaint writer identify at least one rule they allege has been violated. Witnesses are questioned and findings are crafted, knowing what elements of fact must be included to establish the alleged infraction.

Findings are usually not adopted and recorded if no charges will be applied, although occasionally findings are composed and recorded anyway. This may happen if the JC anticipates that School Meeting might later question their decision not to file charges, or if a serious allegation has been made and the investigation vindicates an accused party, or if the investigation was lengthy but inconclusive and its findings might be useful to a future investigation.

If findings support charges, and unless the JC decides that justice will be better served by inaction, then the JC votes to charge (i.e., indict) one or more defendants with violation of specified rules.

The JC has good reason to develop accurate findings that strongly support the charge. If a defendant pleads not guilty, the JC must present the case to a trial jury — which typically requires significant effort to prepare and can go either way. The JC would much rather have the defendant agree that the findings are fair and accurate and agree that the findings establish violation of the specified rule.

## Arraignment and Sentencing

After the charges are voted, the runners summon the defendant as directed by the JC Chair. The defendant is then arraigned. First the Scribe reads the findings to the defendant. If the defendant wasn't part of crafting the findings, or if there is any doubt, the Chair asks the defendant if the findings are accurate. If the defendant objects to aspects of the findings, the JC may consider changes. If the defendant simply repeats a denial that has been contradicted by other evidence, the JC is unlikely to discuss it further, already having made a determination.

The Chair then informs the defendant of the charges made by the JC and reads to the defendant the text of each law charged. If the law is lengthy, the Chair may read only the relevant portion, and the defendant may waive the reading of the law. Repeat offenders sometimes interrupt and recite the text, having heard it many times.

Next the Chair asks the defendant "How do you plead?" and expects a response of guilty or not guilty. Some schools allow a plea of "no contest" (or *nolo contendere*), which has the same effect as a plea of guilty but admits no guilt.

Sentencing proceeds regardless of the plea. If the plea is not guilty, then the sentence does not go into effect until and unless the defendant is found guilty at trial. If the plea is guilty (or no contest), then the sentence begins on the defendant's next day of attendance unless the JC explicitly directs otherwise.

Sentences are determined by vote of the JC, following suggestions and discussion among JC members. Some people use the term "sentence," and others prefer "consequence." Some are determined to find sentences that "fit the crime," and others are satisfied with no connection at all. Sentencing philosophies variously aim for punishment, socialization, behavioral modification, restoration, therapy, and helpful reminding. There is no mandated approach, although there are common patterns. For example, if there has been property damage or monetary loss, the sentence will almost always include an order to pay for repair or restitution.

Sometimes sentencing is completed before the defendant is arraigned, perhaps while waiting for the runners to get the defendant. Sometimes sentencing discussion is interrupted for arraignment when the defendant arrives, and then the discussion continues after the plea is taken. Some JC Chairs, especially the young and the new ones, take things one distinct phase at a time, and the JC spends a lot of time waiting between steps.

The Scribe, having a computer at hand, looks up the defendant's record of prior convictions — the rap sheet — at the beginning of the sentencing discussion. The JC is not permitted to examine or discuss prior convictions until *after* charges are voted, so that the JC's judgment of culpability in the case at hand is based only on the facts of the case and is less likely to be influenced by knowledge of past charges. Of course, in our small community, JC members often do have knowledge of past charges anyway, especially knowledge of repeat offenders. Consideration of past convictions is relevant in sentencing, with repeat offenses bringing more severe sentences.

For example, the first time you are convicted of running in the narrow halls, you will almost certainly get a warning. If your second conviction happens the next day, you may be sentenced to "baby steps ROT" — meaning for the Rest Of Today, each step you take must not exceed the length of your foot, thus imposing slow movement and requiring persistent attention. A third conviction in the near future might get you "baby steps NDA" (Next Day of Attendance). Keep it up and you might be banned from entering the upstairs hall for a day or more.

This year, little Noah goes running down the hall so many times every day that most people now just ignore it. JC sentences don't slow him down for long, and anyway JC would get quite bogged down if he were written up every time. He's small and agile, his collisions are few and inconsequential, and he'll probably grow out of it soon, so we mostly sigh and tolerate his running. There's usually a Noah every year (at least one), whose spirit cannot abide walking when there's such a big world to explore and so many adventures beckoning — and admittedly that pleases me.

## Judicial Case Examples

To summarize: Findings are a statement of facts as determined by the JC after taking testimony and examining evidence. After findings are adopted by vote of the five JC members, charges are determined and voted separately. Sentencing, also by vote, takes into account the findings, charges, mitigating factors that may or may not be in the findings, and the defendant's history of convictions.

The following examples of JC findings, charges, and sentences are taken from recent cases (with names changed). Charges are shown here as the "short name" of the violated law. The full text of the law, which can be lengthy, may be read to the defendant. After charges are made, but not before, the JC examines the defendant's record (i.e., computerized rap sheet) before deciding on a sentence. If it's a first offense, the sentence may be simply a warning. The more offenses, the greater the sentence is likely to be. Here are examples, with my comments in *italics*:

FINDINGS: Marianne pushed Bobby after he told her that her time was up on the computer.

CHARGES: Marianne: Unwanted forceful physical contact.

SENTENCE: No computers ROT and NDA.

———❈———

FINDINGS: Lucas and Johanna weren't at the front door to pick up their pizzas when the delivery person arrived.

CHARGES: Lucas & Johanna: Food delivery acceptance.

SENTENCE: No ordering delivery food for the rest of the week.

*Comment: When the buyer isn't there to receive and pay for the food, someone has to go find them — usually the office staff — and the delivery person is kept waiting.*

———❈———

FINDINGS: Rob threw a stick through the open back door that was larger than one inch in diameter, thus breaking his consequence given in case #041801, which states that he may not touch sticks larger than one inch in diameter for the rest of the school year. He has broken that consequence at least two times previously.

CHARGES: No projectiles through windows. Follow JC sentences.

SENTENCE: Recommended one-day suspension.

*Comment: Breaking a JC sentence ("consequence") is a serious viola-
tion. Combined with the defendant's lengthy rap sheet, the JC found
this justified a suspension. Unlike other sentences, JC cannot impose
a suspension, but can only recommend it. In this case, School Meeting
accepted the recommendation and voted the suspension. School
Meeting accepts about half of JC's recommendations, and votes an
alternative sentence in the other half.*

———— ∞ ————

FINDINGS: Anna brought two live crickets inside and put them in a
Science Corporation bug jar intending to release them after a couple of
hours, which she did not do. The crickets would have been in the Science
Room overnight if JD hadn't released them.

CHARGES: Cruelty to animals.

SENTENCE: She may not capture any animals ROT and NDA-2
*[Next 2 Days of Attendance]*.

*Comment: The defendant had prior convictions of the same charge,
different creatures, indulging curiosity but not intending cruelty.*

———— ∞ ————

FINDINGS: Tom B. was playing music in the Publishing Room. The
song contained the lyrics "I don't give a f***, I don't give a f***," and it was
loud enough to be heard through the closed Publishing Room door to the
downstairs hallway. Tom knew the lyrics before he played it.

CHARGES: Excessive vulgarity.

SENTENCE: No screens for the rest of the week.

———— ∞ ————

FINDINGS: Lori was yelling from the [upstairs] Publishing Room to get
Cord's attention in the [Downstairs] Kitchen.

CHARGES: Yelling, screaming, shouting prohibited indoors.

SENTENCE: No upstairs for the rest of the day, except for doing
her chore or retrieving personal belongings.

———— ∞ ————

FINDINGS: Juni and Evan were slamming the doors in Room 1A loud enough to disturb Ellen in the Office.

CHARGES: Sound levels may not interfere with others.

SENTENCE: They must help JD do touch-up painting on the Room 1A doors.

———∞———

FINDINGS: In the Playroom, Ann and Ben S. dumped a drawer of the school's plastic toys on Aydan and Jibran's heads without provocation. Jibran required a Medical Responder *[for comfort but not first aid]*. Ann and Ben S. tried to bribe Jibran with $5.00 so he wouldn't write a complaint.

CHARGES: Ann and Ben: Appropriate use of materials. No influencing JC with intimidation and bribing. Unwanted forceful physical contact.

SENTENCES: No Playroom and no physical contact with anyone, ROT and NDA.

Democratic schools base public justice on democratic law-making, rule of law, and due process. Democratic law-making means all students and staff members have equal rights of voice and vote in adopting, amending, and repealing school laws. Rule of law means you can be held accountable for compliance only with laws that have been adopted by the democratic process and published for all to see. Due process means everybody has certain legal rights that must be respected as laws are enforced in judicial proceedings.

With peace, fairness, and compassion in mind, we think our judicial system is quite imperfect but probably does justice at least as well as the world beyond school, and we keep striving to do better.

## A Mock JC

At an evening event, our judicial team demonstrated for the school community how the wheels of justice go 'round at school. Simulating what we do every day, they investigated complaints of law-breaking — real cases from the past, with names changed. The players — five Judicial Committee members, two runners, and numerous witnesses — were only lightly informed of the cases ahead of time, and their briefings were as inconsistent as the original testimony, thus preserving the spontaneity, ambiguity, contradiction, and surprise that are so common in our judicial proceedings. One witness says it happened in the yard, another says on the front porch, neither is lying, that can't be, but life is often like that, isn't it? If nothing else, Judicial Committee members — that's all of us here, taking turns — daily confront the woven texture of facts and stories: zoom in close enough and you find space between the threads. You discover that earthy truth is a loose weave and always partial.

## Formal Governance

Democratic school governance is formal, not informal. This might seem surprising for small communities and children, but a degree of formality is an essential feature of democratic schools, no matter what the size. Formality doesn't mean stiff and stuffy, or even complicated. Formality means we thoughtfully design and agree on governing procedures that accomplish our aims, such as equality of rights, authority, and responsibility. Then we write down the agreed procedures, publish it for all to see, and stick to that template with confidence that we are covering all the bases. When we discover a flaw or an opportunity to improve, we change the procedures and that becomes the new form of governing. *Formal* just means *conforming* to a certain *form* that has been duly adopted by public government.

Formality is predictable, contributing to a culture that feels stable, secure, and fair — a solid base from which children freely explore the world with confidence. Formalizing the rights, authority, and responsibility of students also avoids the usual default condition in which rights, authority, and responsibility are concentrated in adults. Formal government helps to position the school as a public commons shared by all.

For example, public law-making helps protect students from arbitrary power — a universally valued protection. Our society is accustomed to adults making rules for children, and it is unusual for children to be democratically empowered. If we didn't insist on law-making according to clearly agreed public procedures — if our law-making happened *informally*, that is "without form" — children and adults might both tend to slip into the socially accustomed mode of adults directing everything. Democratic schools insist on shared authority and responsibility. Formal systems are how we do it.

## Legal Structure

There is much variety among democratic schools in forms of organization and corporate structure — particularly in the relative powers of the Board of Trustees and School Meeting. I'll explain The Circle School's legal structure and then mention other configurations.

The Circle School Corporation (operating as The Circle School) is chartered as a nonprofit Pennsylvania corporation, with a 501(c)(3) tax-exemption granted by the U.S. Internal Revenue Service. The tax-exempt designation, which is customary for nonprofit schools, has two important effects: the school is exempt from paying most taxes, and donations to the school are tax-deductible by the donor.

The Circle School Corporation Bylaws, which are legally binding and enforceable under Pennsylvania law, define three governing entities: School Meeting, Board of Trustees, and Membership. (See the figure.)

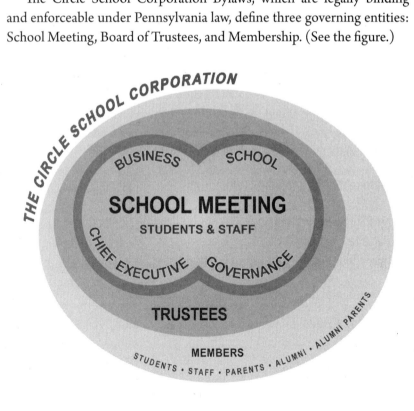

Article Three of the Bylaws lays out a dozen statements of ideals, called "Ends We Seek" (listed in Part One of this book). For example, one statement says "Students enjoy civil liberties such as freedoms of speech, press, thought, attention, religion, privacy, movement, association, and peaceable assembly." Another says "Students are free of curricular coercion." Ends We Seek (or just "Ends") are conditions that all agencies of school government must seek to achieve and maintain, sometimes loosely compared to the American Bill of Rights, which is binding on all units of American government.

Bylaws enumerate powers and duties of each of the three governing entities, roughly summarized as follows: *School Meeting* manages the school as a business and governs the daily program as a society. *Trustees* preserve the school's democratic structure, students' civil liberties, and the school's long-term assets. The *Membership* ratifies or vetoes proposed Bylaws amendments.

## School Meeting

The school is both a business (nonprofit) and a self-governed civil society. The School Meeting functions as chief executive of the business and head of government. Students and staff (but not parents) are automatically members of the School Meeting. Bylaws list 15 powers and duties of the School Meeting; the first two summarize nicely:

7.2.1 School Meeting shall manage school operations; shall conduct day-to-day business and affairs of the school to achieve Ends through acceptable means; shall comply with all applicable local, state, and federal laws and regulations; and shall abide by, uphold, and implement the Bylaws, and policies and decisions of the Trustees.

7.2.2 School Meeting shall govern the daily school community according to and exemplifying the Ends enumerated in Article Three. School Meeting shall determine its systems of governance, offices, officers, meetings, quorum, voting, rules of order, laws, judicial process, and other matters.

As authorized and constrained by Bylaws, School Meeting performs or oversees the functions of a chief executive, governor, legislature, and judicial system.

## Board of Trustees

The Board comprises seven elected trustees, typically but not necessarily drawn from the school community. School Meeting, alumni, and the Membership each elect one trustee annually for a 1-year term. Trustees elect one trustee annually for a 4-year term, typically someone who has served a 1-year term already. Thus, at any time, there are four trustees who have been elected by the trustees, and one each by the other three groups. After ten consecutive years of service, a trustee must cycle off the board for at least a year.

Any person can be elected to any trusteeship by any of the four electing groups. For example, School Meeting sometimes elects a student to the board, and sometimes a parent, alumn, or alumn parent. By design, and now preserved in culture and tradition, all trustees are at-large; no trustee is regarded as representing the body that elected them. For example, the trustee elected by alumni — who may or may not be an alumn — is not viewed as "the alumni trustee," nor expected to emphasize alumni interests, nor to act as a spokesperson to the board on their behalf. The 1-year terms filled by School Meeting, alumni, and the Membership are instead regarded as feeder positions, a way for new trustees to try it out before committing to a 4-year term.

This "interchangeability" of trustees has beneficial results. Consider the school's natural constituencies that could be represented on the board: students, staff, parents, alumni, alumni parents, donors, and the general public. Each is defined by a particular relation to the school and a corresponding perspective and nominal set of interests that differs from the other constituencies. If each trustee were a representative of a constituency, the board's policymaking might be more likely to devolve into partisan politics and competitive dysfunction. In addition to diminished effectiveness, it would make board service less satisfying and thus make it harder to recruit new trustees.

This year the Board of Trustees includes two alumni, two parents of current students, two parents of alumni, and one staff member (who is also an alumn parent). Through a nominating committee, the Board and School Meeting collaborate and coordinate their appointees to achieve continuity, balance, and needed skills and perspectives, according to current perceptions of needs.

The Bylaws list 18 powers and duties of the Trustees, performed "on behalf of all persons everywhere and throughout time who support the [school's] purposes." This broad constituency, and distance from the daily school program, tend to give the Board a long-term, big-picture perspective. Their most important duties are to "secure School Meeting's governing autonomy, students' civil liberties, and the school's long-term assets." More specifically, Bylaws call on Trustees to do the following:

- Establish policies defining standards of prudence and ethics
- Defer to School Meeting on conduct of operations, management of day-to-day affairs, governance of the daily school program, hiring of school staff, and control of operational policies and procedures
- Monitor School Meeting's adherence to policies and Ends We Seek
- Intervene if School Meeting breaches policies or Ends
- Propose Bylaws amendments (by supermajority of 5 out of 7 Trustees)

Board policies tend to be broad, such as "School Meeting shall not acquire or dispose of real property" (i.e., land and buildings) and "School Meeting shall not receive, process, or disburse funds except under controls that meet the school's auditor's standards." There are currently ten of these "limits" policies. Board policies, by custom, are worded in the negative — prohibiting rather than prescribing — in order to maximize School Meeting's freedom to achieve the desired outcome by any legal means, a principle taken from the formal theory of organizational governance known as Policy Governance (associated with John Carver). Here are the titles of current limits policies: Cash Controls, Policy on GAAP Accounting, Funds in Federally Insured Accounts, Real Property, Borrowing, Investment Accounts Controlled by the Board, Designated Funds, Budget Adherence, Deficit Prohibited, Policy on Terms of Contracts. All are intended to preserve long-term assets.

Trustees are required to intervene if School Meeting violates policies or Ends. Happily, that has not happened. In case it does, the Bylaws prescribe a three-step process to be followed by the Board: (1) conduct investigation, (2) communicate to School Meeting a detailed and specific "statement of breach" and give School Meeting a chance to fix the problem, and (3) assume control of operations and funds "to the minimum extent necessary to cure the breach." What would trigger intervention? It's hard to imagine such circumstances, but I suppose something like School Meeting voting to require math classes of all students (violating an End) or to pay out a dividend of $1,000 to each student (misappropriating funds).

The school's three-body structure and division of authority are unusual among private organizations of all kinds. Nearly all boards — profit and nonprofit — have absolute, unconditional control of every aspect of the organization. Boards commonly delegate much authority to an executive, who then delegates to staff, but the board can always direct or override executive actions, or revoke its delegation.

In contrast, The Circle School's board is strictly limited in its authority. Its role is not comparable to that of an executive, legislative, or judicial branch of government, but combines limited elements of all three. The board is required to defer to School Meeting and may not make School Meeting laws, but the board is also required to intervene if School Meeting violates fundamental principles (as expressed in Ends We Seek). In effect, the board's most important role is to guard and preserve. Trustees are entrusted as protectors of the school's most basic principles. They guard the kingdom's jewels. But who guards the guards?

## Membership

Students, staff, and trustees are automatically part of the Membership of The Circle School Corporation. At a minimum, then, the Membership is the union of School Meeting and the Board. In addition, parents, alumni, and alumni parents are eligible to opt into lifetime membership. This represents a potential Membership of around 2,500 now, although only a small fraction are active at any given time.

The Membership has limited but important formal authority. Its key power is to ratify or withhold ratification of proposed Bylaws amendments. In effect, the Membership guards the guards. The Membership cannot initiate Bylaws amendments but can veto them by voting against ratification.

Only the Board can initiate Bylaws amendments. In doing so, the Board is required to solicit the School Meeting's written response (which is adopted by vote of students and staff in School Meeting). Both the proposed amendment and School Meeting's response are disseminated to the Membership before the proposed amendment comes to a ratification vote (by the Membership, typically at its Annual Meeting). So far, amendments have been viewed as technical corrections and occasional refinements. In all cases, School Meeting and the Board have been in agreement. Ratification votes have succeeded without opposition — partly because School Meeting members and Board members also vote as part of the Membership. In the event of disagreement between the Board and School Meeting, however, the influence of parents, alumni, and alumni parents would probably be decisive. That influence could be through the Membership's vote to ratify or reject, but it seems just as likely that informal and political influence in the community dialogue would come into play and avoid a polarizing vote.

The Membership is thus a stabilizing reservoir of school experience and passionate dedication, vigilant and quiescent in normal times, and vitally important in times of contention and times of change.

## Checks and Balances

School Meeting and Trustees share a strong common interest in the well-being of the school. Their unity of purpose is evident in the harmony we have experienced between the two primary governing entities. Of course, we hope mutual cooperation will continue in the future even if and when conditions become contentious, but our governing structure is intended to guard against political mischief and withstand conflict.

The school has not seen conflict between Trustees and School Meeting, so I cannot speak from direct experience on how the governing structure will bear up under stress. In designing The Circle School's current structure (fall 2007), a large committee tried to imagine the many ways things could go wrong, and how a temporary confluence of circumstances and personalities might cause the school to veer from foundation principles or jeopardize the school's future in other ways. We settled on a system of checks and balances and imagined how each governing body might be hijacked — might try to "go rogue" as we put it. The Bylaws represent our best efforts to stymie attempts to go rogue and spoil the fun.

On the other hand, we want to provide for evolutionary change in philosophy, interpretation, and practice, particularly in response to changes in the world around us. Bylaws amendments may be a crucial part of the response. The aim is to enable such amendments through a carefully considered process that involves the entire school community and a significant span of time for deliberation.

The planning horizon represents another important balance in governance. Immersed in the immediacy of day-to-day operations and practical realities, School Meeting's focus tends to be drawn to short- and medium-term considerations. The average (mean) duration of student enrollments is three to four years (assuming normal family mobility and attrition), and students collectively do not typically take a long view or experienced perspective in planning and managing the school's business. Longer-term perspectives are more often asserted by staff members, some of whom have business administration experience. The Board's powers and duties, on the other hand, require it to focus on medium- and long-term considerations, and keep it at a distance from short-term matters. The contrast of long versus short time horizons produces a healthy balance of perspectives between School Meeting and the Board. As previously suggested, the Membership has little formal role in this balance, but its informal and political influences would undoubtedly come into play if the balance tilted towards conflict between the two.

Somewhat like the game Rock-Paper-Scissors, but not as symmetrical, all three governing bodies hold significant power, and all three are held in check by another. Crucially, none alone can change the rules of the game.

## Other Legal Structures

Other democratic schools implement other legal structures and philosophies of governance, including the traditional board-controls-everything structure and two others that I know: the "old Sudbury" legal structure and the "new Sudbury" legal structure. Even within these structures, there are variations from school to school.

The "old Sudbury" structure has three governing bodies: School Meeting, Board of Trustees, and Assembly. School Meeting's duties are approximately the same as I've described for The Circle School. The Board of Trustees, however, has no powers at all. It is entirely advisory, serving as a sort of in-house think-tank. The Assembly mainly consists of currently enrolled students, parents of current students, and staff (but not alumni and alumni parents, who have no formal role). The Assembly has broad policymaking powers, such as regarding "educational policy" and tuition rates. Unlike a board of trustees, Assembly members have no fiduciary duty to the school — no legal obligation to act in the school's interests — and are instead free to vote their own private interests. The Assembly is compared to a Town Meeting, which is a public governing structure in a handful of American states.

The Circle School was governed by the old Sudbury structure for a time. Without fiduciaries and without a clear statement of principles (such as Ends We Seek), the school seemed to be at risk, both fiscally and philosophically, a view that became widespread. Culture and tradition held the school to its principles, but the legal structure, resembling that of a parent cooperative school, would have permitted a transient majority to radically alter the school's principles and practices. Equally troubling, a transient majority could have appropriated the school's substantial savings (towards a new campus) to fund a tuition reduction for more years than the average family's stay. If our families had voted their own economic interests, the school would have been in trouble. Instead, in order to preserve the school's principles long into the future, our Assembly voted itself out of existence many years ago and adopted the current structure by a nearly unanimous vote in a well-attended meeting. Other democratic schools report they are still doing fine with the Assembly structure.

The "new Sudbury" structure is the simplest of all, first adopted by Sudbury Valley School (late 2011). Some other Sudbury schools have followed suit. In the new Sudbury structure, the School Meeting is the only governing body, with a Board of Advisors having no powers, and no Assembly or other body enfranchising parents or anyone else. Students and staff together manage and control every aspect of the school. Period. Bylaws may be amended at any time by a two-thirds vote of students and staff in School Meeting. Sudbury Valley School, the grand flagship of Sudbury schools, continues to thrive under its new governing structure.

Chapter 11:

# The Chore System

THINK OF THE MANY CHALLENGES of a self-governing community of children, teenagers, and adults — together most of the day, most of the week, sharing space and resources, governing the community, and managing school business. In democratic schools, students encounter a steady stream of life.

The essential experience of democratic schooling includes living by cooperative systems developed in public processes for orderly access to resources and a satisfying community life. Over and over, School Meeting encounters collective challenges and develops responses. Keeping the building and campus reasonably tidy and clean is a big one. The Circle School's chore system offers a good example of how democratic schools approach shared challenges.

Housekeeping is handled in a variety of ways by democratic schools. All have rules about cleaning up your own messes, but that's not enough to keep the school tidy and clean. Some hire a cleaning service or engage volunteers after hours. Some operate a chore system.

The Circle School's chore system illustrates how School Meeting manages the school practically and efficiently, powered by children, teenagers, and adults, while sticking to principles of transparency, fairness, rule of law, and free enterprise. Its purpose is to keep the building and grounds reasonably orderly and clean. Of course, messes and apparent chaos are part of community life, but putting things back together and basic cleaning about once a day helps to make it feel like it is managed and manageable, without unduly inhibiting sprawling imagination and creation.

Over the years, the chore system has been refined many times, completely overhauled several times, and once it was thrown out altogether.

---

## No More Chores?

Some people just don't like to do chores. Feeling their democratic power one day, they brought it to School Meeting: a motion to repeal the law that requires everyone to do a chore. Some were opposed, saying that without daily chores the school would be one great big Mess. But word of the proposal had spread, and what started as hopeless grumbling escalated into a full-scale populist reform movement. The meeting was packed, and it was clear they weren't going to take No for an answer. And anyway, the thought of freedom from chores is appealing to everyone, isn't it? After much discussion, the motion was amended to make it a two-week trial instead of a permanent change. That was the compromise that gave everyone enough of what they wanted. It passed with a large majority and became school law. Chores were out! Hooray! We're free!

Alas, the reality was less glorious than the fantasy. Elves did not show up in dark of night to put things away, wipe the tables, replenish the toilet paper, and remove from the refrigerator whatever that smelly gray thing was. By the end of the two weeks, even the anti-chore voters held their nose and agreed that we needed to go back to daily chores. But we tried. We've been there and done that.

That was 20-some years ago. The chore system hasn't been challenged again. But maybe tomorrow.

---

Today, Section 1600 of the Lawbook ("Chores") says that everyone must do a housekeeping chore every day and lays out how to sign up, when to do your chore, how to get your chore checked, how to opt out of doing your chore, and more.

Section 8417, in the Committees section of the Management Manual, is the Chore Committee's charter, enumerating its powers and duties:

- To maintain the chore list, including detailed and accurate descriptions of each chore, and to set standards for the satisfactory completion of each chore.

- To assign permanent chores [for those who want one] and to train School Meeting members to do permanent chores, rather than signing up for a chore each day.
- To nominate Chore Checkers for election by School Meeting, and to train the elected Chore Checkers [whose job description fills a page].
- To schedule Chore Checker terms, assign them zones of the school to check, and to post this information for public display.
- To set and post prices for chore fines, opting out, and doing extra chores.
- To adjust the school's chore system as changes become necessary, and to inform School Meeting members of these changes.

Section 8235, in the Officials section of the Management Manual, is about the Chore Supervisor, an elected official whose job is to manage the chore system on a day-to-day basis. That section enumerates the Chore Supervisor's powers and duties:

- To maintain all necessary records pertaining to the school's chore system.
- To coordinate and supervise the Chore Checkers, and maintain consistency among them.
- To receive information from the Chore Checkers regarding School Meeting members who have failed to do a chore, and to either fine them or initiate Judicial Committee action.
- To run the fine system, including keeping track of who has chosen the fine system, posting fines, collecting fines, and initiating JC action against those who fail to pay fines.
- To run the opt-out system, including collecting opt-out payments and arranging for chore workers to do extra chores, for pay.

Does this seem like excessive documentation or bureaucracy to you? Or, on the other hand, do you find it liberating to know exactly what is expected of you? Many of us experience it both ways at various times. In any case, it keeps the school reasonably orderly, helping to facilitate access to materials, equipment, and space. And, after many iterations over the years, it feels fair to most people.

Many students are attracted to the money-making opportunity of extra chores — so many, in fact, that the Chore Committee had to adapt.

---

## *Die for Extra Chores*

In an overhaul many years ago, the chore system embraced free enterprise. Don't want to do your chore today? Go see Simon, the elected Chore Supervisor, and pay the opt-out fee, currently $2. Simon is low-key, business-like, tough, gentle, and unflappably calm in the midst of last-minute chore chaos. He has long experience with the job and the Chore Committee, and we will miss him when he graduates soon. (Not only because he does a great job as Chore Supervisor, and not only because he sells freeze pops on the side. We love Simon for other reasons, too.)

Want to get paid to do an extra chore today — earn a buck or two? Okay, do your regular chore and then be near the chore chart this afternoon at 2:00. Simon will determine what chores would not otherwise be done, because of opt-outs and absences, and make them available for pay. If the Chore Committee has collected a lot of cash, Simon may offer special chores, too — deeper cleaning and other jobs that don't need to be done every day.

Once Simon decides what chores are available, whoever is first in line gets first pick. So what chore would you pick? Everyone has their own ideas about which chores are easy and which are hard, so the choice can make quite a difference, and that led to a problem. People started lining up before 2:00 — sometimes an hour before. A crowd would form, and they jostled for position, and it got noisy enough to be a problem in the nearby front office.

The Chore Committee studied the problem in several weekly committee meetings, considered possible solutions, and then acted. They said okay, from now on you don't have to wait in line. You just have to sign up ahead of time and then be there at 2:00. Chores will be given out in the order of sign-up. So each morning they put a sign-up sheet on the bulletin board, with 12 places for names, numbered 1 through 12. At 2:00 Simon would start by offering first choice to the person signed up in the #1 slot, and so on through the list. That didn't work. People started lining up in the morning, waiting for the Extra Chore Sign-up Sheet to be put up. More jostling, more noise, more complaints from the front office.

The Chore Committee was baffled for a while but then hit upon a solution that has lasted for years. They still post a sign-up sheet every morning, and it still has those 12 numbered sign-up slots. But nobody waits in line anymore because there is no advantage to being #1. In fact, you can sign up in any slot. It makes no difference.

Here's why. On the bulletin board near the Extra Chore Sign-up Sheet, there hangs a little plastic bag. Inside the bag is a 12-sided die, with sides numbered from 1 to 12 (from a set of RPG dice; that's "role playing games"). At 2:00 each afternoon, Simon takes out the die and rolls it. Whatever number comes up, that's where he starts on the Sign-up Sheet. That person gets first pick, and then the choice proceeds in sequence from there, wrapping around from #12 to #1. No matter what slot you sign up in, you have the same chance of getting first pick as everyone else!

On most days this year, all 12 slots are filled. People love chores after all. Or maybe it's the money.

---

Each democratic school approaches chores and other challenges with its own unique culture and character. Solutions vary. What's mostly constant and consistent across democratic schools, though, is illustrated nicely by The Circle School's chore system and its evolution. A mixed-age, mixed-values community collaborates to develop ways of thriving together. We experience a collective itch and scratch it together, knowing that whatever we come up with today is likely to itch again before long, and knowing that that's okay because we get used to itching and scratching as a basic human condition.

Chapter 12:

# Safety, Safety, Safety

SAFETY AND SECURITY ARE ESSENTIAL support for children's free-dom to explore, experiment, and innovate. Of course, parents and family must provide a base of safe, secure intimacy, freeing children to venture out into the world, confident of anchorage at home. Building on that foundation, the school presents a matrix of safety and security: laws and limits; order and access; recourse to justice; transparency in gover-nance; dependable adults; and a culture of compassion and respect.

In democratic schools, students and staff share responsibility for safety, security, and supervision, just as students and staff share respon-sibility for every aspect of managing the school's affairs. Schools vary in the safety challenges posed by the campus and surroundings — think of differences, for example, between city settings and rural settings. Schools and their communities of families also vary in their relative tolerance of risk of various kinds, and therefore the standards reflected in laws and practices.

Because safety conditions, standards, and practices are so varied and specific to each school and community, I'll discuss features of The Circle School and avoid generalizing about democratic schools.

## Standards

Generally, The Circle School strives to set standards of safety similar to those of a prudent parent, adapted to our school campus and surround-ings, and taking into account principles of democratic education.

In many matters of business, School Meeting discussion includes considerations of safety, for example as it relates to pending legislation, judicial cases, field trips, special events, new activities, proposed equipment purchases, and so on. Safety standards are forged and evolved in this public process. The planning and discussion are just as important, and sometimes more so, than whatever actions are voted.

Often the School Meeting strives to weigh the *risk* of injury against the likely *severity* of injury, to arrive at a prudent risk management strategy. Specifically, if the risk of injury is low and the likely extent of injury is minor, then little or no regulation is required. On the other hand, if the risk of injury is high and the likely extent of injury is severe, then outright prohibition is appropriate. Of course, the School Meeting struggles most with circumstances in between — which seems to be almost everything that comes up!

We often use the "gut test" as a guide to safety. A gut-wrenching reaction to a particular circumstance calls for intervention or prevention, perhaps indicating the law under debate is inadequate to the circumstances. Typically, when a new activity shows up at school — a new way to put ourselves at risk of injury — there are lots of informal discussions to develop shared understanding of standards. Sometimes that leads to a proposal for a new law in the Lawbook.

An important part of growing up is coming to understand one's own physical limitations. Discovery of physical limits involves minor injuries — occasionally for some children and frequently for others. Thus, it is not the school's aim to eliminate minor injuries sustained in wholesome activities.

## Laws

Of course, the Lawbook is an important tool for keeping the school safe. A general rule requires each person to intervene in any circumstances when necessary for safety. Nobody is expected to put themselves in harm's way, but everybody is expected to do what they reasonably can.

Many laws address specific safety issues. For example, there are laws prohibiting each of the following: running indoors; rowdy play indoors; unwanted forceful physical contact; hostile physical aggression; bullying; exploitation; verbal assault; excessive vulgarity; harassment; conspiracy to harass; sexual harassment; use of fire; uncertified knife use; smoking; anything illegal by local, state, or federal law; influencing judicial process through intimidation, retaliation, bullying, bribery, or other coercive or corrupting methods; sexually oriented speech and other sexual behaviors that violate prevailing standards of the school community or the larger community; unauthorized entry into an area designated as restricted. This list is representative and includes only a small fraction of the Lawbook. Scan through the full list of laws in Appendix A to see dozens more laws related to various aspects of safety.

## Safety Practices

The school expects students of all ages, and staff, to generally comply with school laws and community norms of safety and behavior. Expectations are embedded in cultural awareness and enforced in judicial systems. The school holds students to higher standards in this regard than standards commonly held in other kinds of schools, where adults bear most of the enforcement responsibility. Students generally meet the school's expectations and higher standards, as parents and observers often comment.

The benefits of cultivating safety awareness and self-responsibility in children are great. Children who assume active responsibility for their own safety and security are better prepared for today's world than children who passively rely on others for safety and security.

In addition to cultivating personal self-responsibility and collective responsibility, safety considerations are pervasive. Here are some notes about selected aspects of safety.

### Medical Officer

The Medical Officer is an elected official, typically a staff member who is certified for first aid and CPR and may have other training or relevant experience (but is not a medical practitioner). The Medical Officer manages the school's response to illness and injuries, manages secure storage of prescription and nonprescription medications, assists students in taking medications in accordance with medication plans, and coordinates with outside health-related agencies and officials.

### Medical Officer Response Team

Students and staff may qualify as medical Responders who are authorized to respond to incidents of injury and illness. To become a Responder, a candidate must be certified by the American Red Cross or American Heart Association for first aid, child CPR, and adult CPR; memorize a list of ten situations in which to call for help; complete training with the Medical Officer, including an apprenticeship of at least four weeks; demonstrate knowledge and skills of crowd control, confidentiality and privacy, appropriate touch, sensitivity to emotional distress, and relevance of age; and be appointed by School Meeting as a Responder, with the Medical Officer's recommendation. Responders treat scrapes, bruises, scratches, and minor cuts, applying treatments such as cold packs, rinsing, reassurance, and bandages. Every year a new batch of students work hard to become Responders. This year 15% of students are Responders. The youngest is 10 years old.

## School Nurse

A school nurse visits the school periodically to examine student health records, ensure and enforce compliance with state health regulations, administer vision and hearing screenings, and advise the school on health-related issues. The school nurse is a public employee, not a school employee.

## Tree Climbing

By long-standing tradition, tree climbing is permitted at The Circle School. Obviously, tree climbing can be dangerous, as there is potential for falling from a height, which could cause significant injury or death. At present there are no laws or certifications directly regulating tree climbing.

Tree climbing safety is encouraged by an informal tradition of "No Help Up!" According to this tradition, students climb trees only to the extent they can do so without help from others. Giving someone a boost or a push is discouraged because it increases the possibility that they will reach a height or position that is too difficult for their climbing skills. Verbal instructions and physical demonstrations are common and are sometimes the focus of intense student-to-student tutoring.

## Hazardous Equipment, Materials, and Supplies

Like most schools, ours has equipment, materials, and supplies that are hazardous — such as cleaning supplies, science chemicals, dissection scalpels, sharp kitchen knives, motorized pottery wheel, stovetop and oven, and numerous other items. All of these things, and others that are deemed hazardous, are regulated and managed by School Meeting officials, committees, and corporations. Safety precautions vary, but the following are some examples, provided to convey a sense of the school's risk management practices:

- The Facilities Manager stores cleaning supplies in a closet with a latch located six feet off the floor.
- The Art Corporation stores sharp instruments on high shelves in the Art Room closet.
- The Science Corporation stores dissection tools, chemicals, and other hazardous items in high locations.
- The Science Corporation posts a caution sign in the vicinity of any experiment or activity that poses a safety risk and requires observers to wear goggles or take other precautions.
- The Medical Officer maintains first aid kits, some for use at school and others reserved for field trips.
- The NRG Corporation requires that some participants on every overnight backpacking trip be Red Cross certified in first aid and CPR.
- The Cooking Corporation administers a certification process to authorize use of sharp knives for kitchen projects.
- The Cooking Corporation requires that every kitchen project be supervised by a designated and properly certified head cook, who has dictatorial authority over the Kitchen during the project.
- To qualify for certification to use the stovetop, Cooking Corporation rules require that the user stand at least 55 inches tall (because shorter people cannot safely reach across the burners to the controls).
- The Chore Committee individually trains students and staff in their individual housekeeping chores, partly to ensure safe and proper use of cleaning supplies and equipment (and of course partly to ensure a clean building).

## Fire Drills

Fire drills are conducted monthly. New students are trained in fire alarm response procedures by the Facilities Manager. Following most fire drills, a short debriefing and review is conducted while everybody is together.

For the last fire drill of the school year, on a nice spring day, we take advantage of the quiet gathering, with willing cooperation, to get our all-school photo for the yearbook and slideshow.

## Visitors

Other than parents briefly dropping off or picking up their children, adult visitors in the presence of children are required (by state law and school law) to be within supervisory sight of a staff member at all times. From time to time, School Meeting grants permission for unsupervised adult visitations, subject to three background checks: State Police Criminal Background Check, FBI Fingerprint Search, and Child Abuse Database Clearance.

## Staff Presence

The student-staff ratio is approximately 17 to 1 at The Circle School. Students are not required to follow any schedule of classes, and freely move about the premises, indoors and out. Adult staff members are continuously present on school premises and immediately available to students. Adults do not generally direct students' activities unless requested but remain easily accessible to them.

Each staff member has a "home base," typically a desk and computer. Staff stations are distributed strategically throughout the building, so that most locations in the building are within earshot of one or more. Some staff stations are positioned near windows overlooking the schoolyard. Some staff members are heavily scheduled with meetings and other commitments and may be present at their desk for only a small fraction of the day, while others are more often generally available. There is usually a staff member in the school office at the front door, sometimes engaged in office work and sometimes engaged with students. Generally, but not necessarily, at least one staff member is involved with each committee and corporation.

## Transparent Doors

Interior doors have windows, except for lavatories and closets. High visibility facilitates student and staff access to activities, people, and resources and also cultivates a public sense of transparency and openness. Windows in doors also reduce the disruption that would otherwise be caused by frequent opening and shutting by people who want to peek in.

## Corporations, Committees, and Elected Officials

As already mentioned, certain equipment, space, and activities at school are managed by corporations, committees, and elected officials. Each such agency manages safety within their respective domains. For example, persons seeking to use equipment and materials under a corporation's jurisdiction must first receive training and certification or must be supervised by a corporation designee (who could be a student or staff member).

## Field Trips

Every field trip includes at least one staff member. If there are more than three students, then at least one other authorized adult attends, too, and the ratio of students to adults may not exceed seven to one. Field trip participants are required to become field trip certified (by the Field Trip Committee) prior to their first field trip each school year.

Field trips are also subject to the lengthy Field Trip Policy. My favorite provision of the policy makes the attending adults absolute dictators and requires students to instantly obey staff commands, with no rights of voice, vote, or due process. No pesky democracy on field trips! The rationale is that when we venture off campus, we face unknown conditions and hazards, sometimes beyond the experience or likely awareness of students and sometimes requiring quick action. Staff members and other adults, feeling a natural duty to keep students safe, would be reluctant to agree to go on field trips if their safety-related decisions were subject to debate and vote.

## Official Goodbye

On pickup at the end of the day, students who are not leaving by school district busing are required by school law to leave only in accordance with their Authorized Dismissal List (of people they can leave with) signed by a parent. Younger students are typically limited to departure with only their parents and a few other adult relatives or close friends. Many older students are authorized by their parents to leave on their own.

Our "official goodbye" law requires each person to notify a staff member or the elected Bus Supervisor just before leaving (in addition to signing out). Saying "official goodbye" satisfies the law and has become the standard practice. Ideally, the official goodbye is a reminder to leave only as allowed by parents. It also helps staff loosely keep track of who's gone and who's here and is often definitively reassuring when someone asks or a parent calls. The sign-in-sign-out sheet tracks departure times formally, but sometimes people neglect to sign out, perhaps in the (chronic) rush to catch their bus. Personally, I find official goodbyes a sweet tradition — a ritual parting and ceremonial closure to each person's day.

Chapter 13:

# Moving On: College and the World

TODAY THERE ARE MANY PRODUCTIVE LIFE PATHS available beyond high school. With or without college, democratic school graduates pursue interests and enjoy fulfilling careers in self-directed lives. Democratic schools serve young people of all ambitions and support young people bound for all sorts of adult life experiences.

The transition from The Circle School to what comes next can unfold in many different ways, with some common patterns. In their last couple of years here, students occasionally arrange for internships or part-time work in nearby businesses or other organizations, sometimes exploring a career interest and sometimes easing into or just checking out the adult world of employment and money. Some take a class or two at any of several nearby colleges, sometimes out of interest in a particular subject and sometimes to see what college is like. The school's External Resources Coordinator assists with the arrangements for internships and off-campus classes.

Most of our students go on to college — 91% of our "lifers" in a recent comprehensive study. College is crucial for entry into many careers and industries, and college is formative and satisfying for many young people. For some, college follows immediately after high school. For others, a year or two of maturation and experience after high school provides a clear focus for college.

Most of our college-bound students take SAT exams as part of their college admissions campaign. Because the school's culture is so verbally intensive, both oral and written, some students find they need little preparation for the reading and language sections of the SAT; some seek instruction and practice in essay writing. Nearly all students, though, do some concentrated preparation for the math sections — some for a year or more and some for a few months. Some prepare on their own, typically using online resources, and some prepare in classes and tutoring at school.

## High School Diplomas

Many of the democratic schools I know award high school diplomas based on a months-long process of writing and speaking, in which the candidate asserts that they have "prepared themselves for responsible adult life," or something similar. The wording of the thesis and the details of the process vary from school to school. Typically, the diploma candidate prepares a written statement and presents it to a thesis committee, who then question the candidate and decide to grant or withhold the diploma.

Unlike other democratic schools, The Circle School does not conduct a thesis defense program and has not awarded diplomas. The Circle School is licensed by Pennsylvania's Department of Education to issue standard high school diplomas. By state law, a student earns a high school diploma by accumulating 21 academic credits that satisfy the state's subject distribution requirements. Each credit represents "120 clock hours" of instructional time. The school's staff collectively hold all the teaching credentials necessary to support this, and the school maintains all the necessary textbooks and other instructional materials.

Although students can earn a high school diploma at The Circle School, no student has yet chosen to do so. In the early years, we expected students to pursue the diploma, but students quickly discovered that the huge investment of time, particularly to create the required documentation, was unnecessary and not the best use of their time.

## College Admissions

So how do they get into college? Actually, even in conventional schools, students typically apply and are admitted to college in their last year of high school, before earning a high school diploma. Absence of a diploma during the college admissions process is thus not unusual.

What is unusual is that Circle School students, like students from other democratic schools, are admitted to college without a traditional high school transcript of courses and credits.

The Circle School issues to colleges a document that says "Student Transcript" at the top, but there are typically no academic credits to list. Many graduates have taken classes during their high school years, but they do so without the protocols and documentation that would be required for award of formal academic credit, so those classes do not appear on a transcript. Typically, then, the transcript lists the basic student information and dates of enrollment, along with this statement (which I believe we copied decades ago from Sudbury Valley School):

> The Circle School requires each student to take full responsibility for his or her own education. The role of the school is to pro-vide the setting and support for the student's self-initiated work. Accordingly, the most meaningful account of the student's work at The Circle School must be obtained from the student directly.

Most of our graduates are admitted to college based on other cre-dentials, personal interviews, personal résumés, test scores, and other demonstrations of achievement and ability.

The résumé approach has been effective for many students. Patterned after job-seeking résumés, our students list offices they have held, commit-tee positions, corporation involvement, internships, off-campus classes, and projects. Some write about a law they worked to get adopted or a major field trip they helped organize. Because democratic school struc-ture is unfamiliar to many college admissions staff, the résumé is usually accompanied with job descriptions and committee missions excerpted from the Management Manual.

Our students' college admissions essays are often striking in their evident self-awareness, community awareness, and sophistication in democracy, justice, and collaboration. Many have an underlying theme of deep personal self-responsibility and self-authorship — for example, when a student describes their intentional efforts to cultivate an aspect of their character. Many student essays demonstrate comfort with diver-sity in age, culture, ideas, and values. Many show a comfortable relation to authority, practice in leadership, and a second-nature sense of organizational dynamics. Many students write about the positions of authority they have held in the school community and insights they have gained in the challenges thereof.

Some students know what they want to pursue in college and have already begun to pursue it. In that case, their college admission efforts may be narrowly focused on a small number of colleges and particular programs — veterinary medicine in one case, audio engineering in another, clinical research with young children in another. College admissions officers have responded especially well when a student presents evidence and well-reasoned arguments why that particular college is where they must attend.

Above all, I think democratic school graduates tend to be well-developed in character, community, freedom, and responsibility. College admissions officers notice that as unusual, value it, and want to seed their college community with it. Our graduates tend to be attentive college students, going to classes prepared, doing the work, and getting their money's worth. They tend to party less on weeknights and are perplexed by their college friends' lack of time management and self-direction. The college freedom thing? Been there, done that. Yet our graduates are not fundamentally different from their college peers in background or native ability. The difference is that they have been self-directing and time-managing from a young age.

Community college has become a common pathway, attending all the way through to a degree or attending for a year or so and then transferring to a traditional 4-year college. Most of our graduates pay some or all of their college expenses from work and loans. Community college can save them tens of thousands of dollars per year. We are fortunate to have an excellent community college nearby, whose students are welcomed as transfer students into 4-year colleges.

Just as for other pursuits, the school's staff and other resources are available to students in support of their college admission efforts. School staff are accustomed to working with college admissions offices to acquaint them with democratic schooling and help them interpret each student's own presentation of credentials and college readiness.

See Appendix C for a list of colleges attended by Circle School graduates.

## Not Going

Students who plan to pursue a college degree don't need a high school diploma, but other students might. Some choose to study for and take the GED tests (General Educational Development) to earn a high school diploma, and the school stands ready to assist.

In Pennsylvania, students have yet another way to earn a diploma: the Commonwealth Secondary Diploma (CSD). Under this program, the state issues a high school diploma to a Pennsylvania resident after completion of 30 semester hours of college study — about a year's study. A student who completes a year of community college and then pauses, for example, can get a CSD.

## College and Degrees

Although I don't know if it is typical of democratic schools generally, a 2015 study of Circle School graduates (available for download from the school's website) found that 84 to 91% continued their education in college (Chart A). Specifically, 84% had attended college, among those who were enrolled at The Circle School at least through four years of high school, for whom data were available. If you assume the unknowns did not attend college, the rate was 78% rather than 84%. Among those who were enrolled at The Circle School for eight years or more, the college attendance rate was 91%, with no unknowns. For comparison, the U.S. Census Bureau reports the college attendance rate for same-age Americans as 60%.

**Chart A: College Attendance by Years at The Circle School**

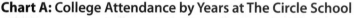
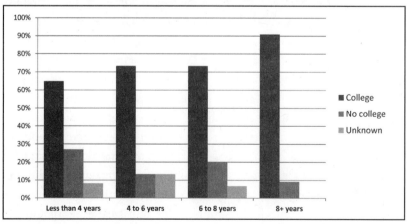

What about college graduation rates? As of 2015, Circle School graduates earned more bachelor's, master's, and doctoral degrees than other high school graduates 25 years and older (Chart B). Overall, 62% of Circle School graduates hold a bachelor's degree or higher (and 21% were still in degree-earning programs), compared with 42% of Americans 25 years and over.

**Chart B: Highest Educational Attainment, 25 years and over**

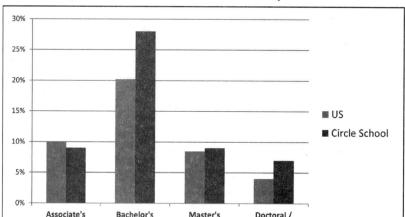

The school's family income profile does not explain these outcomes. Circle School families are representative of the school's catchment area, with median income around $48,000 (Chart C): 30% of households with income less than $30,000 per year, 55% with income less than $50,000, 89% with income less than $100,000. The median income of both the school and its catchment area is slightly less than the national median, which is around $51,000. The Circle School's income profile also stands in contrast to the profile of independent private school families, whose incomes are typically substantially higher (Chart D).

How does this happen in a school with no compulsory curriculum, classes, tests, grades, or homework and serving families from across the socio-economic spectrum? When school is not forceful or frantic about pressing academic studies on children, when school instead immerses students in self-direction, community, and democracy, two relevant patterns emerge. First, children and teens develop fulfilling life skills: self-examination and

## Chart C: Household Income, Region vs Circle School

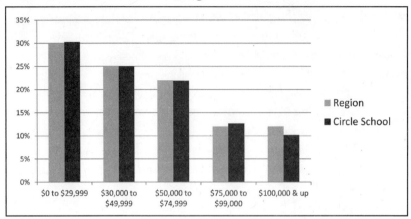

## Chart D: Household Income, Circle School vs Independent Private Schools

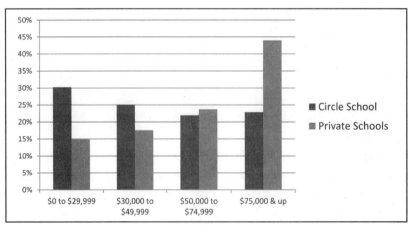

assessment, responsibility to self and others, making culture and community, navigating technology and societal institutions, and critical thinking. Second, the social value and natural appeal of traditional academic pursuits become apparent, untainted by the bad taste of coercion. Building a satisfying life becomes everyday practice, and college is often on the path.

Although these college statistics are well regarded, the school would rather be judged by its graduates' self-actualization, life satisfaction, achievement in self-chosen domains, and productive engagement in culture, community, society, and technology.

## Lisa's First Semester at College

This is Lisa, reporting on my first semester at college. Some students and parents, especially new ones, wonder if The Circle School provides proper education and preparation for college. Relax! I'm here to tell you that it does.

On the first day of a seminar for first-year students, they showed us a slide with this caption: The Difference between High School and College: Freedom and Responsibility. No joking! The instructor said nobody was going to remind us to be in classes, call our parents when we were in danger of failing, or remind us to do homework anymore. This was "real life," and we had to be responsible for ourselves.

This left me both scoffing and laughing inside. Why would society wait until now to teach us this? It seems strange that we are told what to do, led by the hand, and given instructions for almost every activity of our daily lives… until we leave home!

And if college and work is the start of "real life," what were students doing before that? Fake life?

A big question on some parents' minds is whether a Circle School student can produce the grades. Well, yeah! I'm no genius, and I managed to do very well. I got a 3.8 QPA, five As and one B. I did very well and lacked nothing in academic preparedness. Not bad, considering I took no more than two classes in my four years at The Circle School!

I learned so much from reading, conversations, daily experiences, and willing SAT study that I needed no catch-up studying at all. It's a matter of applying oneself. Isn't that what The Circle School is all about anyway?

I'm not saying that every student who attends The Circle School will get straight As at college, or go to classes every day, or even remember to eat breakfast. What I'm saying is that there is nothing lacking in a Circle School education. I will testify to its ability to prepare students for college better than traditional schools. I understand how to apply myself little by little each day.

College, like anything else in the world, gives results depending on how much a person puts into it. This is the classic Circle School lesson. We are all responsible for our own day, and that has definitely stuck with me.

*— Lisa Lightner ('06), writing to the school community*
*a few months into college*

# Part Five:
# Frequently Asked Questions

# Frequently Asked Questions

## Basics

**Q: What's a democratic school?**

**A:** For the purposes of this book, I mean a school that is a free and democratic society, governed and administered by a formal democracy of students and staff, embracing rule of law, due process, student civil liberties, one person one vote, and absence of mandatory curriculum. Students in democratic schools experience personal and community self-determination in democratic liberty, responsibility, and authority. That's the short version.

**Q: Freedom sounds great, but don't children need structure?**

**A:** Yes, structure contributes to the stability and security that set children free to explore their world without fear. Structure is important in democratic schools just as it is in the world beyond school: setting limits for safety and order, guiding us as we go about our business and live our lives. Democratic schools tend to have lots of this kind of structure: formal government, laws, judicial systems, certifications, committees, corporations, dependable adults, anchored culture — and lots of daily, weekly, and yearly rhythms.

American society has similar structures for adults, and that's the point. Let's invite children and teens to join the society and world into which they are growing. Let's immerse kids from an early age in a microcosm of society, with parallel institutions, values, and practices. Let kids practice life and they get really good at it. I know because I've seen it in hundreds of students across four decades.

Yes, democratic schools value structure. The difference is in the *kind* of structure: top-down or bottom-up. If children are trained for 12 years to follow someone else's agenda and orders — top-down structure — then many will tend, as adults, to wait for someone else to direct them. On the other hand, if children are allowed from a young age to direct themselves, mindful of the community around them, then that's what they are more likely to do as adults.

The self-directed person more readily finds satisfying purpose and meaning in life, and is also in greater demand today, particularly by colleges, employers, and clients. Children, families, and society are better served by schools that are structured to enable and demand self-direction and collaboration. That's the kind of structure children find in democratic schools.

**Q: What happens when they go to college and they have to follow the rules of a normal classroom, and study things that don't interest them? How do students adjust?**

**A:** Democratic school graduates tend to adapt to college more easily than their peers from conventional schooling. The pattern is striking, and we hear it over and over. In conventional schooling, students commonly get the message they should sit down, keep quiet, wait for a teacher to tell them what to do, and then do exactly what they are told. These are the messages conveyed by the system itself, communicated to students regardless of teachers' best intentions. In contrast, democratic school students build their lives on intrinsically motivated pursuits, supported and constrained by the community around them, without adults directing and enforcing. They become self-responsible and accustomed to overcoming obstacles to reach goals and build fulfilling lives. The independence and self-responsibility of college come easily to our students, because they've been practicing it throughout their school years. When our graduates go on to college, they adapt quickly and smoothly, sometimes bewildered by their peers' struggles with self-direction and time management.

**Q: Most students will have to submit to authority in a future workplace. Is that a struggle for students from democratic schools?**

**A:** Again, quite the opposite. Students from democratic schools are already accustomed to the combination of formal authority, individual responsibility, and collaborative expectations that are typical of workplaces. Daily they work within the school's many formal structures: school government, judicial system, corporations, committees, certifications, mandatory procedures, and hundreds of rules. Democratic school students develop healthier relationships with authority and better understanding of its various roles and values. They come to know when and how to challenge authority, when and how not to, how to be part of it, and how to share it. From school to college to employment and life, democratic school graduates tend to transition with less turmoil and greater grace.

**Q: How many graduates go on to college and earn degrees?**

**A:** A recent study of graduates of The Circle School may or may not be representative of democratic schools generally, but here's what it found. Graduates go to college at high rates: 84% of those who attended for at least the four high school years, and 91% of "lifers" — those who attended for eight years or more. Nationwide the rate among same-age peers is 60%.

Graduates were also found to have earned bachelor's, master's, and doctoral degrees at higher rates than their high school graduate peers.

Economic advantage does not appear to be a factor. A study a few years ago found that the school's family income profile closely matched the income profile of the surrounding community (30-minute drive time from the school): 30% of households with less than $30,000 annual household income; 55% of households less than $50,000; 89% less than $100,000.

**Q: How do children do in a conventional school after attending a democratic school?**

**A:** Children generally experience smooth transitions to other schools. Most schools are accustomed to receiving children from a variety of educational backgrounds and levels of achievement and knowledge. Families whose children have transferred out of democratic schools into traditional schools often comment that their children's increased confidence and motivation helped them to quickly adapt and excel. It is also common to hear that they are cognitively and socially advanced in comparison to their new classmates, whether or not they are familiar with whatever material is coming up in the conventional curriculum.

## Q: Are democratic schools like homeschooling?

**A:** No, typically the two are worlds apart, but sometimes homeschooling families find they like democratic schooling better. Some homeschooling is motivated by parents' wish to be involved with their children or to control their children's exposure to culture and knowledge. In contrast, democratic schools provide space for children's growing independence from parents and for broad exposure to culture and knowledge. Homeschooling often involves standard curriculum, again unlike democratic schools. But some families welcome their children's independence and engagement in community beyond family, and they homeschool only because they don't like the other alternatives available to them. Many such families have discovered democratic schooling and never looked back.

## Q: Are democratic schools like unschooling?

**A:** There may be some shared values, but the differences are significant. Unschooling is more responsive than standard schools to students' interests and choices and may thus share democratic schools' values of intrinsic motivation and self-direction. Unschoolers abandon formal curriculum altogether, perhaps sharing democratic schools' values of divergent exploration and avoidance of curricular coercion. Unschooling may thus appear to be similar to democratic schooling.

But unschooling is often centered on home and family, an extension of the intimacy and informality of family. Family members commonly tend to indulge and reinforce one another's idiosyncrasies, sometimes including patterns that would be unwelcome in the world beyond family. Families may interact in unnoticed ways that become entrenched, tending to bind children to a self-image, a role, a way of relating to others, and a family culture. Sometimes unschooling complicates children's journey from the dependence of infancy to the relative independence of adulthood.

In contrast, democratic schooling is centered on community beyond family. In democratic schools, kids practice life in a scaled-down society, with relative independence from parents and home. The precious intimacy and informality of family are complemented and balanced. Students find their own ways of navigating the expectations, norms, and constraints of a larger world, sometimes easily, sometimes with constructive friction. Either way, students practice life in a dynamic society beyond family, with daily opportunities to participate in collective self-governance, the making of culture and community, and deep development of original self and identity beyond family. Children are freer to think expansively about themselves and their place in the world.

**Q: Are democratic schools religious?**

**A:** Like most democratic nations, democratic schools value freedom of religion and separation of church and state and thus do not profess any religion or impose religious observances. On the contrary, democratic schools welcome all perspectives: religious (all faiths), non-religious, atheist, humanist, spiritual but not religious, and other varieties of faith and belief. Secular government is an important democratic principle.

Even so, one can infer from self-directed democratic schooling some beliefs and values that are central to some religions and faith traditions. For example, democratic schooling may imply a belief in the sanctity of self-determination and the worthiness or source of the inborn impulse that drives growth.

Most democratic schools are not affiliated with any religion or religious body, but some are, including three I know of that are each formally affiliated with a church. In all three cases, the associated religion is similar to Unitarian Universalism, having in common certain values such as personal search for truth and meaning; embrace of all faith traditions; inherent worth and dignity of each person; importance of democratic process and other forms of social equity.

The Circle School, of which I'm a founder, is not affiliated with a church, but incorporates those foundational values. The school can thus be regarded as religious, spiritual, or non-religious, depending on your own outlook. For what it's worth, my own devotion to self-directed education is rooted in direct experience of, and faith-based belief in, fundamental dimensions of life that are beyond mythic religion, airy metaphysics, and overreaching science.

On the other hand, some democratic schooling advocates are motivated entirely by political, social, and other non-religious principles. For example, some champion the civil rights and emancipation of children, viewing democratic schooling as the next step in extending basic human rights universally. Others value democratic schooling as promoting social justice.

In short, democratic schooling is compatible with a wide range of religious, political, and social views. Democratic schools embrace families of all religious, spiritual, and secular traditions. Children, families, and society benefit from the resulting diversity and pluralism.

**Q: Are democratic schools political?**

**A:** Democratic schools don't advocate for political candidates, don't express political views, and don't aim to nudge the world to the political left, right, or center. They enthusiastically welcome students and families of all political viewpoints. In my vision, the neutrality goes beyond that: democratic schools have no social agenda to "change the world," nor to shape minds or sculpt children to acquire certain traits. The aim is to make culture and society together at school, reflecting basic values of Western civilization: personal freedom, mutual toleration, public government, collective responsibility, and so on. Children bring fresh energy and perceptions to the project and contribute much to the synergy of minds in pluralistic society.

## Curriculum

### Q: No mandatory curriculum? No testing? Really?

**A:** Yes, really. Democratic schools impose no curriculum or classes, no mandatory testing, no mandatory projects, no requirement to keep a log or a journal or any other documentation. Instead, students manage their own time. They pursue activities of their own choosing, and they fulfill civic duties. As 10-year-old Jyles put it, "I just come here and I live my life." Generally, students choose the what, when, where, and who of their time at school. Students encounter a broad variety of subjects and activities — including much that is part of a traditional curriculum and much that is not. In some democratic schools, classes are conducted only when initiated by students, and it's fine if they don't. Because students freely choose their pursuits, learning is generally deeper, more satisfying, and more enduring. Self-motivation driven by personal interest makes the difference.

### Q: Are there optional activities and classes?

**A:** Yes. Democratic schools typically don't centrally plan a schedule, and staff members don't typically initiate classes, but there are dozens or hundreds of activities, groups, events, field trips, and other adventures on

offer. Most fall into one of three categories: affairs organized by participants, activities and events offered by school corporations, and the school
government work of committees and officials.

At The Circle School, the main bulletin board displays signs and
sign-up sheets inviting participation in all sorts of things — discussion
groups, classes, projects, and clubs, for example (see Chapter 9 for more).
Anyone can imagine something and post it. For example, this year there's
a Cultural Studies Group, started by teenagers who enjoy learning about
unfamiliar cultures. They recruited others and reserved a room for twice
weekly meetings. One year there was a popular Zombie Apocalypse
Discussion Group. Studies of math and languages are common.

Corporations (such as Art, Science, and Music Corporations) maintain materials and equipment for anyone to use. You have to follow their
rules, and in most cases, you have to get "certified" (trained) before you
use something for the first time. But once certified, you have free access,
on your own or with others. Corporations offer events, too. The Science
Corporation holds Lego Day, Take-Apart, and Rocket Launch. The
Cooking Corporation holds delicious contests. The Music Corporation
organizes performances and recordings.

School business involves dozens of elected officials and committees,
offering endless opportunities to manage systems and activities that keep
the school running. For example, there are elaborate chore systems and
judicial systems (see Chapters 10 and 11).

In some democratic schools, staff members themselves don't initiate
optional activities, perhaps to avoid over-reliance on adults or to facilitate
emergence of student interests and initiative. In any case, most staff members I know are fully occupied already in the rich and ever-changing mix
of what's going on, with little time available to initiate more.

Sometimes the question about what's offered is rooted in concerns
about kids' exposure to certain subjects and skills. In my experience,
democratic school students are exposed to a wide range of knowledge and
skills, including and extending far beyond a traditional curriculum.

**Q: What if my child isn't self-motivated?**

**A:** Comedian Phyllis Diller observed, "We spend the first year of our children's lives teaching them to walk and talk, and then 12 years telling them

to sit down and shut up." The point is, most children get little opportunity to exercise self-motivation in standard schools.

When children are required to pursue other people's interests rather than their own, it's no wonder they seem to lack motivation. When children's lives are mostly directed by teachers and adults, it's no wonder their skills of introspection and self-direction deteriorate or fail to develop.

Every child begins life with high motivation to learn. Among children who begin their school years in a democratic school, all are motivated. Children who have previously spent years in traditional schools may take time to recover internal motivation and the spirit and sparkle that go with it. They'll get there. Give them the time, space, and community.

**Q: Why doesn't the school impose a curriculum?**

**A:** Three reasons. First, democratic schools avoid curricular coercion simply out of basic human respect. Second, because learning is more efficient and durable when motivated by the child's own interests. And third, because forcing children to "learn" tends, over time, to deaden their curiosity, self-motivation, originality, confidence, and creativity — essential ingredients for highest human achievement. In short, mandatory curriculum is a poor educational strategy, and unnecessary coercion is out of sync with today's values.

In an age of esteem for engineered solutions, we might take comfort in the idea that science and psychology have discovered a treatment process — a standard curriculum — to transform the raw material of children into smart, prosperous adults. Alas, it isn't so. That idea is deeply rooted in the Industrial Revolution when modern schools were first established. The "factory model" of schools that prevails today is based on the assumption that children are all basically the same and can be processed in batches based on their age to produce standardized young adults who meet predetermined specifications. In fact, science and scholarship have thoroughly debunked that idea. Standard curriculum coercively applied is bad science, ineffective education, and unsatisfying life.

**Q: Do most students take regular academic classes?**

**A:** No. Traditional academic studies in formal classes typically make up only a small fraction of activities at school. Formal classes generally happen when initiated by a student or a group. Classes can be organized by anyone at any time, around almost any subject or activity. Some students participate in many classes, some in very few. At The Circle School, math and languages are the most common traditional classes. Many of the older students seek formal instruction to prepare for college entrance exams. Otherwise, most students occasionally initiate or join a class, but students of all ages generally spend only a small fraction of their time in formal academic studies. Some alumni who were here for many years say they never took any classes at all. On the other hand, there are organized gatherings every day — meetings, activities, events — that are mostly not about traditional academic subjects, even though they may look studious and involve instructive materials. See the question above, about optional classes and activities.

**Q: How do students learn?**

**A:** Conventional schooling reduces learning to bite-size curricular objectives packaged into lessons "delivered" to students in classes without experiential context. This is a fine way to study and acquire some knowledge, among many other fine ways. It has some advantages, such as optimizing the expense of teachers' time, and it has some drawbacks, such as being relatively ineffective and boring for many students much of the time. Regrettably, this method dominates in conventional schooling to the exclusion of other methods — so much so, that the word "learning" has come to be widely associated exclusively with this one overused method, applied to the standard academic curriculum.

Democratic schools restore the meaning of "learning" to include many learning methods and many domains of learning. This book identifies some of these new learning modes, methods, and mechanisms, which are mostly unavailable and unknown in conventional schooling: interest groups, self-service systems, systemic or meta-message learning, public process, accelerated culture, near-stage transmission, commerce and entrepreneurship, multiple lines of development, self-balanced development, deep play, and functional apprenticeship. See Chapter 6 (How and What Do They Learn?) for more about each of these and others.

In short, democratic school students sometimes learn in the same ways they do in conventional schools. More often, though, democratic school students learn in a variety of ways, enhanced by self-direction and community dynamics. The result is learning that is more meaningful and enduring and daily life that is more fulfilling.

**Q: What about reading? How do they learn to read?**

**A:** Mostly, children learn to read much as they learn to walk and talk. It's so important, you can't stop them. More than half of our students learn to read without formal instruction, picking it up as they need it in personally meaningful activities. The rest typically ask for "reading classes" at some point, which might last a few weeks and rarely longer than a few months.

Reasons to read are everywhere. If you want to understand the sign-up sheets on the bulletin board — for field trips or events at school — or the inventory list in your Minecraft chest, you better learn to read. Most kids find it vitally important when they see a tray of fresh-baked brownies to read the nearby sign and tell the difference between "For Sale" and "Free — Take One." Each child's process involves a unique mix of reasons, timing, and ways. We find that learning to read is usually quick for children when they come to it on their own, for their own reasons, in their own time.

**Q: What's wrong with mandatory curriculum?**

**A:** Mandatory curriculum harms children's learning, intelligence, and joy of life in many ways: displaces better developmental opportunities, promotes shallow learning, turns kids off to academics, undermines introspection and self-awareness, deadens initiative, fosters passivity, disempowers, alienates, and normalizes coercion. Ouch. If nothing else, democratic schools avoid the damage.

It gets worse. The educational theory of standardized curriculum has been discredited by science and scholarship. Aside from broad patterns, each child's development is unique and unpredictable, influenced by infinite variations in cultural, environmental, and personal factors. The idea that a standard sequence of learning steps will lead every child from kindergarten to college and economic prosperity would be laughable if it were not so deeply entrenched in our institutions of mass education. What's wrong with coercive curriculum? It doesn't work and it causes harm.

**Q: Without mandatory curriculum, what do they learn?**

**A:** Virtually all children who are organically able learn reading, writing, and arithmetic. Beyond that, the possibilities are as vast as human knowledge. Most children learn about many traditional academic subjects and many other subjects as well. Most learn some things more deeply, joyfully, and durably than is likely in standard schools. Generally, kids learn what they're interested in, what they must learn in order to function in their world, and what they must learn in order to achieve self-chosen goals.

What do they learn? In democratic schools, children and teenagers develop cognition, general intelligence, and critical thinking as they practice life in a stew of culture, community, nature, and technology. Instead of worksheets and word problems, or sometimes in addition to, students tackle personally meaningful challenges — social, emotional, physical, intellectual, political, situational, and existential. Self-direction cultivates introspection, self-awareness, initiative, decision-making, and resilience. Community cultivates collaboration, awareness of others, and life skills for navigating society. Collective self-governance and school administration cultivate authority, political sensibility, policy awareness, and public mindedness. Through it all, learning and self-management become fulfilling lifelong practice.

**Q: Is it true that students don't have homework?**

**A:** It is true that the school has no homework requirement, and it is true that most students most of the time do not undertake traditional studies and traditional homework. Some do, sometimes, and traditional textbooks and homework assignments are sometimes involved. More commonly, students voluntarily take responsibility for work to be done on their own, perhaps at home, as part of something they have chosen to do at school — not because of curricular requirements but for their own reasons.

For example, a teenager who was part of a role-playing game group agreed to make a map before the group's next meeting at school and did that work at home. Was that homework? Students who are preparing to take the SATs regularly commit to completing algebra and geometry exercises out of a textbook before their next prep session at school. Is that homework? Or someone may agree to go to the grocery store and buy

spaghetti sauce over the weekend for the Science Corporation's fundraising sale of lunches at school. Is that homework?

But no matter what, the school does not expect *parents* to make their
kids do any sort of homework at all. Students and parents both commonly
find greater satisfaction when parents avoid taking responsibility for their
children's self-chosen commitments at school. School should enhance,
not undermine, family life and parent-child relationships.

## Assessment and Reporting to Parents

**Q: Does the school assess students or issue report cards?**

**A:** No. The school does not test or assess students for reporting to parents.
Although standard schools haven't yet caught up, modern research shows
that required testing harms children's learning — reducing efficiency and
retention. A student might seek assessment, including formal testing, for
their own purposes, but the school does not keep records of it.

**Q: Why don't democratic schools assess students?**

**A:** Absence of mandatory assessment makes several wholesome results
more likely. First, children develop strong self-assessment habits and
introspective skills. Second, they more freely seek and absorb meaningful
feedback, gaining ability and confidence in their original thinking. Third,
children's natural curiosity and motivation are preserved — habits of
growth, rather than action to please adults.

**Q: How will I know how my child is doing?**

**A:** Parents who have paid close attention to report cards in the past are sometimes anxious at first. By the time their children have been enrolled for a year
or two, most say they know them better than ever before and they don't miss
the grades. Sometimes they can't remember why they ever thought they
needed report cards. For some, report cards have been a source of tension
between parent and child, even with "good grades." Removal of the tension comes as a relief, and the relaxed parent-child relationship flourishes.

**Q: Does the school tell me if my child falls behind?**

**A:** Falls behind what? Democratic schools do not assign students to grade
levels, and do not track students' acquisition of knowledge according to a

prescribed curriculum. The school also does not assess students' knowledge compared to whatever grade level expectations might be imposed by other schools. Democratic schools find that the harms of mandatory curriculum outweigh whatever benefits there might be. Science and reason confirm what most parents see for themselves: each child develops uniquely. Parents' own experience of their children's thriving and growth is more relevant and vital than curricular benchmarks. "Falling behind" is an artifact of standardized curriculum. As *Frozen's* Queen Elsa would say, "Let it go."

**Q: Does the school tell me when my child gets in trouble?**

**A:** Only in special circumstances, such as when School Meeting votes to suspend a student following judicial proceedings. In democratic schools, children and teens practice life with relative independence from parents. Thus released from the habits and expectations of family life, they are freer to try out new ways of interacting with people, new areas of knowledge, new mental models of how the world works, new physical feats, and a host of other innovations. Finding and testing limits at school is important to many kids. Getting in trouble in the school's judicial system from time to time can be useful experience. Giving your children the gift of independence may be the hardest thing you do as a parent. Democratic schools help.

## Getting into a Democratic School

**Q: What do democratic schools require for admission?**

**A:** Most democratic schools are open to all children who can function effectively in the school program and who choose to attend. Some schools designate the first few weeks of each enrollment as a "practice period" with family check-in conferences to help the family and school assure a good fit. Others have a "trial week" of attendance before enrollment or other provisions for testing the goodness of fit.

**Q: What about very young children?**

**A:** In young children, minimum requirements are potty training, responsiveness to dialogue, and ability to observe outdoor boundaries. Many children are developmentally ready at 4½ years old. Some schools have a specific age threshold.

**Q: What about children with special needs or giftedness?**

**A:** Admissions criteria are the same for all students: the child can function effectively in the program, and the child chooses to attend. The daily program is the same for all students, with no curriculum or IEP or other remedial work, therapy, or enrichment imposed or monitored by the school. Students with a broad range of needs and conditions thrive in democratic schools. Each child is unique in abilities, interests, aspirations, and idiosyncrasies. The environment and culture fit well for some children with labels and not for others. Democratic schools generally welcome children and families whose needs and hopes are fulfilled by the program, without regard to labels and diagnoses. Democratic schools represent a "mainstream" experience and do not generally hold out any credentials, special knowledge, or expertise in special needs. Regarding gifted, however, you could half-playfully say that democratic schools are experts, finding that every child is uniquely gifted.

**Q: Are democratic schools good for everyone?**

**A:** If I could wave my magic wand and install democratic schools throughout the land, I'd probably do so, replacing coercive schooling with democratic schooling. I would love to live in a society filled with democratic school graduates, each one an original creation and all knowing how to live fulfilling life in diverse community. But I'm committed to pluralistic society and do not believe any one approach to schooling should be imposed on all families and children. Are democratic schools good for everyone? Democratic schools are a win-win for children, families, teachers, schools, society, and humanity.

**Q: Yes, but how can you tell when a student won't thrive in a democratic school?**

**A:** It's more often about the parents than the student. Some parents remain committed to the standard curriculum or a particular school-day program for their child, or they remain fearful of their child "falling behind." If parents' dissatisfaction persists, it undermines the child's experience of school, perhaps resulting in feelings of guilt or diminished self-worth, or subtle fear of loss of parental love. Most parents become comfortable with democratic schooling — some as soon as they learn more about it and some over time as they see their children thrive and grow.

Most children and teenagers thrive in a democratic school — and their families, too — but some do not. For example, a student who lacks the basic cognitive capacity to understand school rules will not thrive. Ditto for a student who abnormally lacks impulse control or is prone to violence or unresponsive to normal dialogue.

For students and families who arrive in a child-related crisis, the school may not be a good fit. The family may regard the child as "broken" and the school as a place to "fix" the child. In that situation, the family tends to view the school as a place of therapy, like a hospital, a place for people who are not healthy. If the child enrolls, parents and child may tend to feel anxious, guilty, and maybe resentful of the school as a symbol of what's wrong. Furthermore, the child is expected to get well as quickly as possible and then leave the school. Yuck. That dynamic undermines the school experience for the family in crisis and others, too.

In crisis situations, sometimes the school will suggest to a family that enrollment be postponed until after the crisis is resolved, perhaps six months after, and then reconsider enrollment as a long-term place of healthy growth and dependable community. On the other hand, sometimes it takes a crisis for a family to see just how broken the conventional school system is. A dear mentor of mine sometimes reminded families that it's the system that's broken, not the child.

**Q: Can I financially afford a democratic school?**

**A:** Tuition costs, financial aid policies, and payment plans vary a lot from school to school. Most democratic schools strive to accommodate a wide range of family financial means.

**Q: Where can I find a list of democratic schools?**

**A:** Visit the website: www.democraticschools.directory.

# Epilogue: Seeking Infinity

I WANT CHILDREN IN SCHOOL TO FIND HAPPINESS. Not momentary fireworks, but the saturating joy of purpose and meaning in life. Not someday, but now, as children.

I've noticed that kids who live fulfilling lives as kids tend to build fulfilling lives as adults. I think personal fulfillment is a learned way of life. It may be easy or hard to learn, but once you do, you never want to stop. You live to capacity, and then you discover more. Fulfillment in one moment tends to lead to fulfillment in the next. It becomes an outlook, an expectation, and a demand on self and life.

Wishing happiness for children is not sentimental or starry-eyed. From the passion of personally meaningful challenge, I see character and intelligence emerge. Practiced with others in bounded freedom and shared responsibility, I see lively culture and supportive community emerge. So I draw a line from children's self-determined adventures to their fulfilled potential, and from there to society's collective advance: fulfilled individuals lead to fulfilled society. Isn't that the purpose of education: elevation of self and society?

I see life as an expression of nature's imperative to seek infinity. In children, it shows up as the inborn impulse to strive, thrive, and grow. In response to never-ending existential needs and situational challenges, nature drives children to seek increasingly effective ways to understand the world and take action. I want schools to sponsor the seeking, finding, passion, and action.

Depending on your perspective and truth-seeking method, you can see nature's imperative and children's inborn impulse as matters of religious belief, or non-religious spirituality, or science. A religious perspective might see human striving as longing for the indwelling Divine, or return to God. A spiritual but not religious perspective might see human striving as realization of one's highest nature, or Unity. A scientific perspective might see striving for intelligence and capability as adaptive behavior, promoting fitness. So, depending on your perspective, the pay-off might be Heaven, Joy, or Survival. Take your pick.

What does all this mean for school? It means we don't need to force children to learn and grow. Nature endows the impulse, and kids take it from there. They walk and talk and then keep going. They make meaning and find purpose. Schools can enhance this power of nature by creating the conditions, holding open the space, and promoting children's agency in community. It's good for kids, families, society, and humanity. So take a look at self-directed democratic schooling. You'll see the spirit and sparkle of kids practicing life.

# Acknowledgments

F ROM TENTATIVE TALKS TO TRICKY CROSSINGS of real and ideal, Beth
Stone and Sue Narten, and dee Holland-Vogt soon after, laid decades
of foundation on which this book rests — beloved heroes between the
lines. Later, when the real had prevailed and The Circle School sought
a better way, Daniel Greenberg, Mimsy Sadofsky, and Sudbury Valley
School appeared with tangible and intangible support, without which
this book would not be. I'm especially grateful for decades of collegial
friendship with Mimsy and Danny. Fellow Circle School staff members
JD Stillwater, Ann Sipe, and Ellen Abbott provided years of front-line wisdom that is baked into the school and this book. Larry Welshon supplied
25 years of challenging questions, perseverance, and once a whiskey and
a cigar. Eugene Matusov, along with Ana Marjanovic-Shane, relentlessly
provoked insights that appear throughout. Gratefully I acknowledge their
vigorous scholarship, intellectual integrity, and warm friendship. Doug
Neidich hid behind the scenes, a steady friend listening intently and offering advice over many a meal. Down-to-earth angels Richard and Barbara
Schiffrin trusted their son to lead the way, and then quietly stayed on.
Thanks to Julia James, JD Stillwater, Jancey Mallory, and Beth Stone for
agreeing to read drafts and offer helpful feedback; and to Juniper Mallory
for reminding me to write for posterity. Special thanks to Jancey Mallory
whose radiant spirit and sparkle enlighten me and this book. Special
thanks to Julia James, who stepped in when the school needed a fill-in
staff member, and stayed longer than she planned. Her influence on me

and this book is beyond words; our collaborations are among the greatest joys and inspirations of my life. Special thanks to the hundreds of children and teenagers across four decades who so vividly drew this book into being. Most of all, I acknowledge profound, loving collaboration with Beth Stone, wife and partner for life who showed me that children are people.

# Appendix A

## The Circle School Management Manual Table of Contents
## (Sections 12 through 59 are the Lawbook)

**8607    Art Corporation**
8607.01  Type of Activity
8607.02  Bylaws
8607.10  General Art Corporation Rules
8607.12  Eager Beaver Certification
8607.    Jumping Giraffe Certification:
30–72    Beads, Crayon Melter, Drawing
         Supplies, Fabric, Glitter, Glue
         Gun, Paint, Paper Rolls & Poster
         Board, Rubber Cement, Sculpey,
         Sewing Supplies, Sewing Tools,
         Stamps, Tempera Paint, Yarn
8607.    Wonderful Whale Certification:
80–89    Acrylic Paints, Beads, Plaster,
         Solid Watercolors, Stone
         Carving Tools
8607.94  Unicorn: Laminator
         Certification
8607.98  Unicorn: X-Acto Knife
         Certification
**8620    Cooking Corporation**
8620.01  Type of Activity
8620.02  Bylaws
8620.10  Using the Kitchen Certification
8620.17  Blender Certification
8620.24  Dishes & Silverware
         Certification
8620.26  Food Processor Certification
8620.31  Griddle Certification
8620.38  Kitchen Knives Certification
8620.45  Mixer Certification
8620.52  Refrigerator Use Guidelines
8620.59  Stove Certification
8620.65  Certification for Certifiers
**8633    Games Corporation**
8633.01  Type of Activity
8633.02  Bylaws
8633.10  Games designated to the care of
8633.15  General Certification
**8635    Gardening Corporation**
8635.01  Type of Activity
8635.02  Bylaws
**8640    Music Corporation**
8640.02  Bylaws
8640.11  Digital Recording Certification
8640.16  Drum Set Certification
8640.19  GarageBand Certification

8640.21  Guitar Certification
8640.22  Guitar Accessories Certification
8640.25  iMac Certification
8640.30  KORG Certification
8640.34  Microphone — Basic
         Certification
8640.36  Microphone — Professional
         Certification
8640.43  Piano & Keyboard Rules
8640.45  Studio Certification
8640.47  Trumpet Rules
8640.50  Violin Certification
**8646    Natural Resource Group
         Corporation**
8646.01  Type of Activity [Hiking,
         camping, adventure]
8646.02  Bylaws
**8661    Science Corporation**
8661.01  Type of Activity
8661.02  Bylaws
8661.10  BASIC Certification
8661.12  PRIMARY Certification
8661.14  ADVANCED Certification
8661.15  List of BASIC equipment
8661.16  List of PRIMARY equipment
8661.17  List of ADVANCED equipment
8661.18  List of SPECIAL certifications
8661.21  Anatomy Rules
8661.23  Animal Tracks Rules
8661.25  Balls Rules — PRIMARY
8661.26  Battery Charger Rules —
         PRIMARY
8661.27  Big Gyroscope Rules
8661.29  Binoculars Rules
8661.31  Cryogenics Certification
8661.33  Density Cubes Rules
8661.35  Digital Balance Rules
8661.37  Dissection Rules
8661.39  Droppers Rules
8661.41  Electricity Rules — PRIMARY
8661.43  Glassware Rules
8661.45  Graduated Cylinders Rules
8661.46  Handwarmers Rules —
         ADVANCED
8661.47  Household Chemicals Rules
8661.49  K'Nex Certification —
         PRIMARY

# Appendix B

## The Circle School Corporation Bylaws

### Article 1  NAME
1.1  The name of the corporation shall be The Circle School Corporation (the "Corporation").

### Article 2  PURPOSE
2.1  The primary purpose of the Corporation shall be to operate a school, including children and teenagers from preschool through high school, particularly according to these beliefs:
- Children are born with an impulse to grow, create, and strive towards self-actualization;
- Fellowship and community are essential to personal growth and fulfillment;
- All persons are inherently worthy of and entitled to respect and self-determination;

and particularly these values:
- Free and responsible search for truth and meaning;
- Universal community, embracing all faiths and worldviews;
- Increasing realization of physical, intellectual, emotional, social, and spiritual potentials;
- Personal fulfillment and engagement in society;
- Personal and community self-determination;
- Personal and community self-responsibility;
- Liberty, justice, harmony, mutual acceptance and support;

and particularly in pursuit of and exemplifying the Ends We Seek ("Ends") as enumerated in Article 3.

The secondary purposes of the Corporation shall be to promote the Corporation's beliefs and values in education; to operate the school as a model or template that others can replicate or adapt in private and public schools; and to disseminate information about the school.

2.2  The Corporation admits students of any race, color, national origin, ethnicity, religion, gender, and sexual orientation to all the rights, privileges, programs,

251

and activities generally accorded or made available to students at the school; and does not discriminate on the basis of race, color, national origin, ethnicity, religion, gender, and sexual orientation in administration of its educational policies, admissions policies, scholarship and loan programs, and athletic and other school-administered programs.

2.3   No part of the net earnings of the Corporation shall accrue to the benefit of, or be distributable to, its members, trustees, officers, or other private persons, except the Corporation may pay reasonable compensation for services rendered and to make payments and distributions in furtherance of the purposes set forth in Section 2.1.

2.4   No substantial part of the activities of the Corporation shall be the carrying on of propaganda or otherwise attempting to influence legislation, and the Corporation shall not participate in, or intervene in (including the publishing or distribution of statements) any political campaign on behalf of any candidate for public office.

2.5   Notwithstanding any other provision of the Bylaws, the Corporation shall not carry on any other activities not permitted to be carried on (a) by a Corporation exempt from Federal income tax under Section 501(c)(3) of the Internal Revenue Code of 1954 (or the corresponding provision of any future United States Internal Revenue Law) or (b) by a Corporation, contributions to which are deductible under Section 170(c)(2) of the Internal Revenue Code of 1954 (or the corresponding provision of any future United States Internal Revenue Law).

2.6   Upon dissolution of the Corporation, after paying or making provision for payment of all of the liabilities of the Corporation, all of the assets of the Corporation shall be distributed to other organizations operated exclusively for educational or charitable purposes, which shall at the time qualify as exempt organizations under Section 501(c)(3) of the Internal Revenue Code of 1954 (or the corresponding provision of any future United States Internal Revenue Law).

## Article 3   ENDS WE SEEK

3.1   Integral education. Children and youth practice personal fulfillment and engagement in society, in a school program of respect for self-determination, and trust in an inborn tendency to self-actualize.

   3.1.1   Opportunity. Students have abundant opportunity for personal fulfillment and societal engagement.

      a. Community. Students experience fellowship, common culture, collective self-governance, and shared responsibility.

      b. Order. Students experience safety, order, and access to community resources.

      c. Knowledge. Students have opportunity to develop knowledge and skills in self-chosen domains.

      d. Staff. Students experience adults who dependably steward the program's facilities, finances, and business; facilitate student access to resources; exemplify mature practice of personal fulfillment and societal engagement; and anchor school culture to values of interpersonal respect and trust in the natural impulse to self-actualize.

   3.1.2   Growth. Students grow in many dimensions, such as physical, intellectual, emotional, social, and spiritual.

a. Personal fulfillment. Students increasingly actualize personal potentials, and seek satisfaction in self-chosen domains of activity, knowledge, and skill.

b. Engagement in society. Students develop increasingly fulfilling ways of participating in culture, community, and society.

3.1.3    Self-determination. Students enjoy natural rights of life, liberty, and pursuit of happiness, paralleling adult experience in the community beyond school.

a. Civil liberties. Students enjoy civil liberties such as freedoms of speech, press, thought, attention, religion, privacy, movement, association, and peaceable assembly.

b. Curriculum. Students are free of curricular coercion.

3.1.4    Governance. The daily school program is self-governing, with authority and responsibility shared among the governed, students and staff alike.

a. Voice. All members of the daily school program — students and staff — enjoy equal rights of voice and vote in matters of governance and the common good.

b. Rule of law. All members of the daily school program are subject to the authority of school government according to duly adopted laws that are publicly disclosed in writing.

c. Responsibility. All members of the daily school program share responsibility for the common welfare.

d. Protection. All members of the daily school program enjoy equal protection and due process under school law.

3.2    Outreach. Parents, educators, public policymakers, and the general public have access to information about the school and integral education, sufficient to facilitate understanding, replication, and adaptation.

## Article 4   MEMBERSHIP

4.1    Members of the Corporation

4.1.1    Automatic Members. Membership of the Corporation shall include the following persons:

a. Each student who is a member of School Meeting (according to Section 7.1a) and has actually attended the school for at least two months.

b. Each school staff member (according to Section 7.1b).

c. Each Trustee.

d. Each Honorary and Emeritus Member (according to Section 4.3.3).

4.1.2    Opt-in Members. Membership of the Corporation shall include, from among the following classes, those persons who seek membership and agree in writing to abide by and uphold the Bylaws of The Circle School Corporation.

a. Parents. Each parent whose signature appears on the enrollment agreement of a student who is a Member of the Corporation. The term "parent" shall include biological parents, adoptive parents, civil union parents, legal guardians, foster parents, tuition-paying step-parents, tuition-paying grandparents, and tuition-paying domestic partners of any of these.

b. Alumni. Each alumna and alumnus who attended the school for at least a year, and is at least 18 years old. Each Alumni Membership shall continue for life or until terminated in writing by the Member.

c. Alumni parents. Each person who was ever eligible for Membership as a parent of a person who is or ever was eligible for Alumni Membership. Each Alumni Parent Membership shall continue for life or until terminated in writing by the Member.

d. Trustee committees. Each person appointed to and serving on a committee created by the Trustees, provided the committee's members' eligibility for Corporation Membership under this paragraph is authorized by the Trustees.

e. School Meeting committees. Each person appointed to and serving on a committee created and appointed directly by act of the School Meeting, rather than its agencies or representatives, provided the committee's members' eligibility for Corporation Membership under this paragraph is authorized by the School Meeting.

f. Non-staff employees of the School Meeting and the Corporation who are at least 21 years old.

g. Public Members (according to Section 4.3.4). Each Public Membership shall continue for the term elected, or one year if no term is specified.

4.2  Meetings

4.2.1   An Annual Meeting of the Membership shall be conducted at the school by the Trustees, at least three of whom shall be present, beginning at 7:00pm on the first Monday of December or, if that day is a legal holiday, then the next day that is not a legal holiday; provided the Trustees may, with at least five weeks' notice, establish a different date and time.

4.2.2   Special Meetings of the Membership may be called at any time by the Trustees. Any business may be conducted at Special Meetings, except ratification of amendments of the Bylaws and Articles of Incorporation.

4.2.3   Virtual Meetings of the Membership may be called at any time by the Trustees, each consisting of a single contiguous period of time, up to a maximum of one month, during which business may be transacted by remote communication modes such as but not limited to the following: telephone, U.S. postal mail, fax, email, Web, and other Internet and electronic technology. Any business may be conducted through remote communication modes, except ratification of amendments of the Bylaws and Articles of Incorporation. Quorum requirements shall apply, counting Members participating rather than Members physically present. Provision shall be made in virtual voting to accommodate Members who have limited or no access to the applicable communication modes.

4.2.4   Notice of each Annual, Special, and Virtual Meeting shall be issued at least ten days in advance of the Meeting, or five weeks in advance of certain Annual Meetings as provided in Section 4.2.1. Notice shall state the date, time, and place of the meeting; identify nominees for Trustee election, if any; state the full text of proposed amendments of the Bylaws and Articles of Incorporation, if any; and state or summarize, by class, who is eligible for Membership (as enumerated in Section 4.1). Notice shall be issued by email to each Member's email address as recorded by the school; and shall also be posted prominently at school; and shall also be posted to an online venue operated by the school for communication to or among members of the school community, such as a social media website, if any such online venue exists. Members may individually waive their right to notice, before or after a meeting. Notice to Members of the Corporation who are also members of the School Meeting shall be satisfied if notice is issued to the School Meeting at least ten days in advance and school is open for at least three days during the ten days prior to and including the day of the meeting. A meeting that is adjourned to a certain time and place shall not require another notice.

4.2.5    A quorum at any meeting shall consist of ten members present in an Annual or Special Meeting, or ten members participating in a Virtual Meeting. The continued presence or participation of a quorum shall not be required for the transaction of business.

4.2.6    Each Member present in a physical meeting or participating in a virtual meeting shall have one vote, and there shall be no voting by proxy. Except as otherwise specified in the Bylaws or by parliamentary authority, all matters shall be decided by a majority of the votes properly cast.

4.2.7    Unless otherwise established by the Trustees, the parliamentary authority for physical meetings shall be *Robert's Rules Of Order Newly Revised* (*The Scott, Foresman Robert's Rules of Order Newly Revised* (1990 Edition, Ninth Edition, ISBN 0-673-38734-8)), and the parliamentary authority shall apply in all cases to which it is applicable and in which it is not in conflict with the Bylaws. In Virtual Meetings comparable parliamentary principles, such as protection of minority views and mechanisms to exclude duplicate votes, shall apply with adaptation to the communication modes, with the Trustees as final authority.

4.2.8    Agenda shall be established by the Trustees, except that the Annual Meeting agenda shall explicitly include at least all of the following items, whether or not there is corresponding business to conduct:
- Trustees' Report to Members of The Circle School Corporation
- School Meeting Report to Members of The Circle School Corporation
- Consider and vote on questions put by the Trustees (if any)
- Consider and vote on questions put by the School Meeting (if any)
- Ratify amendments of the Bylaws and Articles of Incorporation (exactly as stated in meeting notice)
- Annual election of Member-elected Trustee (as stated in notice)
- Special elections of Trustees (as stated in meeting notice)
- Members' remarks

4.3  Powers and duties
4.3.1    The Membership shall elect one Trustee as provided in Section 5.1.1.
4.3.2    The Membership may ratify amendments to the Bylaws and Articles of Incorporation as provided in Article Eight.
4.3.3    The Membership may elect Honorary and Emeritus Members for life, by majority of votes cast, following nomination by the Trustees.

4.3.4    The Membership may elect Public Members, by majority of votes cast, following nomination by the Trustees for a certain term or for one year if not specified.

4.3.5    The Membership shall advise the Trustees on questions and matters put to it by the Trustees, and shall advise School Meeting on questions and matters put to it by School Meeting.

## Article 5  Trustees

5.1    There shall be a Board of Trustees ("the Trustees") of seven persons, each of whom shall be at least 21 years old if not otherwise a Member of the Corporation. To qualify to serve, each Trustee at the start of each term of service shall agree in writing to abide by and uphold the Bylaws and the Trustee Code Of Ethics, if one has been established by the Trustees; and failure to so qualify shall leave the Trusteeship vacant, to be filled promptly by Trustee appointment. Each Trustee term shall begin on March 1 and expire on the last day of February or when the Trustee's successor qualifies, whichever occurs later. Each Trustee may serve continuously for up to ten years plus the remainder, if any, of the Trustee's then-current term; and shall be next eligible for Trusteeship after a lapse of one year. Trustees shall be selected as follows:

5.1.1    Members of the Corporation shall elect one Trustee ("Member-elected Trustee") annually for a term of one year. Election shall take place at the Annual Meeting or, at the option of the Trustees, at a Virtual Meeting taking place during any part or all of the period beginning one day before the Annual Meeting and extending seven days after the Annual Meeting. Nominations for the Member-elected Trustee may be made by petition of fifteen Members, and also by a Nominating Committee as provided in Section 5.3.6. Nominations shall be closed two weeks prior to the Annual Meeting, and nominees shall be identified in the notice of meeting. Election shall take place by secret ballot or substantially equivalent method, and election shall be by majority of votes cast, proceeding through rounds or other process, as necessary to secure a majority.

5.1.2    Alumni shall appoint one Trustee ("Alumni-appointed Trustee") annually for a term of one year, according to procedures determined by an organization of school alumni sanctioned by the Trustees upon recommendation by School Meeting; provided the appointment shall be made and communicated to the Trustees between November 1 and January 1. In the event there is no sanctioned alumni organization or the alumni organization does not appoint a Trustee or does not communicate the appointment to the Trustees by January 1, the Trustees shall promptly arrange for appointment of a Trustee by a committee of five or more alumni and/or School Meeting members, or by School Meeting, and the alumni organization shall forgo Trustee appointment for that year.

5.1.3    School Meeting shall appoint one Trustee ("School-Meeting-appointed Trustee") annually for a term of one year, according to procedures determined by School Meeting, provided appointment shall be made and communicated to the Trustees between October 15 and January 15. In the event School Meeting does not appoint a Trustee or does not communicate the appointment to Trustees by January 15, the Trustees shall promptly arrange for appointment of a Trustee by a committee of five or more School Meeting members and/or alumni, and School Meeting shall forgo Trustee appointment for that year.

5.1.4  The Trustees shall appoint one Trustee ("Board-appointed Trustee") annually for a term of four years, with four Board-appointed Trustees in all, having staggered terms to expire one per year.

5.2  Meetings

5.2.1  Regular meetings of the Trustees shall be held at times and places established in Trustee policies or determined in other Trustee actions.

5.2.2  The President or any two Trustees may call a Special Meeting of the Trustees at any time.

5.2.3  Notice of each meeting shall state the date, time, and place of the meeting. Notice shall be issued reasonably in advance of the meeting, and in any event shall be sufficient if mailed by first class U.S. postal mail at least one week in advance, or if delivered and acknowledged at least 48 hours in advance by any means, verbal or written or electronic. Trustees may individually waive their right to notice, before or after a meeting.

5.2.4  A quorum shall consist of a majority of Trustees serving. Each Trustee shall have one vote and there shall be no voting by proxy. Regardless of the number of Trustees present or participating, business shall be transacted by consent of a majority of Trustees serving, except as otherwise provided in the Bylaws, and shall not be transacted by the lesser standard of majority of votes cast.

5.2.5  Business shall be conducted according to rules and procedures established by the Trustees and not in conflict with the Bylaws.

5.3  Powers and duties

5.3.1  Governance. On behalf of all persons everywhere and throughout time who support the Corporation's purposes as elaborated in Articles Two and Three, the Trustees shall strive to ensure fulfillment of purposes through acceptable means. Through the following actions, the Trustees shall secure School Meeting's governing autonomy, students' civil liberties, and the school's long-term assets:

a. Stewardship. The Trustees shall cultivate regular discourse with, and at least annually seek the advice of, persons who support the Corporation's purposes, in order to better govern on their behalf.

b. Ends. The Trustees shall monitor fulfillment of purposes, especially achievement of Ends; shall intervene in the event School Meeting acts contrary to Ends; and may propose amendments to Ends according to Article Eight.

c. Limits. The Trustees shall establish policies defining standards of prudence and ethics, binding on School Meeting and all other agencies and representatives of the Corporation, particularly regarding but not limited to business, finance, administration, government regulation, safety, and security; and shall intervene in the event School Meeting breaches limits of prudence or ethics established in Trustee policies.

d. Operations. The Trustees shall generally defer to the School Meeting on conduct of operations, management of day-to-day affairs, governance of the daily school program, hiring of school staff, and control of operational policies and procedures.

e. Monitoring. The Trustees shall establish policies defining interactions between the Trustees and School Meeting, such as but not limited to communications, periodic reporting, and monitoring procedures.

f. Governing. The Trustees may establish a Trustee Code of Ethics, binding on Trustees, and shall establish policies and procedures to guide, direct, and constrain Trustees in the proper and orderly business of governing.

g. Intervention. When required to intervene in School Meeting affairs, as provided in Sections 5.3.1b and 5.3.1c, the Trustees shall proceed in the following sequence, by voted action of the Trustees at each step, until the cause for intervention is cured: (i) conduct investigation; (ii) adopt and communicate to School Meeting a statement of breach, including findings of fact, specific identification of breached Ends or Limits, statement of remedy sufficient to cure the breach, and reasonable deadline for reply and/or cure except when delay is likely to lead to irreparable harm to school interests; and (iii) assume supervision and control of operations, funds, campus, and other assets, to the minimum extent necessary to cure the breach and restore non-breaching operations.

5.3.2   The Trustees may delegate or assign powers and duties to School Meeting, in addition to the powers and duties assigned to School Meeting by the Bylaws.

5.3.3   The Trustees may accept delegation of powers and duties from School Meeting as requested by School Meeting, and may serve operational functions as requested by School Meeting.

5.3.4   The Trustees shall determine the school's tuition, fees, annual budget, and other fiscal policy; shall have unconditional access to all records, facilities, and resources of the Corporation and its agencies; shall exercise all the powers of the Corporation not expressly assigned to others by the Bylaws; and may conduct any business that is legal.

5.3.5   The Trustees may conduct business in physical meetings and may permit or require conduct of Trustee business through remote communication modes, such as but not limited to the following: telephone, U.S. postal mail, fax, email, Web, and other Internet and electronic technology. Business conducted through remote communication modes may include any or all business that may be conducted in physical meetings of the Trustees, such as but not limited to adoption of policies, appropriation of funds, and election of Trustees. Advance notice for business conducted through remote communication modes shall be no less than that required for business conducted in physical meetings. Quorum requirements shall apply, counting Trustees participating rather than Trustees physically present.

5.3.6   The Trustees shall annually appoint a Nominating Committee to nominate one candidate or, at the Trustees' option, more than one candidate, for election of one Trustee by Members of the Corporation for a term of one year.

5.3.7    The Trustees shall annually appoint one Trustee for a term of four years.

5.3.8    The Trustees shall promptly fill unexpired Trustee terms that become vacant; and shall promptly fill Trusteeships left unfilled after exhausting the provisions of Sections 5.1.1, 5.1.2, and 5.1.3.

5.3.9    In the event the number of serving Trustees falls below four, for any combination of reasons, the Trustees shall without delay arrange for appointment or election of at least three additional Trustees by the Membership, School Meeting, or a committee of at least five alumni who are not Trustees, in any combination; and shall in the meantime refrain from enacting substantial policy changes.

5.3.10   The Trustees shall appoint Officers as provided in Article Six, and shall promptly fill vacated offices.

5.3.11   [REPEALED]

5.3.12   [REPEALED]

5.3.13   The Trustees may create, charge, and discharge committees ("Trustee committees"); may appoint Corporation Members to such committees, and may appoint non-Members who are at least 21 years old; may appropriate funds for and delegate authority to such committees; and may specify that committee appointees be eligible for opt-in Corporation Membership under Section 4.1.2d. Each Trustee's committee memberships shall terminate when the Trustee's Board membership lapses, unless otherwise directed by the Trustees. Other committee memberships shall terminate when the committee member's Corporation membership lapses or after two years from appointment to the committee, whichever comes first, unless otherwise directed by the Trustees.

5.3.14   The Trustees may sanction an organization of alumni upon recommendation by School Meeting, and the Trustees may revoke such sanction only with School Meeting consent.

5.3.15   Amendments to the Bylaws and Articles of Incorporation
a. The Trustees may propose amendments to the Bylaws in accordance with Sections 8.1 and 8.3.
b. The Trustees may propose amendments to Articles of Incorporation in accordance with Sections 8.2 and 8.3.

5.3.16   The Trustees may nominate Honorary and Emeritus Members of the Corporation, for election by the Membership.

5.3.17   The Trustees may nominate Public Members of the Corporation, for election by the Membership.

5.3.18   The Trustees may remove a Trustee who is unable or unwilling to serve, or for other cause, such as but not limited to breach of the Trustee Code Of Ethics.

5.3.19   The Trustees may designate a Trustee who may attend any and all meetings of the School Meeting, provided that if no Trustee is designated, then the President may attend or designate another Trustee.

5.3.20   [REPEALED]

5.3.21   The Trustees shall establish and maintain a Conflict of Interest Policy, and shall publish the policy for the school community, either continuously on the school's internal or public website, or annually by other means.

5.3.22   Indemnification. The Corporation shall, to the extent legally permissible, indemnify each person who may serve or who has served at any time as a Trustee or employee of the Corporation against all expenses and liabilities, including, without limitation, counsel fees, judgments, fines, excise taxes, penalties, and settlement payments, reasonably incurred by or imposed upon such person in connection with any threatened, pending, or completed action, suit, or proceeding in which he or she may become involved by reason of his or her service in such capacity; provided that no indemnification shall be provided for any such person with respect to any matter as to which he or she shall have been finally adjudicated in any proceeding not to have acted in good faith in the reasonable belief that such action was in the best interests of the Corporation; and further provided that no compromise or settlement shall be made without approval by a majority vote of Trustees who are not at that time parties to the proceeding. The indemnification provided hereunder shall inure to the benefit of the heirs, executors and administrators of persons entitled to indemnification hereunder. The right of indemnification under this Section shall be in addition to and not exclusive of all other rights to which any person may be entitled. No amendment or repeal of the provisions of this Section which adversely affects the right of an indemnified person under this Section shall apply to such person with respect to those acts or omissions that occurred at any time prior to such amendment or repeal. This Section constitutes a contract between the Corporation and the indemnified Trustees and employees.

## Article 6   Officers

6.1   The Officers of the Corporation shall be a President, a Secretary, and a Treasurer.

6.2   Officers shall be appointed annually between March 1 and July 1 by the Trustees from among their number, provided that no two offices shall be simultaneously held by the same person, and Officers shall be at least 21 years old. Each Officer shall continue in office until their successor assumes the office or their Trusteeship lapses, whichever comes first. Vacated offices shall be promptly filled by the Trustees.

6.3   Powers and duties

6.3.1   President. The President shall preside at meetings of the Trustees; shall preside or appoint another Trustee to preside at meetings of Members; may participate in debate and all other Trustee business as any other Trustee; and may call Special Meetings of the Trustees. Unless another Trustee has been designated by the Trustees, the President may attend any and all meetings of the School Meeting, or designate another Trustee.

6.3.2   Secretary. The Secretary shall record in Minutes all actions and meetings of the Trustees and the Membership; shall ensure proper notice of meetings of the Trustees and the Membership; shall ensure proper care and custody of Minutes; and shall perform other duties assigned by the Trustees.

6.3.3   Treasurer. The Treasurer shall have custody of all the funds and securities of the Corporation and shall deposit same in institutions as authorized by the Trustees; shall make investments, other than deposits, as authorized by the Trustees; shall disburse funds for other purposes only under the Trustees' authority in pursuit of the Corporation's purposes; shall keep or cause to be kept complete and accurate accounts of all financial transactions; shall at all reasonable times exhibit the Corporation's account books to any Trustee upon application; shall submit a full financial report, including at least a Balance Sheet and Statement Of Revenue And Expenses, to the Trustees annually and at other times as directed by the Trustees; shall perform other duties assigned by the Trustees. Funds of the Corporation may be withdrawn or disbursed only on the signature of the Treasurer or other persons expressly authorized by the Trustees. The Trustees may direct that the powers and duties of the Treasurer be discharged by the Treasurer alone, or by the School Meeting, or by the Treasurer and one or more other persons jointly.

## Article 7  School Meeting

7.1  Membership of the School Meeting shall include the following persons:

  a. Students, each beginning on the first school day of their enrollment and ending on the last school day of their enrollment.

  b. Staff, consisting of employees who are subject to school government and are substantially engaged in the school program, as determined by School Meeting.

7.2  Powers and duties

  7.2.1  School Meeting shall manage school operations; shall conduct day-to-day business and affairs of the school to achieve Ends through acceptable means; shall comply with all applicable local, state, and federal laws and regulations; and shall abide by, uphold, and implement the Bylaws, and policies and decisions of the Trustees.

  7.2.2  School Meeting shall govern the daily school community according to and exemplifying the Ends enumerated in Article Three. School Meeting shall determine its systems of governance, offices, officers, meetings, quorum, voting, rules of order, laws, judicial process, and other matters.

  7.2.3  School Meeting shall assume additional powers and duties as delegated by the Trustees.

  7.2.4  School Meeting may, with consent of the Trustees, delegate powers and duties to the Trustees; and may, with consent of the Trustees, engage the Trustees to perform operational functions that would otherwise properly be performed by School Meeting.

  7.2.5  School Meeting shall pursue no ends or purposes other than those enumerated in Article Three, except as delegated by the Trustees.

  7.2.6  School Meeting may suspend or expel from the school any member for cause, following investigation and process under School Meeting rules.

  7.2.7  School Meeting shall annually draft and submit to the Trustees an annual budget, according to a schedule and in a manner prescribed by the Trustees; and shall manage the school's annual budget as established by the Trustees.

  7.2.8  School Meeting may hire Staff, and other employees, who agree in writing to abide by and uphold the Bylaws.

7.2.9   School Meeting shall annually appoint one Trustee, according to Section 5.1.3.

7.2.10   School Meeting may create, charge, and discharge committees ("School Meeting committees"); may appoint Corporation Members to such committees, and may appoint non-Members who are at least 21 years old; may appropriate funds for and delegate authority to such committees; and may specify that committee appointees be eligible for opt-in Corporation Membership under Section 4.1.2e.

7.2.11   School Meeting may recommend to the Trustees an organization of alumni to receive the Trustees' sanction, and may withhold consent for the Trustees to revoke the sanction.

7.2.12   [REPEALED]

7.2.13   [REPEALED]

7.2.14   School Meeting shall adopt and present, in a digitally archivable form, a Report to Members of The Circle School Corporation at the Annual Meeting of the Membership, including items of business and interest as it sees fit.

7.2.15   In the event the Trustees intervene in School Meeting affairs as provided in Section 5.3.1g, School Meeting shall promptly cooperate with the Trustees' investigation, promptly respond to statements of breach, and promptly yield operational control as directed by the Trustees.

## Article 8   Amendments to the Bylaws and Articles of Incorporation

8.1   The Trustees may propose amendments to the Bylaws by affirmative vote of five Trustees, provided amendments shall take effect only when ratified by the Membership of the Corporation by majority of votes cast at the next Annual Meeting following the Trustees' vote, subject to Section 8.3.

8.2   Articles of Incorporation may be amended only by affirmative vote of five Trustees, followed by ratification of the Membership by a majority of votes cast at the next Annual Meeting of the Membership following the Trustees' vote, subject to Section 8.3.

8.3   The Trustees shall submit the full text of proposed amendments to School Meeting at least 60 calendar days prior to the Annual Meeting, including at least 20 school days, and shall publish School Meeting's written statement of response, if provided by School Meeting, in Notice of the Annual Meeting and all other presentations to the Membership of the proposed amendments.

# Appendix C

## Colleges Attended by Circle School Graduates

Allegheny College
American University
Arizona State University
Babson College
Bard College
Bennington College
Brown University
Bucknell University
Central Pennsylvania College
Community College of Vermont
Culinary Institute of America
Davis & Elkins College
Duke University
Dutchess Community College
Edmonds Community College
Eugene Lang College of Liberal Arts
Franklin & Marshall College
Full Sail University
George Mason University
Gnomon School of Visual Effects
Hampshire College
Harcum College

Harrisburg Area Community College
Harvard University Extension School
Indiana University of Pennsylvania
Institute for Social Ecology
International Language Institute
Lebanon Valley College
Marlboro College
McDaniel College
Millersville University
Montgomery College
Old Dominion University
Pennsylvania State University
Prescott College
Recording Workshop
Rochester Institute of Technology
Saint John's College
Saint Louis University
Saint Mary's Public Honors College
Sarah Lawrence College
Shippensburg University

Slippery Rock University
Temple University
Thaddeus Stevens College of
   Technology
Thomas Edison State College
Tidewater Community College
Union Theological Seminary
Universität Heidelberg
University of Colorado
University of Maryland University
   College

University of Pennsylvania
University of Pittsburgh
University of Rochester
University of South Dakota
University of Virginia
Washington University in St. Louis
Western Governors University
Widener Law School
Worcester Polytechnic Institute

# Index

# About the Author

J IM RIETMULDER IS A FOUNDING STAFF MEMBER AND EDUCATOR at The Circle School in Harrisburg, Pennsylvania, a pioneering democratic school, where he has worked for 34 years. With his support, students at The Circle School practice freedom and responsibility in a scaled-down version of the larger world, becoming experts at life, liberty, and pursuit of happiness. Jim also tutors students to take college entrance exams, plays mixed-age soccer at every opportunity, and anchors the daily Critical Thinking Discussion Group. Prior to, and overlapping with, The Circle School's early years, Jim was a history magazine editor, business analyst, independent software developer, and management consultant to manufacturers. Jim is married to co-founder Beth L. Stone and is the father of two Circle School graduates. He lives in Lewisberry, Pennsylvania.

## A Note about the Publisher

NEW SOCIETY PUBLISHERS is an activist, solutions-oriented publisher focused on publishing books for a world of change. Our books offer tips, tools, and insights from leading experts in sustainable building, homesteading, climate change, environment, conscientious commerce, renewable energy, and more — positive solutions for troubled times.

We're proud to hold to the highest environmental and social standards of any publisher in North America. This is why some of our books might cost a little more. We think it's worth it!

- We print all our books in North America, never overseas
- All our books are printed on 100% post-consumer recycled paper, processed chlorine free, with low-VOC vegetable-based inks (since 2002)
- Our corporate structure is an innovative employee shareholder agreement, so we're one-third employee-owned (since 2015)
- We're carbon-neutral (since 2006)
- We're certified as a B Corporation (since 2016)

At New Society Publishers, we care deeply about *what* we publish —but also about *how* we do business.

Download our catalogue at https://newsociety.com/Our-Catalog or for a printed copy please email info@newsocietypub.com or call 1-800-567-6772 ext 111

---

## New Society Publishers
### ENVIRONMENTAL BENEFITS STATEMENT

For every 5,000 books printed, New Society saves the following resources:[1]

| | |
|---:|---|
| 30 | Trees |
| 2,695 | Pounds of Solid Waste |
| 2,965 | Gallons of Water |
| 3,867 | Kilowatt Hours of Electricity |
| 4,899 | Pounds of Greenhouse Gases |
| 21 | Pounds of HAPs, VOCs, and AOX Combined |
| 7 | Cubic Yards of Landfill Space |

[1]Environmental benefits are calculated based on research done by the Environmental Defense Fund and other members of the Paper Task Force who study the environmental impacts of the paper industry.

---

MIX
Paper from responsible sources
FSC
www.fsc.org   FSC® C016245

new society
PUBLISHERS
www.newsociety.com